Labor and Global Justice

Labor and Global Justice

Essays on the Ethics of Labor Practices under Globalization

Edited by Mary C. Rawlinson, Wim Vandekerckhove, Ronald M. S. Commers, and Tim R. Johnston

Foreword by Edward S. Casey

LEXINGTON BOOKS
Lanham • Boulder • New York • London

Published by Lexington Books
An imprint of The Rowman & Littlefield Publishing Group, Inc.
4501 Forbes Boulevard, Suite 200, Lanham, Maryland 20706
www.rowman.com

Unit A, Whitacre Mews, 26–34 Stannery Street, London SE11 4AB, United Kingdom

British Library Cataloguing in Publication Information Available

Library of Congress Cataloging-in-Publication Data

Labor and global justice : essays on the ethics of labor practices under globalization / edited by Mary
C. Rawlinson, Wim Vandekerckhove, Ronald M. S. Commers, and Tim R. Johnston.
pages cm.
Includes bibliographical references and index.
ISBN 978-0-7391-9369-3 (cloth : alk. paper) -- ISBN 978-0-7391-9370-9 (electronic)
1. Labor and globalization--Moral and ethical aspects. 2. Labor market--Moral and ethical aspects. 3.
Employee rights. 4. Social justice. 5. Industrial relations. I. Rawlinson, Mary C.
HD5706.L2174 2014
174--dc23
2014026734

♾ ™ The paper used in this publication meets the minimum requirements of American
National Standard for Information Sciences Permanence of Paper for Printed Library
Materials, ANSI/NISO Z39.48-1992.

Printed in the United States of America

Contents

Foreword

Laboring in the Darkness of Global Justice

Edward S. Casey

Rather than the light promised by the rhetoric of global justice, conditions of labor today everywhere are characterized by the darkness of a conspicuous lack of effective criteria for judging just actions in the workplace. At least this is so for virtually all countries of the world today, most conspicuously those dominated by the regime of late capitalism. Questions of justice that go beyond lip service to "workers' rights"—rights that in their abstractness do not touch upon the concrete realities of labor—and the invocation of a purely formal framework inscribing an ethos of "fairness" are more often marginalized in contemporary debates about labor practices than they are considered for their substantive content. Neoliberal regimes—private and governmental alike—may *speak of* equity and even treatment, equal hearing for workers' demands, and a just distribution of wages, but in actuality these tenaciously held rhetorical ideals cast an enormous shadow upon the realities of human labor.

The scene of labor itself, famously distinguished by Arendt from anything like creative work, may be regulated by expectations and demands of just practices that claim global scope and sanction; these strictures may be rigorously enforced on the job while deficits in wages and benefits are passed over in silence. These shortfalls include women's labor in the homeplace and immigrants' toiling in the fields. In one case, the labor is taken for granted—is part of the "natural contract" of marriages arranged to advantage the primary wage-earner, all too often a man; in the other, the labor is a matter of life and death—given the dearth of options for those who have come to a host country on the basis of forced migration from a home country where there are no longer any significant prospects of earning a living from ordinary jobs.

Two kinds of places are here at stake—one in the interior of a residence, the other in the exteriority of open fields where crops are raised and harvested—but they share a common subjection to exploitation by existing structures of power, whether marital or corporational.

Both forms of exploitation just mentioned—along with myriad instances of ordinary jobs that do not offer a living wage—consider themselves to be self-justifying. Doesn't uncompensated and unrecognized housework come as part of the "bargain" of marriage, especially marriage pursued under the regime of compulsory heterosexuality? What would these poor Mexican laborers be doing were they not working in these fields? And that kid who labors at the local ice cream shop for sub-minimal wages: shouldn't he be grateful for finding any work at all? In all such cases, there is a self-congratulating air of righteousness on the part of employers. So long as this is the case, there is no motive to consider more effective standards of just employment. Why bother when the system seems to be working, at least for those in control and who profit from it: if it doesn't appear to be broken, why try to fix it?

But the system, in both home and field (not to mention the shop), *is* broken. In the absence of an effective ethics of interpersonal care and concern, any sense of the unjust treatment of those who labor under duress and who are inadequately paid is cast into the shadows of the unreal to which Plato consigned cast-off reflections under the heading of *eikasia*. On this tacit but powerful paradigm, undeniable material signs of human suffering (exhaustion, increased susceptibility to disease, depression, shortened lifespan) fall under the sharp-edged scythe of the *eidetic*, the formally real. They are somehow *less than real*, passing symptoms. After all, isn't the system eminently fair when it comes to strict standards of justice?

Laboring in this realm of shadows, there is no light left for the re-envisaging of all too abstractly formulated ideals of human rights and fair practices. Such rethinking would entail an appreciation of a genuinely place-based and people-specific ethics of nonexploitation in which the fierce Moloch of late modern capitalism would yield to a serious reflection on a new ethics of the finite, intermediate spaces in which laboring actually exists: a reflection on the daily realities of the workplace *as a place* and laborers as *people-in-that-place*. The global would need to take account of the vicissitudes of the local—which is where labor in fact occurs. Exploitation occurs there too; but any thoughtful consideration of labor practices must start just there—in the home, the field, and the shop.

The chapters in this volume delineate the space of just such a reflection. Each contribution addresses a different aspect of the neglected problematic of labor in a global economy and politics that are increasingly under the sway of neoliberal ideologies. Taken together, these chapters break new ground in what is a desperate need of the present moment: how to bring global thinking from an empty universalism into human-scale models of justice for all those who labor under unjust conditions—in whatever city or nation or region they obtain, granting their very great differences in detail from each other. Where are we to look for fully and finally concrete universals of labor justice?

This timely and singular text takes major steps toward diagnosing the current predicament of labor in a variety of settings, offering meaningful alternatives to repressive practices. It goes a long way toward moving from the shadows of the current dilemma into the light of a truly caring and just treatment of laboring forces wherever they are to be found.

Introduction

Wim Vandekerckhove

With this volume, the editors had one aim: to put labor back on the agenda as the focus of analysis within debates around global justice. Over the past two decades, the field of global ethics, or global justice, has evolved into a proper academic domain, as well as a policy discourse, as evidenced in the conferences and journals carrying these terms in their titles, as well as international networks and policy programs.

While the debates in this field center around notions of cosmopolitanism, equity, global redistribution, and migration, we missed in the language and debates on global justice the explicit questioning of labor practices and labor market policies as these have been affected by globalization. The chapters collected in this edited volume together begin to fill this lacuna.

The need for this book—putting labor back into global justice—is made evident in two introductory chapters, providing the conceptual context for the other essays, which focus more specifically on the politics and policies of labor under globalization. In the first of these introductory chapters, Ronald Commers presents a critique of the "global justice"/"global ethics" stream of narratives. He insists on a more radical view concerning the social power relations worldwide. The conflict between labor/capital is too hidden in global justice narratives. For example, the global compact narrative addresses forced and compulsory labor only by proposing the abolition of child labor, as if only children are subject to forced labor.

Commers recalls Marx's metaphor of the Juggernaut of capital accumulation wheeling at full speed to argue that the primitive form of capital accumulation is still at work: pauperization and enrichment go hand in hand through social fractures, austerity policies and drastic cuts in public services, and coordinated campaigns against trade unions. These themes run through the chapters presented in this volume.

1

In the second introductory chapter, Mary Rawlinson demonstrates the dependence of a just state on meaningful work. She draws on Franklin D. Roosevelt's Four Freedoms speech, in which he identifies the right to work as fundamental to citizenship, health, and happiness. On this account, international community, security, and peace depend on the extent to which the right to work is realized within and among countries. Rawlinson draws on Nussbaum and Sen to qualify GDP as a meaningful measure of growth, arguing that it only becomes a meaningful measure when other variables like income distribution across race, class, and gender are put into the equation. The reality, however, is that growth of the global economy increases inequity and produces forced migration, as well as the dispossession of traditional homes, lands, and practices.

What the common measure of global economic growth—GDP—fails to count is the benefit of domestic and agricultural labor performed predominately by women. In Roosevelt's analysis, the valorization of moneymaking results in an alienation of destiny as citizens of a free republic. Rawlinson brings an analysis of how the alienation of destiny and disrespect for labor is gendered.

Rawlinson argues that the alienation of labor is inherently linked with the loss of respect for others: currently, education reproduces this alienation instead of preparing people for meaningful work. Globalization in its current form fails to produce and sustain the "international generosity" and transnational collaboration that Roosevelt foresaw as necessary to both global security and prosperity. For Roosevelt and Rawlinson, a more generalized prosperity depends not on a confidence in "free markets," but on a respect for labor.

CITIZENSHIP, DEMOCRACY, AND GLOBAL JUSTICE

The first part of the book contains chapters that examine the role and meaning of work for citizenship and democracy. Labor migration and cosmopolitanism both undermine nationally bounded understandings of how work and citizenship constitute democracy.

Franc Rottiers advances the proposition that, if the world is global, then participating in that global community is only possible if certain conditions are met. More precisely, you need to be a global citizen, and citizenship requires a subjectivity that is both participatory and acknowledged as contributing to the communal welfare. Rottiers argues there are not enough access points to this realm of participation and integration. His chapter can be read as a critique of what "work" and "contribution" are understood to be and an account of how restrictive definitions limit access to citizenship, and, thus, to justice.

The chapter by John Pearson analyses how different theories of global justice understand the role of trade unions. His chapter demonstrates how a failure of theories of global justice to appreciate the role of trade unions undermines debates about global justice. Pearson's method is to take the main positions one by one and to derive from these positions general concerns relating to the collective organization of labor. More precisely, specific rights, institutions, values and norms need to be in place for trade unions to function effectively in promoting social justice. He analyses communitarianism, social liberalism, liberal internationalism, and cosmopolitanism to show how a republican approach to collective organization might be developed to address the deficiencies of other approaches. One thing is clear from Pearson's account: theories of global justice and the debates around them cannot remain neutral with regard to countries' choices on the collective organization of labor. Theories must account for each country's need to fashion and implement industrial relations structures that match its traditions.

József Böröcz's chapter analyses what happens in terms of labor migration when these "traditions" of industrial relations are broken. He notes that a steadily growing proportion of the world's labor force crosses state boundaries and becomes immersed in the exploitation process in states with which they have no citizenship relation, so that the exploitation process is even more oppressive and abusive. More precisely, Böröcz shows how the experience of state socialist societies that have recently exited state socialism is relevant for discussions of global labor migration. The question guiding his analysis is the following: if the conditions of post-state-socialist labor are so deeply disadvantaged, and if opportunities of exit are so clearly available, then why is labor from the former-state-socialist states not "flooding" the labor markets of the European Union, the United States, and other wealthy economies? He looks at EU and US visa policies to answer this question, but also points out that the disintegration of the region's three federal states—Yugoslavia, Czechoslovakia, and the USSR—implied changes in rights, principles, and practices regarding citizenship. These changes had deep effects on labor, as they created noncitizen labor pools by administrative fiat. These people became labor migrants overnight, whilst having close familiarity with local conditions, excellent language skills, work skills and habits that are compatible with local customs, and extensive informal networks. Hence, they exhibit characteristics opposite to those of east European labor migrants in western Europe. This leads Böröcz to conclude that citizenship, or the denial of it, is a "perfect" structural condition for the transformation of fellow-citizens into undocumented "migrants."

JUSTICE ACROSS BORDERS?: MIGRATION AND TRAFFICKING IN THE GLOBAL ECONOMY

The chapters in the second part of this book deal explicitly with labor migration policies: regular labor migration, undocumented labor migration, and human trafficking.

For Patrick Loobuyck labor migration is—in ideal circumstances—a triple win for home countries, host countries, and migrants and their families. However, the real situation shows a stark difference from the ideal one. Labor migration can increase unemployment, create unfair competition, or distort the labor market otherwise. Migrants often end up in flexible or informal employment, working long hours for low wages. Controlled labor migration can avoid these negative consequences and make it work toward a more ideal picture. Loobuyck reviews the European labor migration policy after the EU enlargement of 2004. His analysis shows that the intentions of the EU on labor migration are in line with the minimal principle of justice, which stipulates that a policy should not make anyone worse off. However, one challenge for the future is to implement these intentions in concrete and effective policy measures. Another is to devise a more organized and corrective international policy to address the social-economic root causes of forced migration, through fair trade and redistribution. Also, perceptions of migration within the EU and its member states need to be brought in line with reality. Currently, member states see migration as a security threat, while Eurocrats seem to be more sympathetic toward migration, emphasizing the link between migrant rights and international development.

In her chapter for this book, Zahra Meghani takes up one form of labor migration, undocumented direct care workers (DCW) in the United States, and analyses how this group is treated from the perspective of the epistemic dimension of justice. She starts by identifying the key characteristics of the female undocumented DCW population and gives a brief account of the political, economic, and social factors that shape their decision to work in the United States. She argues that Benhabib's approach for addressing the problem of the unjust treatment of noncitizens—by disaggregating political rights from citizenship status and hence affording a political voice to noncitizen residents—may not be effective in liberal democracies such as the United States (or the European member states) where a "vision-distorting" type of nationalism is mainstream. Such a distorted vision creates the belief that their right to engage in self-determination as a democratic polity gives citizens the right to treat undocumented workers as falling outside local concepts of justice. Similar to Mill's understanding that the experience of living in a patriarchy has a corrupting influence on the character of males, Meghani argues that liberal democracy distorts both the vision of the oppressed and the self-understanding of those who benefit from the injustice. Meghani decodes these oppressive ideologies, showing their complicity with public democratic deliberations about what constitutes just treatment of undocumented workers. Her critique of nationalism and its interaction with other systems of oppression opens the way for a more just approach to undocumented workers.

Ramona Vijeyarasa's chapter analyses a particular system of oppression. Her chapter shows how victims of trafficking are not adequately represented by data on trafficking and, hence, how their labor exploitation remains hidden. The case study reveals the methodological challenges that determine both the scope of trafficking in Vietnam, as well as the socioeconomic characteristics of Vietnam's trafficked population. Vijeyarasa makes a number of recommendations for a more nuanced and accurate approach to data collection as a precondition for addressing the exploitation and global injustice involved in labor trafficking.

LABORING FOR JUSTICE: THE ROLE OF LABOR IN ACHIEVING SOCIAL EQUITY UNDER GLOBALIZATION

The third part of this book focuses on what the role of organized labor currently is or could be in order to achieve more social equity across borders.

Stephen Bouquin's chapter shows how French sociology systematically exaggerated and then discounted strategies of labor resistance. Bouquin argues that the role of unions in resistance to work is related to worker identity. Against contemporary depictions of labor as fragmented, self-interested, and lacking solidarity, Bouquin identifies productive points of resistance and diagnoses the blindness of theory and policy to the real capacities for solidarity.

Charles Umney follows with a chapter looking at the ambiguous relationship trade unions have with the concept of global justice. Unions may resemble global justice actors in the context of international framework agreements or corporate codes of conduct, but when looking at a more local level, it is not always possible to see how their actions are compatible with the notion of global justice. Umney does this exercise for British unions. He asks what the motivations for unions to act internationally are and what forms such activities take. Is internationalism motivated by material interests or by trade union norms? In any case, internationalism has often failed among grassroots union members and has remained consigned to union elites. Union members are more directly menaced by threats to employment conditions than their leaders; union officials on the other hand are committed to normative principles of workers' solidarity, transcending short-term interest representation. Umney finds that a union's capacity to fulfill the role of global justice actor reflects underlying material conditions. Union members caught up in multinational economic structures may find workers abroad to be a source of solidarity, but they may also represent a competition for jobs. Hence, internationalism will be fraught with tension. Strengthening international activity will be possible if international resources can be used to support local material disputes. Oddly enough, when organizational activity is not linked to international economic structures (e.g., in the public sector) and internationalism is hence of only limited interest to members, there might be more space to develop wide-ranging "global justice" programs at an elite level. Umney concludes, however, that internationalism in unions is always driven "from above."

The final chapter in this book, by Lefteris Kretsos, brings us back to where we started: the Juggernaut at full speed, or how austerity measures can be read as an intended and orchestrated strategy of pauperization. Kretsos discusses the impact of austerity policies (as a response to the Greek crisis) on living and working conditions. He points out the visible and nonvisible political dimensions of resistance to austerity politics. The crisis in Greece is a Greek manifestation of a global problem. Kretsos gives examples of new grassroots movements in Greece and argues how these can be Greek manifestations of a more global mobilization of workers.

CONCLUSION

Together these chapters attempt to transform debates around global ethics and global justice by demonstrating how the concept of labor and the formulation of labor practices and policies are central and essential to these debates. This agenda has three dimensions. First, these chapters question core concepts of global justice, such as citizenship and democracy, and show how these concepts must be reconfigured around a respect for labor. Second, these chapters clearly reveal the necessity of formulating cross-border policies from a labor perspective. Finally, the agenda of these chapters reveals how resistance or alternative globalizations can be organized through labor movements.

If the academic and policy debates of philosophers and other social scientists are to contribute to the creation of a more inclusive and equitable world, then their narratives and analyses, and the institutions in which they are presented, need to take labor and respect for labor as a focus of analysis. The chapters presented in this volume aim to show some ways in which this can be done.

Chapter One

Putting Labor on the Global Justice Agenda

The Juggernaut of Capital Accumulation and the Global Assault on Labor Standards

Ronald M. S. Commers

THE LABOR ISSUE IN GLOBAL ETHICS: A CRITIQUE

In surveying the domain of the admirable research and scientific communication efforts, and reflecting upon the worldwide "global ethics" movement from the last two decades of the twentieth century up till now, it appears to me that labor and work condition issues were and are somewhat underrated. It is beyond doubt that human rights are crucial to what one scholar recently has called "the work of global justice" (Kurasawa 2007).

Conferences on the subject are taken on with two approaches mainly. The first: an inventory of questions and issues concerning labor and employment, exploitation, work conditions, gender, trafficking, and bondage systems, all of them in relationship with economic globalization and the institutionalization of "global governance." The second: the search for a reasonable, realistic, general theory of decent work and fair trade, in relationship with the UN Millennium Development Goals and the related UN Development Programs, and the UN Global Compact.

The UN Global Compact, remarkably enough announced by UN Secretary-General Kofi Annan in his address to the World Economic Forum (Annan 1999), led to the international efforts to encourage capitalist economic

players (corporations, business sectors, industries, etc.) to commit themselves to normative principles such as: sustainability, social responsibility,
respect for human rights in work and employment situations, environmental
awareness, and anti-corruption. Concerning labor, four principles are mentioned (the principles 3, 4, 5, and 6):

• Freedom of association and the effective recognition of the right to collec-
  tive bargaining
• The elimination of all forms of forced and compulsory labor
• The effective abolition of child labor
• The elimination of discrimination in employment and occupation

Right from the start it was acknowledged that these principles couldn't have
any regulatory force. They were meant to be advice giving and are consultative only, lacking a legal framework to support the enforced application of
them.

   Nevertheless, in affirming these principles it was recognized that world
capitalism, going through its new globalization processes, was marked by the
old problems of the relationships between labor power and capital. I will
return to this semantic formula subsequently, insisting upon a more radical
view concerning the social power relationships worldwide, which are hidden
by what I consider to be a typical moralistic step in the globalization narratives.

   In advising the elimination of all forms of forced and compulsory labor,
one was affirming the existence of forms of forced and compulsory labor
worldwide. In recommending the effective abolition—and pay attention to
the adjective—of child labor, the Global Compact creators have confirmed
the continuing existence of child labor in different regions of the capitalist
world system. In counselling the freedom of association and the effective
recognition—again the adjective has been taken up—of the right to collective
bargaining, the Global Compact writers admit both the partial nonexistence
of a bargaining system and the current dispensing with existent bargaining
systems.

   Could that be stated more candidly than it was done? It is quite clear that
endemically something is going wrong in the capitalist world system. Ever
more this seems true as the system went into a new globalization period and
stage. Can our global ethical research be satisfied with justice discourses
based on the defense of human rights only? I doubt it. More is asked from us
in defense of global justice. Though theoretical efforts in terms of Global
Resources Dividend (see Pogge 1998), Global Distributive Justice (see Follesdal and Pogge 2005; Beitz 1973), Tobin Tax (Tobin 1978; Ul Haq et al.
1996), Fair Trade for All (Stiglitz 2006), and Global Citizenship (Habermas
1994; Meadows 1991; Dower 2003) have great value for all of us, yet it

might be doubted whether they are conclusive for a critical and constructive view on the normative approach of a fair world order.

Indirectly, the creators of the Global Compact admitted that it would not be enough. "If another world is possible" (cf. Stiglitz 2006), it will neither be reached by theoretical reflection on global distributive justice, nor by armchair proposals coming from academics and international organization officials considering the issues of corporate social responsibility and Global Compact. Again, though I am supportive of the moral sense underneath these endeavors, it is obvious to me that the most important issue is left out of the picture: labor exploitation under the conditions of recent globalization processes in world capitalism.

I agree with those who say that labor migration is not the first and foremost problem. Rather, it is the uncontrolled, unrestrained, and so to speak severe exploitation of workers, which confronts working people with massive existence problems. To command the respect of human rights and to stand up for citizenship should not be our only concern in putting forward a global ethics research agenda and program. We should direct attention toward the duty to ban by all legal means degrading labor exploitation mechanisms, which are triggered by the present-day globalization processes. Poverty is the consequence of these degrading labor exploitation mechanisms. To eradicate poverty means to deal with those worldwide labor exploitation mechanisms. Stated otherwise: our business should be to investigate the suppression of the one-sidedness in the social power relationships between labor and capital. Whatever our disquiet regarding rights and our uneasiness on the subject of fairness, the labor standard issue is pressing itself on to the forefront of our theoretical and practical concern.

WORLD CAPITALISM AND THE PROCESS OF PRIMITIVE ACCUMULATION OF CAPITAL

There is an issue, which time after time seems to worry international organizations: the world's failure to get rid once and for all of forced labor, bondage, and informal degrading work processes.

My question is: can world capitalism do without these primary—or primitive—forms of capital accumulation? I prefer to state this subject matter in concepts that are too easily forgotten. The answer to the question is negative. All along the history of world capitalism, forms of inappropriate profit realization reappeared. The fight against them is an endless one. It will go on as long as world capitalism is alive. This is not a pessimistic point of view. On the contrary, it is meant to be realistic, and I put it at the heart of my way to think ethics globally.

Consider what Vladimer Papava, a senior fellow of the Georgian Foundation for Strategic and International Studies in T'bilisi (Georgia), has to say on the question of transitional economy in a post-state-communist country:

> The corruption is a secondary phenomenon, because there are economic preconditions causing it. Unless the achievement of macroeconomic stability and the formation of the institutions appropriate to a market economy reach their logical ending, both of them may become the cause of corruption in the post-Communist transformation of the economy. In order to restrict corruption and establish the institution of private property, it is necessary to legalize the existing results of primary accumulation of capital, which will let it "act" in the public interest. Such an approach does not exclude the punishment of all the lawbreakers according to the law. (Papava 2006)

History repeats itself, so it seems, when we tag along Papava in his candidly stated diagnosis. Regulating and legitimating primitive (or primary) mechanisms of profit making, in order to achieve a regular and legalized capitalist accumulation process, that is what this former minister of economy and member of parliament of Georgia "explains" and defends "in the public interest." Ideology never lies. In the veneration of economic reality, ideology reveals the delusions of human belief.

For the idea of the ever-ongoing processes of primitive (or primary) accumulation of capital—what refers to an offensive and criminal profit realization and a reprehensible reproduction of capital—we may rely on the analysis of the Marxist scholar Ernest Mandel. In *Der Spätkapitalismus*, one of his major contributions to Marxist political economy, he writes that primitive accumulation is part of the "uneven and combined development" of world capitalism. Even in the core of the capitalist system, phenomena of blameworthy profit making are by and by reappearing, whereas in the so-called developing countries they play their terrorizing role. Throughout these mechanisms of capital reproduction and the related phenomena, the profit realization properly speaking can continue its process securely. Without bribery, corruption, unashamed privatization, land confiscation, robbery of local agricultural means and areas, and last but not least, forced labor, bondage, child and women exploitation (both in domestic work and sex work), this proper profit realization cannot proceed in world capitalism today.

Scholars who investigate the intricate relationship between free labor and forced labor have put forward the very similar idea. Not only "there," in the so-called undeveloped countries, but also "here" at the center of world capitalism, proper and improper accumulation of capital carry on side by side. It is mere illusion to think that in the rich West, people are set free from what wrongly is considered as a transitory phase of so-called "primitive" profit realization. Time and again, primary accumulation processes are started up and continue to give the basis for the actual accumulation of capital, by means of more regular profit-making activities.

As critical scholars have argued, the aggressive expansion of capitalist profit making goes hand in hand with a seemingly legitimated profit making. Primitive accumulation resembles a Dracula, who together with the naïve vampire killer victoriously rides the coach from the woodlands to London town, to refer to Roman Polansky's motion picture *The Vampire Killers.*

The compulsory expansion of capitalist markets seldom stands equal with forced labor, slavery, bondage, particularly debt bondage, child and women labor, and migratory labor. This is probably what Mandel meant by the simultaneity of "original accumulation of capital" and "actual accumulation of capital" (Mandel 1972, 42–69):

> We are thus dealing with a double process, and the two sides of this process have to be combined if we are to understand both the genesis and subsequent self-development of capital. Primitive accumulation of capital and capital accumulation through the production of surplus-value are, in other words, not merely successive phases of economic history but also concurrent economic processes. Throughout the entire history of capitalism up to the present, processes of primitive accumulation have constantly coexisted with the predominant form of capital accumulation. (Mandel 1998, 46)

More recently, in his *Historical Capitalism*, Immanuel Wallerstein has drawn attention to the concurrence of the two types of capital accumulation process in recent history of world capitalism. He thereby recalls the "law" Rosa Luxemburg had phrased in her book *The Accumulation of Capital.* Only when no more domains for surplus-value production (profit making) are left, historically capitalism will fail at last. But in the long historical interval we are going through, capitalists will seek eagerly to regain the lost terrain, either by pushing large parts of population into misery, bondage, and brutal slavery, if necessary, or by lowering the standards of living and of labor at the center of the system. Concentration camps in Nazi Germany were an example of the former. Today, we see how somewhat corresponding types of human labor exploitation reappear and persist in China, in North and South Korea, in Indonesia. Perhaps this was what Marx meant when he foresaw either a noncapitalist future for mankind or barbarity.

THE PERSISTENCE OF INAPPROPRIATE LABOR EXPLOITATION IN WORLD CAPITALISM: FACT OR FICTION?

Daily we can read in the newspapers how unacceptable labor exploitation measures are implemented. The evidence is growing. The consequences for working people are disastrous. Today we are not only facing massive unemployment and irreversible impoverishment, but also the total collapse of people's *Lebenswelt*.

September 2012, Spanish and international newspapers reported that the impoverishment of the Spanish laboring people has increased to such a degree that house eviction has become a daily custom. They reported how Spanish workers nowadays consider the living conditions to be better in Mali, while Muslim fundamentalist militia terrorizes this African country by persecuting their opponents and instituting sharia law. Pauperization provokes a wave of suicide in Madrid and elsewhere in the country, anytime people do not see an exit for their misery and poverty. Yet people from the lower and middle classes are not exempt from this despair, when they also are left without financial resources to pay their mortgage debts whilst the banks threaten to sell their houses.

In the intervening time rich people in France are changing residence from their country to Belgium, a country considered by them as a tax paradise. Social and fiscal "incivism" is becoming the rule among the wealthier citizens, as their reaction to a more equal fiscal policy is to escape tax paying. A Belgian newspaper reports that in 2012 a Brussels-located real estate office sells one luxury stay each day to French rich people. Their peers legally advise them: lawyers, notaries, and investment bankers. The report speaks of six hundred to two thousand clients on a monthly basis.

All over Europe social fracture can no longer be denied. Exactly as it was in the nineteenth-century and the twentieth-century interwar period, the law of capital accumulation works in such a way that pauperization and enrichment go together in an inversely proportional way. Social exclusion is well organized to the advantage of the wealthiest, all the way through international governance institutions like IMF, World Bank, and OECD. Governments are pushed toward austerity measures by cutting into social security and public services, and by attacking trade union organizations and basic labor rights. This equals a massive economic and social drawback, at the loss of the laboring classes globally.

It is not mistaken to write that the Juggernaut of capital accumulation once more wheels undisturbed (see below for this amazing concept). September 2012 the organization Students and Scholars against Corporate Misbehavior (SACOM) reported on the labor conditions in the Chinese Foxconn Corporation. Foxconn produces components for Apple products (such as the iPhone). The workers are facing harsh working conditions. These include excessive and unpaid overtime, meager wages, arbitrary relocation of labor force, occupational health and safety problems, inhumane management practices, and crackdown on strikes. It is exemplar for the unequivocal affirmation of the "absolute exploitation rate" mechanism, which Marx described in the first volume of his *Capital*. Corporations do not hesitate to advance into the direction of a global diminishing of labor costs, despite the fact that workers cannot meet their needs and aren't able to support their families. In China, workers are recruited throughout the country. They are obliged to leave the countryside to go to live in the cities, where the industrial plants are situated. They are housed in huge buildings with communal sleeping rooms. The management decides on their private and social time and existence, for the workers cannot escape the subjecting corporate requirements, which accompany the global mechanism of capital accumulation.

It is often observed that even at the center of the capitalist world system, degrading forms of labor exploitation have not disappeared. Time and again these humiliating forms of exploitation reappear in the process of capital accumulation. In 2011, the British newspaper the *Guardian* reported that Marks and Spencer's, Next, Ralph Lauren, DKNY, Gap, Converse, Banana Republic, Land's End, and Levi's do have something in common. They all rely on sweatshop labor internationally. They are responsible for shocking working practices, to which most of the time female workers are obliged to earn their living and that of their families.

Undoubtedly, these practices are mostly widespread in countries such as the Philippines, Indonesia, and Sri Lanka. Nevertheless, allegedly forced labor is also used in the United States of America, such as both Steven Fraser (of the *New Labor Forum*, author of *Wall Street: America's Dream Palace*) and Joshua B. Freeman (author of *American Empire*) described in discussing the return of prisoners' penal labor. With 2.3 million prisoners, the United States holds 25% of all the prisoners on the planet. On a website, commenting on Fraser's and Freeman's observations, we can read what follows:

> What began in the 1970s as an end run around the laws prohibiting convict leasing by private interests has now become an industrial sector in its own right, employing more people than any Fortune 500 corporation and operating in 37 states. And here's the ultimate irony: our ancestors found convict labor obnoxious in part because it seemed to prefigure a new and more universal form of enslavement. Could its rebirth foreshadow a future ever more unnervingly like those past nightmares?
>
> Today, we are being reassured by the president, the mainstream media, and economic experts that the Great Recession is over, that we are in "recovery" even though most of the recovering patients haven't actually noticed significant improvement in their condition. For those announcing its arrival, "recovery" means that the mega-banks are no longer on the brink of bankruptcy, the stock market has made up lost ground, corporate profits are improving, and notoriously unreliable employment numbers have improved by several tenths of a percent.
>
> What accounts for that peculiarly narrow view of recovery, however, is that the general costs of doing business are falling off a cliff as the economy eats itself alive. The recovery being celebrated owes thanks to local, state, and Federal austerity budgets, the starving of the social welfare system and public services, rampant anti-union campaigns in the public and private sector, the

spread of sweatshop labor, the coercion of desperate unemployed or underem-
ployed workers to accept lower wages, part-time work, and temporary work,
as well as the relinquishing of healthcare benefits and a financially secure
retirement—in short, to surrender the hope that is supposed to come with the
American franchise.

Such a recovery, resting on the stripping away of the hard won material
and cultural achievements of the past century, suggests a new world in which
the prison-labor archipelago could indeed become a vast gulag of the down-
wardly mobile. (Fraser and Freeman 2012)

If this were true, we are obliged to acknowledge that forced and slave labor
still remains the outspoken tool for an improper—primary—capital accumulation process going hand in hand with the regular and genuine accumulation
of capital. A 2011 report in the *Guardian* says, "Sweatshops are still supplying high street brands," and "[T]hings seem to be getting worse, rather than
better. Employment is becoming more precarious as more workers are put on
to temporary contracts, day labor, on call" (Bunting 2011). It gives employers the means to impose compulsory overtime, lower wages and higher production targets on workers. Certainly this has been going on for almost three
decades in poor countries, but surprisingly, nowadays it is progressing at the
center of the capitalist world system.

The German weekly *Der Spiegel* reported, September 2012, that Germans
fear poverty after a life of work:

> Von der Leyden, a member of Chancellor Angela Merkel's conservative
> Christian Democratic Union (CDU), released data showing that, in two
> decades, the statutory pension will only be enough to guarantee a life on the
> edge of poverty, even for average earners. To make matters worse, what Ger-
> mans have managed to save during the course of their working lives is in
> danger of evaporating in the chaos of the global financial and debt crises. (Boll
> et al. September 2012)

All this goes together with the decline of earnings in the sector of the "so-
called low-wage sector, which includes poorly paid seasonal work, bogus
'self-employment' schemes and 'mini-jobs' which allow people to work
part-time and earn a limited amount of money without paying taxes or social
security contributions" (Boll et al. September 2012). The same laboring people are further endangered by political measures to combat the so-called
social fraud. The *Der Spiegel* report says:

> [T]here is a rising number of low-wage earners. There are now some 8 million
> German employees who work for an hourly wage of less than 9.15 €, as
> revealed by a study conducted by the Duisburg-based Institute for Work, Skills
> and Training (IAQ). Researchers found that 1.4 million employees even
> earned less than 5 € an hour in Germany, which has no statutory federal
> minimum wage [*sic*]. Figures from the German government's new report on

provisions for old age, to be published in November, show that of the roughly 25 million employees in the country between the ages of 25 and 65 who make social security contributions, more than 4.2 million earn a gross monthly salary of less than 1,500 €. This only entitles these individuals to the legally guaranteed basic social security.

Despite the fact that people recently are working more, they are earning less, and it is quite clear that there is yet no end to the tunnel. Working conditions and earnings are further deteriorating, even in Germany, afflicting increasingly those who are obliged to accept low-qualified labor as a consequence of the unemployment perspective. As a result, "the gap between wages of people with good and bad qualifications has grown in recent years" (Boll et al. April 2012):

> [T]his growing chasm between the top and the bottom is not only growing in Germany, but also in many countries across the world, according to organizations such as the International Monetary Fund (IMF) and the Organization for Economic Cooperation and Development (OECD).

UNMASKING THE "LOGIC" OF LABOR EXPLOITATION VS. MORALIZING THE MISERY OF LABOR CONDITIONS: TWO FACES OF THE JUGGERNAUT OF GLOBAL CAPITAL ACCUMULATION

In the nineteenth century, Charles Dickens wrote about similar labor conditions to which the working poor of his time were subjected. He himself experienced these conditions. Still a young boy, he was obliged to work in the Warren's Blacking Factory (Hungerford Stairs, in the neighborhood of Charing Cross Railway Station) following the debt imprisonment of his father. One author correctly perceived the coincidence of Dickens's and Marx's writings on the consequences of capitalist accumulation. He did so in his paper "Capitalism with a Conscience":

> Both Dickens and Marx observed the aches and pains, the groaning and suffering of an industrializing Europe . . . Both could see that capitalism without a conscience was a cultural dead-end that would lead the masses into alienation from each other and the world around. (Garber 2010)

Facing an obvious similar misery today, Steven Garber, surprisingly, preferred a spiritual escape, proudly asserting that "eventually I was drawn even more so into a vision of the kingdom of God" (Garber 2010). Whether this would have comforted a strongly moralizing novelist, such as Dickens, remains doubtful. Yet the resemblance, Garber noted, between Marx's and Dickens's observations, and the contemporary meaning of it for our reshaping the language of labor and global justice today, is cautionary. That is why I used the expression of the Juggernaut, which Marx introduced in his unravelling the process of capital accumulation.

For Karl Marx labor force is a commodity, which is the very expression of the worker's own life—a life activity sold to anyone who can and will come up with the money for it, a person who intends to use labor force the way he or she likes. For the worker, Marx further explained, this life activity is but a means of securing his own existence. What he brings forth—a service or a product—is for him not the aim of the activity. The aim is securing his life. After he has done so, time and again, the worker goes free.

This is what makes the difference between the worker as an owner of labor power and the slave who belongs to the person who makes use of the slave's labor power. Additionally Marx developed this idea:

> The worker leaves the capitalist to whom he has sold himself—understood as: his life activity—as often as he chooses, and the capitalist discharges him as often as he sees fit, as soon as he no longer gets any use . . . But the worker, whose only source of income is the sale of his labor power, cannot leave the whole class of buyers . . . unless he gives up his own existence. He does not belong to this or that buyer, but belongs to a group, a class. (Marx 1993 [1891])

This is the way the relationship between wage labor and capital works. This relationship, from a general point of view, is a socially embedded power bond. In particular situations and contexts of power distribution, the relationship varies over time and place. Depending on supply and demand, the price of the labor power will vary. Within the limits of the fluctuations, the price of labor power will be determined by the cost of producing the labor power. And what is the cost of producing it, other than the cost required for the maintenance of the worker as a worker, including the cost for his training and instruction as a worker.

Marx added something dreadfully clear:

> [T]he shorter the time required for training up to a particular sort of work, the smaller is the cost of production of the worker, the lower is the price of his labor power, his wages. In those branches of economic activity and business in which hardly any period of apprenticeship is necessary and the mere bodily existence of the worker is sufficient, the cost of his production is limited almost exclusively to what is necessary for keeping him in working condition . . . the necessary means of subsistence. (Marx 1993 [1891])

This is true each time the conditions determining the relationship between wage labor and capital is so that there is plethora of labor power. Whenever scarcity of labor power or when the power relationship between wage labor and capital is at the advantage of the bargaining position of labor power, capital can benefit in seeking new reservoirs of labor power.

> And here again, the author comes up with a lucid observation:
> The minimum price for labor power—the minimum wage— . . . does not hold good for the single individual, but only for the species. Individual workers, indeed, millions of workers, do not receive enough to be able to exist and to propagate themselves; but the prices for the labor power of the whole working class adjust themselves . . . to this minimum. (Ibid.)

In fact, this is what is meant by the expression "power relationships between wage labor and capital."

Karl Marx gave a sharp analysis of the dominant socioeconomic power relationship early in his 1847 lectures for the Association des Ouvriers Allemands de Bruxelles, afterward brought out as articles in the *Neue Rheinische Zeitung* (dated 1848). His close collaborator and friend, Friedrich Engels, published the collected articles in a booklet, *Lohnarbeit und Kapital*, and he translated the text in English (*Wage Labor and Capital*). In further developing the theme and the analysis in his major work, *Capital*, volume 1, chapter 23, "The General Law of Capitalist Accumulation," Marx used the metaphor of the Juggernaut.

Marx explains how in part IV of *Capital* he analyzed the production of relative surplus value within the capitalist system. He gives a list of the consequences for the working people. I summarize his rather austere description in what follows (for which I base myself on his text of which an English-speaking person can find a good translation on the website I mentioned, 1973, 1995):

a. Methods to raise the labor productiveness are brought at the cost of the worker.
b. The means necessary for the development of production are measures of domination over those who produce, the workers.
c. These measures degrade the worker personally, making him an attachment of the machinery employed in the process of production.
d. They destroy what is left of the work-pleasure, the proper enjoyment in being a creative person.
e. They turn the work into detested toil, something one wants to get rid of by all means when the occasion presents itself.
f. They alienate him from human intellection, in pace with the instrumentalization of scientific wisdom, intellection and wisdom both essentially linked with human creative activity.
g. These measures transform the worker's personal existence into labor time.

h. ". . . and they drag his wife and child under *the wheels of the Jugger-naut of Capital.*"

He concludes:

> [T]hat is the way capital is accumulated (on a worldwide scale), whereby the extension of the accumulation process equals the speeding up of the *Jugger-naut*. In the same way, the accumulation process of capital brings forward the growth of misery. At one pole, the advance of wealth; at the opposite pole, the accumulating increase of misery, toil, slavery, ignorance, brutality, and mental degradation.

At the very onset of this worldwide expansion of the accumulation process, early modern political economists (from the Venetian monk Ortes, to the cameralist Heinrich von Storch, and the Swiss-born Jean Charles Léonard Sismondi) vindicated this process. In the somewhat exaggerated view of Marx, they glorified human misery, which they thought beneficial for the development of wealth. The Church of England parson Joseph Towsend, anticipating the thoughts of Thomas Malthus on poor relief, called establishing hunger and poverty beneficial for the economic progress of the nation. He considered it "a natural motive for industry," writes Marx, for he spoke of "a law of nature that keeps the poor improvident." And Marx goes on ridiculing this Methodist political economy in writing that God and Nature are collaborating in a friendly manner to get the capitalist nation rid of the Poor Laws, or of any other legal confinement of the accumulation process, to the profit of the wealthy few. He writes: "Finally Destutt de Tracy, the fish-blooded bourgeois doctrinaire, blurts out brutally: 'In poor nations the people are comfortable, in rich nations they are generally poor'" (Marx 1973, 674–677; see also 1995).

It is well-known that the metaphor has been used repeatedly thereafter, emptying its meaning and referential quality. While Marx was indicating a concrete social process of exploitation and alienation—partly granted by his contemporary Charles Dickens, the moralizing novelist of the Victorian Age—sociologists today are using the metaphor far more vaguely and am-biguously (without reference made to Marx). It even entered literature and the entertainment industry.

Is it not frightening that today, as a consequence of the deep crises of the capitalist world system, the Juggernaut, Marx depicted, is wheeling again at full speed? I would like to answer the question in the affirmative. Further-more, I there see the necessity of a radical conceptual change in dealing with global justice matters in relationship with human labor. In the above sections, I primarily tried to outline a background for such an urgent conceptual shift. I now turn to some concluding remarks on this latter issue.

CONCLUSION: FROM RIGHTS TO DUTIES

Early in 2009 the North-South Movement Belgium (also called the 11.11.11 nongovernmental organization) started an action program, "Work in Dignity." The organizers did not use the "fairness" concept. They preferred to speak in terms of dignity instead. At the 2009 Center for Ethics and Value Inquiry Conference, various speakers, among them Christien van den Anker and Steve French, requested a far-reaching concept change. Concept change in the global justice discourse is part of my methodological and epistemological endeavors. In the approach of justice issues related to labor exploitation, such a drastic semantic shift might be brought forward by the substitution of duty concepts for right concepts. Corporations do have duties, and decent work expectations shouldn't be formulated in terms of rights of the workers only. They should be devised and expressed in terms of the duties large companies, multinationals, and of governments (which are acting to the advantage of big business) have toward stakeholders and working people. To make these duties compulsory undoubtedly will be the subject of political and social power relationships. But by stating them unequivocally and straightforwardly, we will bring forward profiles and formats to facilitate coordinated social action, both on a national and a transnational scale, not to forget the local level.

In the defense of dignity prior to fairness, and duties in advance of rights, we might effect a necessary change in the action and policy of trade unions and local community organizations. The rights and fairness discourses have a prominent "defensive" import. It is, metaphorically speaking, begging for little pieces of bread, whereas people should petition for their full part of growth and development.

Dignity- and duty-centered discourses might lead us to additional "offensive" (or assaulting) allegation, which on its turn can lead us to more conflicting action research perspectives. On this subject, I respond to Christien van den Anker for asking a sweeping change in the content and method of global ethics, though I would like to go even further than she already urged us to do. I am not suggesting that a semantic of human rights is worthless. I only assert that the almost exclusive emphasis on rights instead of duties is obstructive to restate a refreshing and enlarged global ethics agenda.

When the writers of the "Work in Dignity" program of the North-South movement called for decency, they grasped the importance of such a conceptual change. Collective bargaining, social dialogue, recognition of the self-organization of the workers, recognition of the democratic representation in trade unions and local community action groups, social protection in cases of illness, unemployment: they all refer to the duties the buyers of the labor force have when they act in the worldwide labor market. Corporations, companies, and the political institutions have the duty to stop the "race to the bottom." The "race to the bottom" stands for the ongoing downgrading of labor standards in the capitalist world system. Today all this seems even more important as we are confronted with a deep economic crisis in the capitalist world economy and with the rebirth of the severe worldwide impoverishment of large groups of people. Listening to governments, conservative and liberal newspapers, professional company organisms, and CEOs, invariably we can hear the same thing: the cost of labor must be lowered. Labor cost stands for the cost companies are forced to spend on salaries. The argument consistently sounds like this: to stay competitive on the world market of capitalist goods, salaries must go down. Worldwide we can hear this same complaint uttered by businessmen, shareholder corporations, and company executives. They chuck it down over the heads of people who are obliged to sell their labor force to capitalist organizations in order to acquire the means of existence both for themselves and their families.

But is this well-organized universal weeping not wide of the mark? If all of them, whether in the United States, or in Germany, in Brazil or in Japan, do have complaints on the subject of their competitive status, under the assumed free market conditions, aren't they stirring up a worldwide deterioration of the working people's part in "the wealth of nations"? And aren't they herewith promising capital owners an ever-greater part in society's riches?

To conclude, let us get closer again to what happens in Europe nowadays. In the progressing extinction of industrial activities in the European Union, many a company CEO proudly acknowledges that new industrial plants are to be constructed outside the European Union. Seemingly a paradox, for the explanation repeatedly is as candid as can be: the general overcapacity of the buyers' market, while the markets are displaced from the Union countries to Far-Eastern countries, to Russia, to India, and to Brazil, where only the labor costs and logistic expenses are far less than in Europe. Obviously this, and not so much the overcapacity, is the main reason for closing down factories and for displacing industrial plants from the Western countries toward former third-world regions. The displacement operations are shamelessly related to a seemingly justified general degradation of the standards of living of laboring people worldwide.

In my opinion, all this blocked the way to the effective execution and accomplishment of the rather ill-conceived program of the Millennium Development Goals. Global Justice, if it means anything comprehensible, obvious, and appealing, should be linked with a challenging labor agenda. The "wealth of nations," unquestionably, will remain empty and insincere, as long as the fulfilment of decent labor standards in the whole of the world economy has not been guaranteed. The set of eight aims to eradicate poverty is from this point of view a big lie. That this is not an exaggeration is proven by the fact that the United Nations itself took a different direction from 2005 onward, after having ascertained that the Millennium Development Goals could not be accomplished. From that time on, their executives and administrators recognized the importance of labor issues for these goals.

BIBLIOGRAPHY

Annan, Kofi. 1999. "Secretary-General Proposes Global Compact on Human Rights, Labor, Environment." World Economic Forum, Davos, January 31.

Beitz, Charles. 1973. *Political Theory and International Relations*. Princeton: Princeton University Press.

Boll, Sven, and Sebastion Brauns, Markus Dettmer, et al. 2012. Trans. Paul Cohen. "Penson Armageddon: Germans Fear Poverty Even After Life of Work." *The Guardian*, September 13. Available at: http://www.spiegel.de/international/germany/germans-fear-poverty-in-retirement-even-after-life-of-work-a-855352.html.

Boll, Sven, Markus Dettmer, Catalina Schroder, Janko Tietz, and Florian Zerfass. 2012. Trans. Christopher Sultan. "The High Cost of Germany's Economic Success." *Der Spiegel*, April 13. Available at: http://www.spiegel.de/international/business/german-labor-reforms-create-greater-gap-between-rich-and-poor-a-830972.html, part I, "The High Cost of Germany's Economic Success."

Bunting, Madeleine. 2011. "Sweatshops Are Still Supplying High Street Brands." *The Guardian*, April 28. Accessed at: http://www.theguardian.com/global-development/povertymatters/2011/apr/28/sweatshops-supplying-high-street-brands.

Dower, Nigel. 2003. *An Introduction to Global Citizenship*. Edinburgh: Edinburgh University Press.

Follesdal, Andreas, and Thomas Pogge (eds.). 2005. *Real World Justice: Grounds, Principles, Human Rights, and Social Institutions*. New York: Springer.

Fraser, Steve, and Joshua B. Freeman. 2012. "Sweatshop Labor Is Back with a Vengence." *Mother Jones*, http://www.motherjones.com/.

Garber, Steven. 2010. "Capitalism with a Conscience." *The Washington Institute*, http://www.washingtoninst.org/.

Habermas, Jürgen. 1994. "Citizenship and National Identity: Some Reflections on the Future of Europe." In *The Condition of Citizenship*, ed. Bart van Steenbergen. New York: Sage Publications.

Kurasawa, Fuyuki. 2007. *The Work of Global Justice: Human Rights as Practices*. Cambridge University Press.

Mandel, Ernest. 1972. *Der Spätkapitalismus*, II. Kapitel. Frankfurt am Main: Suhrkamp.

———. 1998. *Late Capital*. New York: Verso.

Marx, Karl. 1962. *Travail salarié et capital*. Paris: Editions Sociales.

———. 1973. Das Kapital. *Kritik der politischen Ökonomie*. Berlin: Dietz Verlag.

———. 1993 [1891]. *Wage Labor and Capital*. Trans. Frederick Engels. Available at Marxist Internet Archive, www.marxists.org .

———. 1995 [1887]. *Capital*. Trans. Samuel Moore and Edward Aveling. Marxist Internet Archive. www.marxists.org.

Meadows, Donella H. 1991. *The Global Citizen*. Washington DC: Island Press.

Papava, Vladimer. 2006. "Corruption and Primary Accumulation of Capital in Transitional Economies." Available at http://www.papava.info/PapavaEng.html.

Pogge, Thomas. 1998. "A Global Resources Dividend." In *Ethics of Consumption: The Good Life, Justice, and Global Stewardship*, ed. D. Crocker and T. Linden. New York: Rowman & Littlefield, 501–536.

Stiglitz, Joseph. 2006. *Making Globalization Work*. New York: W. W. Norton and Company.

Tobin, James. 1978. "A Proposal for International Monetary Reform." *Eastern Economic Journal* (Eastern Economic Association): 153–159. Retrieved January 31, 2010.

Ul Haq, Maqub, Inge Kaul, and Isabelle Grunberg. 1996. *The Tobin Tax: Coping with Financial Volatility*. Oxford: Oxford University Press.

Chapter Two

Meaningful Work

Labor, Gender, and Justice after Globalization

Mary C. Rawlinson

On January 6, 1941, eleven months before the bombing of Pearl Harbor, with Hitler in possession of Europe, imperialism expanding around the globe from South Asia and China to Latin America, and the massacre of six million Jews well underway, Franklin Roosevelt delivered an unprecedented third inaugural address to a US Congress and a country that still hoped to avoid going to war against fascism and Nazism. A people, with a tradition of noninvolvement, who sent soldiers to the distant slaughter of World War I only to see the same corrupt imperialist and colonialist powers arise again afterward, like a reshuffled deck, might not be inclined toward a new involvement in international affairs, in Europe or anywhere else. A people who had barely begun to emerge from what would prove to be the worst economic catastrophe of their century might be forgiven for being unready to assume the costs and rigors of war, however necessary the cause. A politician, calculating votes, might have been expected to talk of peace and the need for negotiation or to strike an isolationist tone by focusing on domestic issues, assuming a silence on international affairs that Roosevelt's contemporaries would have found neither unusual, nor disturbing.

Instead, in what has come to be known as the Four Freedoms speech, Roosevelt announces a moment "unique" in American history, when "our actions and our policies" should be devoted "exclusively" to foreign affairs, "[f]or all our domestic problems are now a part of the great emergency" (Roosevelt 1965). The speech foresees a globalized world, which, Roosevelt insists, is coming in some form, no matter what. Isolationism will be impossible. The survival of the American Republic, Roosevelt argues, will depend on the character of the relations that bind it to foreign powers.

Roosevelt foresees, on the one hand, the "dictator's peace" in which "law lacks mutuality in its observance," and, therefore, becomes an "instrument of oppression" in a world without freedom of expression or religion. The aggressive tyrant who rules by fear and violence waits only for a tactical advantage to launch his attack. Roosevelt reinscribes the unsteady peace Americans hoped to sustain as unreadiness before an inevitable assault. As Hobbes argued, a state of war exists, even without actual conflict, when the *disposition to fight* makes war inevitable (Hobbes 1996, 88–89). Peace is impossible with tyrants and dictators because they will always resort to force to secure their authority and interest. Roosevelt tells his listeners not only that they must go to war, but that they are already at war in all but the formal declaration and actual attack.

On the other hand, he lays out a "vision" for Congress and the American people of genuine peace. Roosevelt reimagines basic infrastructures of life in America in order to secure the health and happiness of its citizens. In his vision, justice, as well as security and freedom, depend on full employment and on securing the conditions under which each citizen can flourish in meaningful work. Issuing a call to action, he articulates a list of specific policies that need to be enacted in order to free citizens from fear, so that they are free for the "joy" of meaningful work.

Roosevelt locates these domestic concerns, however, in an international frame. A republic of free citizens, if it wishes to survive, must seek a world of other such free republics. The "antithesis" of the world of tyranny, where power sustains itself through fear, propaganda, and violence, a community of free nations exists on "international generosity" and constitutes "the return of true independence." The realization of this world of free nations bound by reciprocity and respect depends, Roosevelt argues, on the achievement of full employment "everywhere in the world." From his first inaugural address in 1933, Roosevelt develops an analysis of work as the locus of freedom and happiness. Collaborating toward a world where everyone has an equal opportunity to find the "joy of achievement" in meaningful work, Roosevelt insists, is not only necessary to international security and liberty, it is "even good business."

GLOBAL INEQUITY: INVISIBLE LABOR, BLIND CONSUMERS, AND THE MYTH OF THE "FREE MARKET"

Michael Pollan argues that if "consumers" in the United States knew how their food was produced, they would not eat it (Pollan 2006, 244–245). Consumer "ignorance" features as an essential ingredient in the business model of industrial agriculture. A similar blindness proves essential to labor practices under globalization.

To some degree, the exposure of abusive labor conditions, as well as related catastrophes and loss of life, puts pressure on large global corporations to improve labor practices in developing countries like Bangladesh or China. What remains invisible to the consumer in the smartphone or clothing that he purchases is that the exploitation of cheap labor in emerging economies is essential to globalization, not an exceptional circumstance that might be remedied. Invisible in these products as well is the evisceration under globalization of the postwar contract between labor, business, and the state that yielded unprecedented increases in social equity and mobility in the United States and Europe.

The cheaper products touted by globalization as its chief justification regularly hide costs, both to the health and security of labor and to the environment. Global agribusiness, for example, justifies itself by its cheap prices, at the same time that it aggressively hides its conditions of production. In the United States, agribusiness has successfully lobbied to block investigative reporting on CAFOs (concentrated animal feeding operations) and other industrialized animal farming operations so that the public is uniformed about the maltreatment of animals, as well as the serious environmental risks posed by these operations (Paulson 2013). The health threat posed by the wide use of antibiotics in industrial animal operations is not visible in the consumer's burger. The threat to the environment from agribusiness's reliance on artificially cheap and highly polluting fossil fuel consumed in producing its fertilizers and in its transportation is not visible in the consumer's fast food. Consumers see only the immediate price tag, and the real costs of globalized production, to labor, to the environment, and to citizens' health, remain invisible. Due to this blindness, the citizen becomes complicit in the very system that exploits him, both as consumer and as labor.

In both developing and developed countries, globalization has produced widening social inequity. The structural inequity associated with globalization results not from differences in individual effort or talent, but from features of the economic and political systems themselves, which favor the concentration of privilege and wealth. Hobbes described money as the "ensanguination" of the body politic: it must circulate freely to all members if the body is to be healthy. The contemporary global financial system thrives on a metaphorics of free circulation. Its markets, however, favor capital, not labor, so that a very small percentage of the population owns a rapidly increasing share of resources. In the United States 35.4% of wealth is owned by the top 1%. The bottom 80% own 11.1% of wealth. The wealth of the bottom 80% has decreased by 7.7% since 1983 (Wolff 2012). In 2006 the United Nations' World Institute for Development Economics Research reported that 10% of the world's population owns 85% of its wealth, while the poorest 50% own just 1%. "Free" markets are, in fact, highly regulated and subsidized to serve this concentration of capital and are accessible only to privilege. Ordinary citizens, who have been led to think of themselves as "investors," have neither the information nor the scale of capital to compete successfully in these markets. [1]

Public policy analysis that relies on macroeconomic indicators operates at a scale under which the real effects of policy on ordinary citizens remain invisible. Measures of GNP may indicate "growth," but they are sufficiently aggregate to hide concentrations of privilege and wealth or increases in social inequity. As Martha Nussbaum remarks, the GNP "fails to provide an adequate basis for normative thinking in large part because it is not individualistic enough: it does not look at people one by one to see how each one is doing" (Nussbaum 2000, 65; Baudrillard 1998). Macroeconomic indicators or analyses that focus on aggregated classes or social units make invisible the real conditions of experience for specific individuals. In treating the family as a basic social unit and basing evaluations of welfare on its economy, public policy and economic analysis can remain blind both to the systematic deprivations women may endure in the family structure (less food, less education, less health care) and to the positive contributions of their labor to the welfare of the family and community.

Drawing a distinction between development and growth, Amartya Sen argues that, while an expansion of GNP, other things being equal, should enhance the living conditions of people, there are in fact always other variables that determine those conditions. Things are never equal. Growth under globalization is rarely distributed equally across income groups. "It is possible . . . for a country to have an expansion of GNP per head while its distribution becomes more unequal, possibly even the poorest groups going down absolutely in terms of their own real incomes." Sen notes the necessity for looking at income distributions in relation to racial, regional, and class groups, a list to which sexual difference should be added, as Sen acknowledges elsewhere (Sen 2008, 161–162). The growth of the global economy both increases inequity and inflicts heavy costs on the least well off, such as displacement or forced migration and the dispossession of traditional homes, lands, and practices. [2]

Sen also demonstrates how many benefits and costs remain invisible to the market. He notes the lack of recognition of environmental costs or the underpricing of natural resources in market calculations. He might also have noted the failure to count the benefit of domestic and agricultural labor performed predominately by women. This labor remains invisible to GNP and other macroeconomic indicators. As Vandana Shiva argues,

> Growth in the global economy has led to the destruction of nature's economy—through which environmental regeneration takes place. It has also destroyed the people's sustenance economy—within which women work to sus-

tain society. Ironically, this hard, unpaid labor is frequently denied the name of work. (Shiva 2005)

The degradation of nature's generativity and the invisibility and discounting of the generative labor of women are not separate problems, but symptoms of the same biopolitical structure of inequity. In Shiva's analysis, macroeconomic actors, such as the World Bank and WTO, regularly favor large, multinational corporate interests at the expense of the local, "informal" economy, particularly small farmers who are mostly women.[3] While failing to calculate the environmental costs of agribusiness, or the cost of its extensive subsidies, or the cost of the artificially low-priced nonrenewable energy on which it depends, these global agents, at the same time, give no credit to the benefits of women's generative labor in the home and the field or to the informal economies of which it is a part. The methodologies used by these agents of global capital to measure "growth" are complicit with the systematic inequity that increasingly concentrates wealth and privilege in the hands of a few.

The "structural reforms" required of developing countries by these agents of globalization invariably fall most heavily on the poor and tend to fall disproportionately on women and children, as these policies consist largely in eliminating or reducing funding for education, health care, food subsidies, unemployment benefits, and pensions. In developed countries, several researchers have chronicled the struggle of women to support themselves and their children in the minimum wage and part-time employment that is available to them under globalization (Ehrenreich 2001; McMillan 2012). Globally, economic distress regularly leads women to the sex trade as a means of survival. In an environment where the value of anything is determined by money, human beings, mostly women and girls, become commodities to be bought and sold in well-developed global markets.[4] Sex trafficking is the most common form of modern-day slavery, and its victims are overwhelmingly women and girls. No woman really wants to do this work, to turn the intimacy of her generativity into degrading violence.[5]

Under globalization, labor, particularly women's labor, is discounted and disempowered, even invisible. The 1,100 Bangladeshis, mostly women, who died in the Rana Plaza disaster, were invisible to consumers while they were inside the factory making clothing for Benetton or Primark. Their horrific working conditions and poor compensation were invisible in the clothing marketed to Western consumers, until the factory building collapsed. A brief outrage follows, along with a promise by complicit companies to do better, but these commitments quickly fade, as the exploitation of this labor is essential to the economics of globalization (Hossain 2013). What lies behind the label "Made in Bangladesh" or "Made in China" must remain invisible.

The conditions under which workers make the T-shirts and smartphones of globalization would be intolerable to the consumers who buy these products.

The economic mobility afforded by globalization belongs to capital, not to labor. Global corporations move factories from countries where labor, through collective bargaining, enjoy rights and benefits, to countries where labor has few if any rights and little bargaining power. The global labor market is characterized by low pay, abusively long hours, a failure to pay for overtime, dangerous working conditions, surveillance, and physical intimidation or abuse. Complaints or attempts to organize are regularly met with and punished by beatings or other physical threats.[6] When these practices come to light through investigative reporting or a catastrophe like the Rana Plaza collapse, companies address the public relations problem, but little seems to change for the garment workers themselves. The purpose of moving to Bangladesh or Haiti was to cut costs, so that products can be cheap and profit margins high. If workers in Bangladesh or China enjoyed the same safety rules and benefits as an American worker, the factories would still be in Detroit or Pittsburgh. The economic model of globalization depends on consumers' blindness, both to the exploited labor embodied in the products they buy and to the way in which their own identity as workers and the world of labor itself is threatened by globalization's reliance on renewable pools of cheap, unprotected, and unorganized labor.

Globalization exacts invisible costs on ordinary citizens that do not figure in its accounts of "growth." It is associated with environmental degradation and health risks, as well as increasing inequity, physical and social displacement, and economic dependence. While pretending to advance the free circulation of ideas, goods, persons, and wealth, globalization produces widening social inequity, forced migrations and confinements, and workers who, whether documented or undocumented, cannot expect the sort of policies that reflect respect for their labor. Globalization cannot supply the sort of "international generosity," nor the forms of transnational collaboration that Roosevelt foresaw as necessary both to security and prosperity. As Peter Buffet insists: justice requires "concepts that shatter current structures and systems" (Buffett 2013). Justice requires reconfiguring the relation of labor and the state, not by pursuing isolationism or barriers to genuinely free trade, but by exposing the deceptions of globalization's metaphorics of "growth" and "free circulation," its threats to the environment and human health, and its devaluation of labor, particularly the generative labor of women. Such a critique opens the way for a concept of justice based on respect for labor.

LABOR AND THE JUST STATE

Both Plato and Roosevelt define justice in the state in relation to the labor of each citizen. For Plato, justice is a matter of "minding one's own business," in the sense of performing on behalf of the community the tasks, actions, or services to which the citizen's particular talents are suited (Plato 2004, 370c, 433a).

Each citizen, Plato argues, will be healthier and happier engaged in pursuits that are both appropriate to his or her endowments and clearly appreciated by the community as worthwhile. The just state's twofold duty is to insure the security of its citizens and to educate them properly so that their talents are discovered, developed, and deployed for the benefit of all.

For Plato the most serious impediment to attaining justice in the state is *pleonexia*, a kind of greediness in which the citizen fails to stick to his own business. Such a citizen arrogates to himself an authority that properly belongs to others. Pleonexia may take many forms, as when an unqualified politician seeks higher office or a poor craftsman makes rickety tables. They attempt tasks for which they lack the requisite skills or abilities, with unfortunate results for all (Plato 2004, 350b).

The most serious form of pleonexia, however, arises from a confusion around money. Using medicine as his example, Plato argues that when a physician puts "moneymaking" above patient care, he ceases to be a physician. Injustice results when one fails to mind one's own business by substituting the aim of making money for the true aim of excelling in one's appropriate labor. Labor that alienates itself from its own task in favor of profit will prove unhappy.

On Plato's analysis, labor, unlike money, has intrinsic value and commands respect, because it is productive of the good in every register of life: a clean, safe street; a cured patient; a steady table. Meaningful work promotes the flourishing of the worker and her community by adding value. Virtually every good, except the beauty of nature and the laughter of children, is the result of some worker's industry. Labor is good for the laborer as it allows her to realize her talents and become who she is, assuming that she has been properly educated and minds her own business. Justice depends on an educational program adequate to identify and nourish the true labor of each and all. Health and happiness are generated by minding one's own business in a state where everyone else is doing so too.

Having secured its citizens' safety, the primary task of the just state is to install an educational program adequate to identify and nourish the true labor of each and all. In Book Five of the *Republic* Plato argues that every citizen should have an equal access to the education that will allow the citizen to flourish as a laborer in the collaborations of the community. This identification of citizenship with meaningful work trumps even the prejudices of gen-

der. At a time when women were considered property and confined to domestic spaces and the care of the body, Plato argues that because some
women are smarter or stronger than some men, citizens must be judged
according to their talents and capacities, not their sex. Some women will
make better warriors or scientists or, even, philosophers than some men. It is
the task of the educational system to make these identifications and to nourish each citizen according to her own talents.

Plato also insists on the elimination of private property and on the dissolution of the family as the locus of private property in order to insure that
each member of the state identifies himself with the whole community, rather
than some part or faction. In the just state, where each citizen minds her own
business, you are what you do to contribute to the health and happiness of the
whole. Justice in the state requires recognition of and respect for the labor of
each and all. To respect means to *see* in the mode of *"looking back."*[7] Justice
requires that I see the worker in the dress that I wear or the meal that I eat.
The other work looks back at me in her work, and I am obliged to acknowledge that vision by looking back. The cashier or the cleaner or the cabbie is
not just a functionary or a cost factor in a production line. Their labor is a gift
on which the community depends. Each citizen in the just state labors for
herself and for all. Each citizen enjoys with other citizens a reciprocal relation of "looking back," as they collaborate toward the mutual ends of health
and happiness. The invisibility of labor under global capital violates this
ethical requirement and facilitates the material mistreatment and disenfran-
chisement of labor under globalization.

To the extent that the excellence of her labor is compromised by the aim
of making money, the citizen ceases to be who she is and disturbs the whole
community with the degraded work. An opera singer may select one engagement over another because of a larger fee, but to the extent that the choice
requires an aesthetic compromise, she demeans herself and deprives the community of her special contribution. When a legislator votes for one bill and
not for another because he is serving the interest of campaign contributors, he
abdicates his authority to govern in the name of the people. He substitutes the
expedient for the right, and the people suffer for it through lax regulation or
expensive subsidies. When a physician pays more attention to turnover rates
and revenue generated than to the specificity of each patient, he elevates
moneymaking over his medical labor and the good it serves. While making
money isn't bad, taking moneymaking as an aim in itself tends to corrupt the
real work.[8]

Under globalization, the most spectacular wealth accrues to those who
perform no labor whatsoever, except moneymaking or gambling in the markets. The hedge fund manager or investment banker works for no one except
himself and his privileged clients, and he produces nothing but monetary

wealth or credit with the house. Yet his wealth is vast in proportion to most workers.

Under globalization, corporations are judged, not by the excellence of their product or service, but by their stock price and market share. Excellence and share price may be related, but the former is regularly sacrificed to the later. Moreover, when moneymaking is privileged as the paradigm of productive activity, labor is transformed from a positive value, commanding collective respect, as in Plato's just state, to a cost, to be "kept down" and "contained" as much as possible. In the last four decades, in the developed world, particularly in Britain and the United States, a relentless assault on labor has left most workers with stagnant wages, no pensions, and rapidly reducing, if any, benefits. Only at the upper reaches of the pay scale, in the thin crust of upper management, do salaries, bonuses, and perquisites seem capable of inflating infinitely.

Plato thought that minding your own business would generate a hierarchy of expertise in which the best ruled and each citizen labored for himself and all. The educational system, not democracy or the market, would determine one's place in the order. Plato envisions a ruling power that descends vertically, controlling both freedom of expression and religion in order to cultivate communal commitment and an identification with the state over personal interest. Nussbaum suggests that Plato's analysis, or at least Platonism, proves inadequate as a theory of justice insofar as it gives little credit to the knowledge of experience. Even if Plato does recognize perception and craft as forms of knowledge, he values stability over creativity and does not see how knowledge might be generated and circulate horizontally, through collaboration, rather than vertically through authority. Moreover, while experience may be a source of knowledge, a strict hierarchy of experiences means that knowledge and authority are concentrated in a privileged few. All experience is valuable, but some much more than others.

Like Plato, Roosevelt takes the productive employment of a well-educated labor force to be the central mission of a just state, but he embraces freedom of expression and religion as essential to justice, as well as to the creativity and initiative that make "good business." Instead of concentrating authority and privilege in an elect few, Roosevelt invests authority in democratic processes and in "the hands and heads and hearts of . . . millions of free men and women." What citizens love and what they can do is as important as what they think. In Roosevelt's vision, the knowledge of heart and hand informs thought and judgment, especially in public policy. Policy should promote a "civilized society," collaborating toward health and happiness.

Of the "basic things" a citizen can justly expect of the state, the most important are "equality of opportunity" and "jobs for those who can work." Roosevelt recognizes that the prosperity and stability of the state depend on securing these aims. "The inner and abiding strength of our economic and political systems is dependent upon the degree to which they fulfill these expectations." Unemployment is a prima facie indictment of the state's injustice, as well as a threat to its security and the health and happiness of its citizens.

Taking full employment as the standard of the just state, Roosevelt takes aim at the financial interests that would undermine it. The health of the just state is properly measured not by growth in GNP, but by its ability to facilitate those collaborations that will secure the welfare of its citizens. Companies that exploit differences in wages and benefits to reduce labor costs or corporations that exploit tax law to shelter profits are not only "bad for business" to the extent that they serve the concentration of wealth and privilege rather than the free circulation of knowledge and goods, but, in Roosevelt's view, they are deeply unpatriotic. He warns against a "small group of selfish men who would clip the wings of the American eagle in order to feather their own nests." He foresees how the concentration of wealth and privilege threatens justice by devaluing the work of the many in favor of the interests of the few. If as Peter Buffett argues, we need to "shatter our current structures . . . that have turned the world into one vast market, one strategy would be to reorient economic policy around the aim of full employment and the universal access to education that it requires" (Buffett 2013).

While Plato limits justice to the domestic state and foresees no end to tribalism and the inevitability of conflicts among states who vie over territory and wealth, Roosevelt understands domestic justice and security to depend on a new international order. The "cooperation of free countries" will be required to secure freedom, including freedom from want. Roosevelt seeks international collaborations around policies aimed at insuring full employment globally: "economic understandings which will insure to every nation a healthy peacetime life for its inhabitants—everywhere in the world." Capital ought not to be able to exploit poverty or to take advantage of social inequity. Global institutions, as well as states, ought to make freedom from want and the full employment it requires the first aim of all economic policies. Roosevelt foresees that no state on its own will be able to achieve the justice of full employment. International solidarities will be required to create and secure the conditions under which labor can flourish.

The economic collaborations necessary to insure full employment depend on peace. Only a "world-wide reduction of armaments" can secure the fourth freedom, freedom from fear, on which the other freedoms of expression and religion and freedom from want depend. Roosevelt envisions a world in which "no nation will be in a position to commit an act of physical aggression against any neighbor." What he does not foresee is the degree to which the state and its economy would become hostage, as Eisenhower warned, to the "military-industrial complex" (Eisenhower 1961). While discussions of contemporary economic crises regularly focus on the way in which debt is driven by unaffordable benefits accorded to labor, it is worth noting that in the United States, for example, nearly 20% of the economy is committed to the military and war industry.[9] Without robust international collaborations to insure global employment, economic disparities will produce global violence. Without a secure peace and global disarmament, the next tyrant only waits for his tactical advantage.

HAPPINESS OR MEANINGFUL WORK

"Happiness lies not in the mere possession of money; it lies in the joy of achievement, in the thrill of creative effort." —Franklin D. Roosevelt, first inaugural address, 1933

Roosevelt's strategy for achieving the domestic and international collaborations that he deems necessary to a more generalized prosperity depends not on a confidence in "free markets," but on a respect for labor. In his analysis, the valorization of moneymaking has resulted in an alienation of destiny. Our destiny, as citizens of a free republic, seeking a world of free republics, is "not to be ministered to, but to minster to ourselves and to our fellow-men." Both politics and business have been corrupted by "the falsity of material wealth as a standard of success." It leads the politician to substitute his own pride and profit for the welfare of his constituents, while it produces in banking and business "the likeness of callous and selfish wrong-doing." Like Plato, Roosevelt sees the focus on profit as inimical to justice, as well as to the health and happiness of labor and to its productive activities and products. "The mad chase of evanescent profits" has dulled and obscured the "joy and moral stimulation of work." Repeatedly Roosevelt emphasizes the joy of meaningful work as the core of both happiness and justice. Perhaps, only a few professions offer the "thrill of creative effort," but almost all employment can provide the opportunity for the "joy of achievement."[10]

Roosevelt insists that in a just state this opportunity for joy in work will be equal for all. To secure this equality of opportunity, the state must insure that an effective education is available to all citizens. Without this opportunity early in life to discover and develop her talents, the citizen will not be able to deploy them later on. When poor children attend schools that are significantly poorer in quality than those attended by wealthier students, social inequity is reinforced. Justice in the state requires the universal availability of a state education to match the best of the private sector. In developed countries, inequities in education are linked to inequities in health and life expectancy, as well as economic security. In developing countries, where educational opportunities are limited and girls are often denied education, the future is compromised for the state and its citizens, both in terms of health and economic independence. In both cases, lack of education makes it impossible for citizens to mind their own business, and it robs them of their opportunity to experience the joy of meaningful work. These citizens are more likely to find themselves working long hours for low wages and few benefits, or no wages or benefits at all, in tasks in which they are given little independence or opportunity for the sort of "achievement" through labor that Roosevelt describes as the life of a citizen in the just state. As Gustavo Gutiérrez argues,

> [T]he poor person does not exist as an inescapable fact of destiny. His or her existence is not politically neutral, and it is not ethically innocent. The poor are a by-product of the system in which we live and for which we are responsible. They are marginalized by our social and cultural world. They are the oppressed, exploited proletariat, robbed of the fruit of their labor and despoiled of their humanity. Hence the poverty of the poor is not a call to generous relief action, but a demand that we go and build a different social order. (2004 [1979])

To be meaningful, work must first be life-sustaining. The existence of a class of "working poor," whose minimum-wage or part-time jobs do not pay enough to cover basic expenses, such as food and housing, is a symptom of the state's injustice. Freedom from want, on which the other freedoms depend, requires not only an adequate wage, but also various forms of life support, including health care and a pension. In addition to his general goals of full employment and disarmament, Roosevelt outlines three specific policy goals related to aspects of the "social economy" that need "immediate improvement." First, pensions and unemployment insurance should be expanded. Second, access to adequate medical care should be expanded. Third, the state needs to devise "a better system by which persons deserving or needing gainful employment may obtain it." Meaningful work, then, not only provides at least the basic needs of life, it also secures the worker against sickness, unemployment, and old age. These policy goals were urgent on January 6, 1941. Without these infrastructures in place, citizens are doomed to live in constant fear of economic ruin, through an illness or protracted unemployment or a penurious retirement. It is urgent that every state act in ways to allay these fears, as fear is an invitation to tyranny. As Peter Buffett argues, the current global economy is a "perpetual poverty machine." Heads of state, corporate managers, and economic leaders are "[a]ll searching for answers with their right hand to problems they have created with their left" (Buffett 2013). The current economic system creates vast wealth for a tiny minority whose charity "just keeps the existing structures of inequity in place." From his vantage point as the head of a major foundation, Buffett argues that "money should be spent trying out concepts that shatter our current structures and systems that have turned much of the world into one vast market. Is progress really Wi-Fi on every corner? No. It's when no 13-

year-old girl on the planet gets sold for sex." Buffett calls for the sort of structural change envisioned by Roosevelt, based on a respect for labor and an appreciation of the necessity of social and economic equity to the life of a democratic state.

To be meaningful, work must be worth doing and experienced as such by the worker. Meaningful work answers a real need and produces real value in the world of experience. A mother nursing her infant has no doubt that the work is meaningful. A surgeon saving a life has no doubt that his work is meaningful. Garbage collection may not be glamorous, but those who do it know, like firefighters and police, how essential they are to the safety and security of the city.

Telemarketing jobs focused on conning people into buying things they don't want or need aren't meaningful because they are only concerned with profit. Real estate deals in which shoddily built homes in overbuilt tracts are marketed to gullible consumers aren't meaningful because they are only concerned with moneymaking. The forklift operators, moving aluminum around all day among a series of warehouses because it allows Goldman Sachs to accrue massive storage fees, know that the work isn't meaningful (Kocieniewski 2013).

To be meaningful, work must be visible and recognized as meaningful by the community. The invisible garment workers in Bangladesh do not enjoy meaningful work. The lack of respect for their labor is painfully illustrated when a catastrophic factory fire occurs or one of the shoddily built factories collapses. Thousands die, yet the Bangladeshi garment industry continues to thrive, because the invisible exploitation of this labor is central to the global fashion industry. Similarly, the labor of small farmers, who depend on the informal economy, remains invisible to the metrics of the global economy, making the small farmer vulnerable to the expansionist policies of global agribusiness. If small, indigenous farming can be represented as "unproductive" in global policy discussions, as it often is, then the expansion of agribusiness can be represented as good for the country under "development."[11] This lack of respect for the knowledge and productive labor of indigenous farmers permits agribusiness and policymakers to discount them, and these farmers have little, if any, role in the decisions that affect them. Because global agents fail to recognize and respect their knowledge and expertise, the very way of life of these farmers is threatened, as their lands are turned over to agribusiness or development. Respect for the knowledge accrued over millennia by indigenous farmers ought to be a first principle of global agricultural policy. Justice requires respect for all the labor on which the community depends, from the mundanities of cleaning and washing to the glamours of science and art. In a just state, each citizen contributes in her own way, and all labor deserves respect. Significant social and economic inequity corrodes this respect and promotes factionalism and fear.

Finally, to be meaningful, work must not be demeaning. Work can be demeaning because the labor itself is demeaning, as in sex work or some forms of surrogacy. Or, it can be demeaning because the boss is demeaning, as in individual cases of sexual harassment or racial discrimination.[12] Beyond these particular instances, workers are often demeaned by *structural* forces of sexism and racism. Structural sexism can be at work in individual relationships and in individual judicial cases. For example, a dentist in the United States fired his hygienist based on the claim that her beauty was so great a temptation, it posed a threat to his marriage. He survived judicial scrutiny on the ground that the hygienist was fired not because of her sex, but because of her appearance. The court ignored the structure of sexism that operates here, in which women are injured because men find them a temptation (Kemp 2012). It ignored the injury to the dental assistant, not only in economic terms, but in terms of the loss of what Roosevelt identified as the condition of happiness, her "joy in achievement." She repeatedly described her loss by saying, "I loved my job."

Structural sexism may also create environments in which whole classes or groups of women are demeaned. Female agricultural workers are especially vulnerable given the circumstances of their work, which often involves remote settings with little, if any, oversight or protection. This vulnerability may be compounded for the many immigrants and undocumented workers in agriculture. Women in agriculture are so regularly subject to sexual harassment and rape that these experiences have become structural features of employment (Bergman 2013). The meaningful work required by the just state is inconsistent with this demeaning devaluation of the worker.

Policy in the just state aims at securing meaningful work for all citizens. First and foremost, educational institutions must be established to give every citizen equal access to the opportunity to discover and develop her talents. The educational infrastructure of the just state provides a culture of possibilities in which each citizen can flourish. Inequities in education perpetuate and exacerbate existing social inequities.

Meaningful work is visible and recognized by the community. In the just state, labor elicits the respect of being seen in the mode of looking back, each one acknowledging the work of the other. Meaningful work is worth doing in answering to a real need and producing real value. No one is demeaned by meaningful work.

Freedom of expression and religion, based on freedom from fear and freedom from want. This is the world of meaningful work.

REMEMBERING WOMEN

Unfortunately, Roosevelt does not address "the problem of our time" (Irigaray 1993, 88–89). Whatever his support for women's rights, he assumes the domesticity of women, whose labor has been and remains invisible in the official economy. These women don't "go to work." When they do, the gender division of labor is disturbed in ways that produce significant social crises, from "latch-key children" to an obesity crisis linked to the lack of home cooking. Who will feed and care for the children, the sick, and the elderly, if women abandon their traditional unpaid and unrecognized labor as family caregiver? Families become dependent on fast food, day care centers, and nursing homes. Women's work is being commodified through the expansion of low-wage employment in "service" or "caring" professions like health aide or teacher's assistant. Of course, the women in these positions also have families who may not have access to these services and who also need to be cared for. The United States regularly solves its shortage of nurses by recruiting from the Philippines without wondering about the families that these women have left behind. Instead of enjoying the presence of their mother, the nurse's children receive money, the remittance she sends home every month. Professional women regularly solve the problem of child care by hiring women of color, who are often undocumented, but these women also have children, and what provision is made for them?

Not only labor, but virtually every human institution, has been organized around this distinction between the public world of work and the private world of the family; yet no adequate infrastructures exist to support the integration of the two. For millennia, it was assumed that women would remain in the domestic sphere. When women moved into the world of work in significant numbers, they continued, and still continue, to perform the care labor essential to the family (Breen and Price 2005, 43–57). In the United States, unlike many European countries, virtually no supports exist for working mothers, making pregnancy very difficult for working-class mothers. Maternity leave is minimal and rare, even for professional women. Medical care for pregnancy and childbirth is exorbitantly expensive and erratically priced, and those working in low- and medium-wage jobs rarely have adequate insurance.[13] Mothers regularly experience extreme stress over money and incur significant debt. Workplaces rarely supply childcare. Parental leave is more or less difficult to take. There are no financial supports for working mothers of young children to rely on, other than piecemeal programs for food and housing aimed at the extremely poor.

In France, where the financial supports for motherhood are generous, working women experience a different problem. Once they have children, there is significant social pressure to stay home, and the transition back to the workplace is difficult (Reineke 2008, 91–125). Despite state support for the family, women in France remain underrepresented in the councils that determine the future. They hold about the same percentage of leadership positions in politics, business, and academia as their American counterparts.[14]

Similarly, professional women in the United States, who enjoy educational and economic privilege, also experience the lack of adequate infrastructures for integrating work and family. In the last decade a wave of professional women have attested to the difficulties they face in dividing their time and energy between the two. A recent survey of Ivy League graduates revealed a trend among these women toward domesticity and away from work in the public sphere. These women repeatedly cited the suffering they had witnessed in their mothers as they attempted to achieve at work while striving to care for their families (Hersch 2013; Steiner 2007; Lerner 2010). The suffering of these working mothers, significant enough to turn their daughters away from work, is a symptom of the urgent need for new infrastructures to sustain both work and family. Our time calls for concepts that "shatter our current structures," not only by reconfiguring economic relations, but also by reimagining the infrastructures of space and time to facilitate women's generativity as mothers and workers. How might the built environment be reconstructed and daily schedules revised to support women's labor in all its domains of employment? Until these questions become the focus of policy debates, the state will suffer from the loss of women's labor in the public sphere and from the damage to both work and family that results from the antagonism between the two.

In many parts of the world, of course, women face far more difficult situations and choices than those of professional women in the West. They are often treated as property and married without consultation at a very young age. They begin their life of labor so young as to almost miss having a childhood. And the labor, hauling water or firewood, for example, is rarely that in which one can find the "joy of achievement." Often denied education, these women are deprived of the skills and ideas that might enable them to imagine a future of meaningful work.

On a visit to Rajasthan in 2010, I was struck by how hard the women worked. At dawn, they climb steep hills to collect firewood. By noon, they descend in groups of eight or ten, each one carrying an enormous bundle of sticks and limbs on her head, usually larger than the girl or woman herself. Several times during the day, they haul the family's water from the local well. At other times, the women are cooking or sweeping the house. They seem to be always working, while the men of the village are occasionally in their shops, but more often drinking chai. A young woman of thirty-five looks fifty, after more than two decades of daily, continuous hard labor and several children.[15]

In a remote corner of Rajasthan, however, I found women engaged in meaningful work and clearly enjoying themselves and their achievements.

As I approached Dastkari Kendra in Ranthambore, I realized that it was the first time in India that I had encountered women laughing. From some distance, I could hear several dozen women of all ages, chattering and laughing with unrestrained joy. The women sat in their magnificently colored saris on the floor of an open porch. Each one had busy hands. One group was making a patchwork quilt. Another was making fans. Several women were drawing designs for block printing. Not far away were a group of potters working at their wheels. And just inside, off the porch, women were tie-dying and block printing fabrics out of which they would make clothes in both Western and Indian styles, table linens, and purses. The Dastkar Craft Community Center provides employment for women and men from agrarian villages who were displaced by the Ranthambore Tiger Park. The land onto which they were relocated could not sustain an agrarian economy, and the Ranthambore Foundation asked Dastkar Society for Crafts and Craftspeople to work with the villagers to create a viable economy in crafts and handiwork.

Not only have the villagers created a thriving economy in Dastkari Kendra, it has changed their lives by introducing them to the joyful collaborations of meaningful work. The women were suspicious at first, and the Dastkar Society organizers understood that its task was to help them "discover their hidden potential." By sending its craftspeople to live in the villages and work with the villagers, Dastkar gained their trust, and within six months more than seventy-five women were participating. Twenty-five years later, more than three hundred craftspeople participate. Dastkari Kendra has changed the villagers' attitudes toward caste, *purdah*, marriage, and religion. Initially, they segregated themselves according to caste or religion, but their joyful collaboration has created a democratic space where people mingle freely across these distinctions. The economic independence of the women has not only improved their material quality of life and that of their children, it has also reshaped gender relations in the villages, with women taking leadership roles, both in the craft collective and in other local institutions. The collective demonstrates how the happy collaborations of meaningful work can overcome inequity and the violence of racism and sexism.

Dastkar quotes the local doctor: "I can recognize a Dastkar craftswoman from half a kilometer away, just by the way she walks and holds her head." These women have found the meaningful work on which, as Roosevelt argued, health and happiness, as well as the peace of the community, depend. They have found the "joy of achievement" along with economic independence and social recognition.[16]

Justice is neither an illusion nor a dream. It is an achievable reality of which material examples currently exist.

States and global actors need to "try out concepts that shatter our current structures." Most importantly, states need to address inequities in education that perpetuate inequities in life and to insure that everyone has the opportunity to experience the "joy of achievement" in meaningful work. These phil-osophical commitments have clear implications for public policy, if the latter can be freed from the myths and rhetoric, as well as the interests, of global-ization. States might begin by making full employment and equity in educa-tion the standard of economic and political success.

NOTES

1. "When the global trend is isolated, we find that in the last two decades, inequality has increased throughout the world in a pattern that cuts across the effect of national income changes. During the decades that happen to coincide with the rise of neoliberal ideology, with the breakdown of national sovereignties, and with the end of Keynesian policies in the global debt crisis of the early 1980s, inequality rose worldwide." Galbraith, James K. "A Perfect Crime: Global Inequality," *Daedalus* 131, no. 2: 11–25.

2. China is currently experiencing a forced "urbanization," as the government pursues a policy of displacing rural farmers in an effort to turn them into urban consumers. See, for example, "China's Great Uprooting: Moving 250 Million into Cities," *New York Times*, June 15, 2013. Large-scale global projects like dams regularly require the displacement of local peoples. See, for example, Asthana, Vandana, "Forced Displacement," *Economic and Political Weekly* XLVII, no. 47–48, December 1, 2012. During the 1990s about ten million people a year globally were displaced by development projects. Cernea, Michael, "The Risks and Recon-struction Model for Resetlling Displaced Populations," *World Development* 25, no. 10, Octo-ber, 1997: 1569–1587.

3. US President Obama's recent $3 billion deal with agribusiness to "develop" agriculture in developing nations is a case in point. While paying lip service to small, indigenous farmers, the agreement clearly paves the way for their displacement by global capital. They do not have a seat at the table in the discussions that determine their future. See IJFAB Blog, May 31, 2013, "Obama and Agribusiness."

4. While the difficulty in obtaining reliable data is regularly cited, most sources suggest that the victims of human trafficking number in the millions annually. The UNODC report on human trafficking estimates that of two to four million cases annually, 80% involve sexual exploitation, overwhelmingly of women and girls. *Global Report on Trafficking in Persons*, United Nations Office on Drugs and Crime, February 2009.

5. A recent study of the "Gilgo Girls," a series of prostitutes abducted, murdered, and buried on a Long Island beach, reveals how these working-class women were driven to work as "escorts" because of the impossibility of actually supporting themselves and their children on the low-wage service jobs to which they had access. Kolker, Robert, *Lost Girls: An Unsolved American Mystery*, New York: Harper Collins, 2013.

6. See, for example, "Buying Overseas Clothing, U.S. Flouts Its Own Advice," *New York Times*, December 23, 2013. The article surveys working conditions at various garment factories in Central America and Asia.

7. Demeter will have nothing less than the living presence of her daughter, Persephone, "looking back."

8. In the 1954 film *Executive Suite* (MGM), two executives vie for control of a furniture company. One is an engineer committed to making the best product possible. The other is an accountant. At one point in the whirl of negotiations leading to the board's decision, the accountant boasts that he can save the firm more money with a little accounting trick than the engineer could ever make with his new furniture designs. Unfortunately, today the global economy seems dominated by the former strategy, rather than the latter.

9. Spiraling health care costs in the United States cannot and should not be addressed by cutting benefits. What is not sustainable is the fee-for-service delivery of medical care or the profits of the insurance industry. The delivery of care needs to be reorganized around *patients*,

not *procedures*. Medicare has been significantly more efficient and cost-effective than private insurers and should be universalized.

10. First inaugural address.

11. Vandana Shiva demonstrates how the supposedly "higher yields" of the Green Revolution "disappear in the context of total yields of crops on farms." Higher yields of wheat or maize were achieved at the expense of straw. Resulting reductions in fodder amounted to "stealing food from animals and soil organisms." *Stolen Harvest*, Cambridge, MA: South End Press, 2000, 12.

12. Multiple women have complained that the current mayor of San Diego is an abusive employer who indulges in various forms of sexual harassment, yet he refuses to resign and has not been charged. The celebrity cook Paula Deen, who built a multimillion-dollar empire on Southern food, has recently been exposed for her indulgence in racist attitudes and for her failure to share her success with the black employees on which her business depended. While these are famous cases, the attitudes of these employers are, unfortunately, common in the workplace.

13. "American Way of Birth, Costliest in the World," *New York Times*, June 30, 2013.

14. In 2013, the French parliament is 18.5% women, while women hold 18.5% of the seats in the US House of Representatives and 20% in the Senate. In both states, women hold about 15% of seats on corporate boards. In both states, women hold about 30% of the positions in higher education, but less than 20% of full professorships, and less than 10% of academic leadership positions.

15. Despite this toil and lack of luxury, no one could be more generous. A stranger walking a road through small farms and villages is repeatedly pressed to stop and share a chapatti. The women admire my red nail polish, and I their bangles. Without sharing any language, we share this small encounter in which I am a curious, but welcome, interruption in their labors.

16. www.dastkar.org/ranthamborep.htm.

BIBLIOGRAPHY

Asthana, Vandana. 2012. "Forced Displacement." *Economic and Political Weekly* 47, no. 47–48: 96–102.
Baudrillard, Jean. 1998. *The Consumer Society*. London: Sage Publishing.
Bergman, Lowell. 2013. "Rape in the Fields." *Frontline*, PBS, June 25.
Breen, Richard, and Lynne Price. 2005. "The Persistence of the Gendered Division of Labor." *European Sociological Review* 21, no. 1: 43–57.
Buffett, Peter. 2013. "The Charitable-Industrial Complex." *New York Times*, Op-Ed, July 26.
Cernea, Michael. 1997. "The Risks and Reconstruction Model for Resettling Displaced Populations." *World Development* 25, no. 10: 1569–1587.
Ehrenreich, Barbara. 2001. *Nickled and Dimed: On (Not) Getting by in America*. New York: Henry Holt and Co.
Eisenhower, Dwight D. 1961. "The Military-Industrial Complex Speech." Public Papers of the Presidents, January 17, 1035–1040.
Gottlieb, Robert, and Anupama Joshi. 2010. *Food Justice*. Cambridge, MA: MIT Press.
Gutiérrez, Gustavo. 2004 [1979]. *The Power of the Poor in History*. Trans. Robert R. Barr. Maryknoll, NY: Orbis Books.
Hersch, Joni. 2013. "Opting Out among Women with Elite Education." *Social Science Research Network*, Vanderbilt Law and Economics Research Paper, no. 13–15, April 24.
Hobbes, Thomas. 1996. *Leviathan*. New York: Cambridge.
Hossain, Emran. 2013. "Rana Plaza Collapse Victims Still Waiting for Compensation." *Huffington Post*, August 6.
Irigaray, Luce. 1993. *An Ethics of Sexual Difference*. Trans. Carolyn Burke and Gillian C. Gill. Ithaca: Cornell University Press.
Kemp, Joe. 2012. "Iowa Court OKs Firing of Female Dental Assistant for Being 'Too Irresistibly' Attractive." *New York Daily News*, December 22.

Kocieniewski, David. 2013. "A Shuffle of Aluminum, but to Banks, Pure Gold." *New York Times*, July 20.

Kolker, Robert. 2013. *Lost Girls: An Unsolved American Mystery*. New York: Harper Collins.

Lerner, Sharon. 2010. *The War on Moms: Life in a Family-Unfriendly Nation*. Hoboken: John Wiley and Sons.

McMillan, Trace. 2012. *The American Way of Eating: Undercover at Walmart, Applebee's, Farm Fields, and the Dinner Table*. New York: Scribner.

Nussbaum, Martha C. 2000. *Women and Human Development*. Cambridge: Cambridge University Press.

Paulson, Ken. 2013. "Ag-Gag Bills Harm Free Speech." *USA Today*, April 17.

Plato. 2004. *The Republic*. Trans. C. D. C. Reeve. Indianapolis: Hackett.

Pollan, Michael. 2006. *The Omnivore's Dilemma*. New York: Penguin.

Reineke, Sandra. 2008. "*In vitro veritas*: New Reproductive and Genetic Technologies and Women's Rights in Contemporary France." *International Journal of Feminist Approaches to Bioethics* 1, no. 1: 91–125.

Roosevelt, Franklin D. 1965. "The 'Four Freedoms' Speech." In *Documentary History of the United States*. New York: Signet/Mentor.

Sen, Amartya. 2008. "The Concept of Development." In *Global Ethics: Seminal Essays*, ed. Thomas Pogge and Keith Horton. St. Paul, MN: Paragon House.

Shiva, Vandana. 2000. *Stolen Harvest*. Cambridge, MA: South End Press.

———. 2005. *Earth Democracy: Justice, Sustainability, and Peace*. Brooklyn: South End Press.

Steiner, Leslie Morgan. 2007. *Mommy Wars*. New York: Random House.

United Nations Office on Drugs and Crime. 2009. *Global Report on Trafficking in Persons*. February.

Wolff, E. N. 2012. *The Asset Price Meltdown and the Wealth of the Middle Class*. New York: New York University.

Chapter Three

Laboring with Others

Franc Rottiers

While we are all citizens of the world; none of us are world citizens, that is, none of us can claim to be part of a global citizenry. To be more precise, none of us possesses a global passport that gives free and unconditional access to any and every group, institute, community, or nation-state within the global realm. Nevertheless, the world we live in today is a world where gaining access to parts of that global realm is conditioned by the expectation that we participate in it *as if* we were global citizens. Such a way of life—and politically sustaining such life—has its consequences. Indeed, what does it mean to live in a world where access to its parts is conditioned by such an *as if* that can be characterized as being both virtual and "ideal" as also actual and "real"? Does participation even compute citizenship, and if it does, can we then still talk about citizenship as such? Is it not so that today citizenship is recognized exclusively through the figure of participation? Is it not so that when citizenship is addressed, participation is not merely one of its attributes but its defining and identifying feature? Is it not so that this feature, which is omnipresent in political discourse, has become almost the equivalent of what it means to be social, and even guides economy, as well as configures citizenship in a very limited way?

For some it might seem odd to pose such questions, certainly when putting them forward from the perspective that citizenship is to be equated with a virtual and ideal notion of participation that begets actual and real "experts" for whom citizenship is about "laboring with one another." However, from the perspective that "expertise" is formed on a day-to-day basis through actual and real contributions that guide what it ideally could mean to be a citizen, these questions can reach another dimension of reflection. In my contribution to this volume, I will show that the figure of participation answers to a specific logic encompassing both an inclusive ideal and also rules for real-life exclusion and that it, consequently, veils the fact that citizenship, rather than through the figure of participation, is configured by contributions that "mutely" voice what it really means to "labor with others" (instead of laboring with one another).

In what follows I will, first, demonstrate that the logic of participation renders imperceptible those contributions that fail "participation tests" checking whether or not one is "laboring with one another." Second, I will indicate how and in what way local contributions indeed are perceivable by referring to my research with undocumented migrants with whom I experienced different ways of "laboring with others" in configurations I have come to name *translation milieus*. It is precisely in these milieus that newcomers are able to gain access and interact with the people present in their environment. Third, I will sketch how, that is, through "culture and arts," or better, through the figure of the *cultural-artistic*, these contributions can become intelligible as meaningful citizenship practices in which the materiality of the different contexts, the particularity of the epistemologies that emerge in these contexts, and the ethical and aesthetical considerations that are tested in them provide the constituting parameters. In conclusion, I will discuss why these parameters should be included in any discussion that concerns global justice.

THE LOGIC (?) OF PARTICIPATION

Goethe once wrote that "[o]ur participation [Anteil] in public affairs is mostly mere philistinism" (Goethe 2010). With this reflection, Goethe accurately pointed his finger to the hostility, indifference, or the plain misunderstanding of culture and the arts when participation in public affairs is at stake. That is, when people engage in public affairs, culture and the arts are not merely considered to be excluded from the prevailing participatory practices; they are affirmatively negated in any matters of public affairs. While Goethe's reflections were inspired by the particularities of his time, his choice of words remains valid in today's world where philistinism remains extant in the logic of participation. While the existence of such a logic is addressed from many different vantage points, two of these stand out, that is, those of Peggy McIntosh and Jacques Rancière.

McIntosh (1995) admirably describes how—the logic of participating in—"white privilege" has engendered discourses of authority toward "nonwhites." The crux of her article is that such discourses prevent "whites," on the one hand, from *recognizing* certain "traits and qualities" that could only emerge in "nonwhite" contexts and, on the other hand, from even *developing* similar "traits and qualities." McIntosh, however, though her idea concerning the failure of recognizing and developing certain traits and qualities is quite powerful, does not mention what these certain "traits and qualities" as developed by "nonwhites" might be. Hers is a task of making her readers aware of the fact that white privilege indeed exists and that it operates as an "unconscious" idea of power both negating and protecting itself. Mine is one of taking not only these traits and qualities into account but in pointing out that these bear the mark of a cultural-artistic contribution.

A similar effort to raise awareness about the logic of participation is addressed by Jacques Rancière. For Rancière, this logic is not restricted to "white privilege" but encapsulates the way the sensible world is partitioned in the "logic of the arche" (Rancière 2001). Though Rancière (2004) does not formulate his address in terms of participation, he does demarcate the partitioning of the sensible and the way this partitioning is governed by what he calls *the police order*, as a realm where participation of its members is necessary and obligatory. To be clear, the police order Rancière refers to is not to be understood as a real police force, but, rather, it represents every effort to protect and sustain the way the sensible world is partitioned. Rancière claims that within such a realm, "politics" is not only lacking omnipresence but it takes place very rarely. To be more precise, politics is that rare event that occurs when the prevailing partitioning of the sensible is repartitioned by those who are "shared out" of that order (Rancière and Hallward 2003). Such a repartitioning, as the one that took place in the struggle of the workers' movement to claim their rights, challenges and changes the prevailing partitioning of the sensible. Moreover, in order to make this challenge and change possible, those that are "shared out" need to perform what Rancière calls *acts of subjectivation*, that is, acts through which those that perform such an act become a recognizable subject. They become such a subject by addressing *a wrong* and in that address take up a role that is not expected from them. The way *dissensus* is voiced through that address is precisely what democracy is about. Traditional politics and the way it currently "distributes" democracy both negate the fact that it partitions the sensible by assigning well-defined parts and places within the police order as it also protects this partitioning by denying "shared-out" people to voice any kind of dissensus; here, too, democracy takes place very rarely (Rancière 2010). Today, democracy is precisely about the opposite of dissensus. Democracy is about reaching consensus and about sustaining or, to phrase it in Rancière's terminology, *policing* that consensus. Policing consensus is precisely an act that abides to the logic of participation. This act takes consensus to be an agreement on some kind of ideal, for example, the European Lisbon agreements that aim at securing work for all, social integration, and participation in the society of knowledge, for which a vast amount of participants are needed. For the consensus to survive and maintain its grip on society, these participants, who each are assigned particular roles, need to be controlled, hence the *policing*. A consensus, such as the Lisbon agreements, aims at substantiating the parameters of citizenship through the figure of participation in work, social life, and the society of knowledge. While the current parameters of citizenship have an aura of endorsing an "inclusive" citizenry, they also imply that those who participate in it need to subscribe to a *privileged citizenship-ideal*. This ideal is operationalized through the figure of participation consequently excluding those who, from the perspective of that ideal, fail to participate. It is precisely this logic of participation that renders imperceptible those traits and qualities that fail the current "participation tests."

While both McIntosh and Rancière address the logic of participation from interesting vantage points, surprisingly lacking in their analyses is precisely the philistinism Goethe already saw emerging in his time. Could the traits and qualities McIntosh refers to but does not qualify further and the Rancièrean acts of subjectivation not be of the cultural-artistic kind? A brief excursion to Adorno will allow me to make a case for my assertion.

In his *Notizen zur Neuen Anthropologie*, Adorno wrote that "being consumed, swallowed up, is indeed just what I understand as 'participation' which is so totally characteristic for the new anthropological type—the lack of curiosity. No longer wanting to know anything new, above all anything that is open and unguarded" (Adorno cited in Buck-Morss 1977, 189). In rephrasing, to participate is about surrendering oneself to a *milieu* that is closed and guarded, and in which nothing new—no new *translations* of concepts and ideas—is allowed to emerge. In relation to the Lisbon goals mentioned above, testing participation can then be decoded as being about testing people on their noncuriosity regarding matters of "work," "social integration," and "participation in the society of knowledge." It is from here on but a small step to present as interesting the case of the undocumented, who are by definition in a position in which they are confronted with these matters, curiously searching for adequate translations to rephrase or understand what these precisely mean in the new context they have come to live in.

In the case study that follows, I will show that the parameters of noncuriosity pertain to administrative—mostly juridical—procedures in which the *curiosity* of the newcomers I have met during my research is clearly denied access. Sometimes denials as these attest to plain injustice, but more often they are a demonstration of either pure ignorance or plain incompetence. It is, in fact, precisely through the emergence of injustice, ignorance, or incompetence that the logic of participation, as a lack of curiosity, materializes as a procedure of negation and self-protection. However, while the people in my research were denied access to challenge and possibly supplement these procedures as such, the people I encountered were indeed able to perform their curiosity in their various "cultural-artistic" contributions as also to the uses of administrations and those that work in them. In these uses and through their contributions, they not only reconfigured, together with the people they met along the road—such as researchers, social service assistants, and all those that came into contact with them and who took a pause to recognize their concerns—the *milieu* as a milieu in which only the "wrong" logic of participation rules into a milieu where a "dissensual" logic of contributions is tested, but also, due to their very presence in this milieu, engaged in acts of *translation*.

RECOGNIZING CONTRIBUTIONS, ANTICULTURE BUT SURELY CULTURAL

During my stay at the Protestant Social Centre (PSC) in Antwerp,[1] I met with many undocumented migrants. While we discussed many issues, what persisted throughout these meetings and discussions was that most of them requested me to write letters to the governmental administrations. Given the fact that a lot of the people who seek assistance already had lawyers who handled their pending asylum or regularization dossier, it seemed striking that most of the questions of the PSC clients were—and to date still are—of a legal or juridical nature. What was even more striking was that similar requests were voiced by the people who had received legal residence documents but found themselves in a new situation of difficulty when trying to exercise the rights they were entitled to. Among those were the rights to apply for financial support and child allowance. The problem there was not that the newly documented, in the end, were not allowed to exercise these rights but that it took several letters to the respective governmental administrations to get things done. Other striking experiences included the case of an Iraqi refugee who, due to relocation from one shelter to another, was denied medical follow-up in the latter after having received medical care in a hospital near the former; the cases of asylum seekers continually being denied asylum but who in their communications toward the center indicated that the democratic situation in their country is more severe than the Belgian authorities wanted to acknowledge; the cases of asylum seekers who indicated that the image they had regarding the respect for human rights in Europe failed their expectations; and the cases of regularized migrants who were not allowed financial support because the residence they lived in did not meet the minimal standards for being taken into consideration *as* legal residence.

Though many more examples of cases can be listed, each of these cases calling for different approaches, what remained a constant throughout this heterogeneity of cases and experiences is that in all of these, ideally, the responsible administrations could or even should have resolved the issues at hand and not so much the PSC. However, as is often the case with the assistance given by the PSC and often voiced by its personnel: "What is supposed to work in theory does not always work out in practice." In theory, asylum seekers are indeed entitled to receive help, such as housing and medical care, from the government. However, in practice this is not always the case. I have listened to many stories from the undocumented who upon arriving at the hospital were denied urgent medical care, which, in Belgium, they are entitled to receive. In most cases this was related to the ignorance of the personnel regarding the procedures, which the undocumented themselves had to explain to the medical staff. In fact, in most of the cases where the undocumented requested me to write a letter to a governmental administration, the undocumented themselves had to point out the particular rights they were entitled to. So why did they need us at the PSC? Maybe because they did not master the Dutch language? That is partly true, but then you have missed the point. Every time I wrote such a letter, it struck me how well these undocumented people performed their duties, both from a social and juridical perspective, as citizens while formally they were not allowed to be citizens. They gave examples about the way they helped the people in the building they lived in; they wrote poetry they were not allowed to write in their home country. They tried to integrate into our society by becoming a member of a sports or other club, tried to set up and support an organization without the cash they would normally need to back them up, or even cleaned the streets because they thought them to be too dirty.

And then, after a while, you receive an answer. Particularly noteworthy are the answers related to an appeal for regularization. Often they are phrased to convey the following message: "You say you obey the law. Of course! Do you not know you are supposed to obey the laws of this country! What did you expect? This is not a reason to allow you permanent residence!"

Now, is this answer correct? Of course it is; we all live in a participatory world, do we not? However, when you do not have the necessary documents that attest to your legal citizenship status and your right to participation, none of your actions will be recognized and acknowledged. But here again the whole point of the personal encounter with the undocumented and the spark of what it means to genuinely contribute is missed. There you had an encounter between two people who tried to labor, not *with one another*, but indeed *with others*. There you had an encounter, not based on creating some kind of joint identity (with one another), but where difference was at play (between others). Other than uniting in a joint state of activism (with one another), we were both laboring with respect for what was to remain "other," that is, with respect for that what was not and would never become part of a soporific participatory citizenship expertise.

What happened there can also be rephrased as follows: You have your culture and I have mine; we are both intrigued by the way you do things in other ways than I do; nevertheless, we both need to get our facts straight regarding what it means to be a citizen here in Belgium or in Europe at large. This encounter is by definition a "cultural" encounter. It is an encounter where "culture" is not blindly adopted but actively made in the confrontation between the way "we" often blindly follow the guidelines of what is "right" as provided by the administration and the way the undocumented approach it from a less dogmatic perspective and thereby constantly question whether what is considered to be unquestionably juridical is really about doing (global) justice.

LABORING WITH OTHERS, AN ART

When I say that "laboring with others" has the quality of being a cultural-artistic contribution, the "cultural" part represents the encounter with "culture" at its ugliest, that is, "culture" as it is claimed and managed by the administration in the name of participation. It is, nevertheless, precisely the ugliness of the way "culture" is upheld and distributed by and through an administration that renders possible a response to it. In one way or the other the world has "necessarily" become what it is. It has, to say it with Leibniz, become the best of all possible worlds. However, to critically respond to such a world with the same discourse, with the same tools that create and re-create the figure of participation as the only one valid, would be, to keep Wittgenstein in mind, complete nonsense. Even art, at least when it is explained from the perspective that it articulates the world from vantage points different than the standard ones, takes part in the creation and re-creation of the figure of participation. But this is not the "art" the undocumented "perform," both in their confrontation with and their response to the administration. It is not the standard (re)creative "art" that requires the obligatory disinterested onlooker. On the contrary. Their art demands an interested onlooker. Moreover, this "art" not only requires an "other"; it also needs an "ugliness." To be more precise, it needs the ugliness Adorno refers to when he states that "art has to make use of the ugly in order to denounce the world which creates and recreates ugliness in its own name" (Adorno 1984, 72). While Adorno most definitively had another kind of artistic form in mind, that is, a modernist avant-garde one, the confrontation and questions the undocumented pose fit his definition impeccably. These questions are of the same order as the following one: "[T]he only possible question we must pose now, so it seems to me, is *an experimental one*: what will become of human beings and their capacity for aesthetic perception when they are fully exposed to the conditions of monopoly capitalism?" (Benjamin and Adorno 2000, 305). While introducing the capacity for aesthetic perception in relation to a confrontation with an administration might not seem evident, taking into consideration that the conditions of monopoly capitalism fit the logic of participation and vice versa, there indeed is an urgency to do so. More closely to the context of my research, the urgency I appeal to has emerged through the fact that while I encountered many talented and creative individuals among the undocumented I walked with, very few organizations that support and/or assist them in their often long journey to obtain permanent residence documents take their aesthetic traits and qualities into account. The reason for this lack of "aesthetic perception" is not so much to be found in a complete illiteracy with regard to aesthetic perception but with an unfamiliarity of attributing aesthetic traits and qualities to the undocumented. This unfamiliarity is caused and conditioned by the fact that for many administrations, ranging from the governmental organizations over nongovernmental organizations to even socio-artistic organizations that assist or work with the undocumented, only the juridical aspect of their status is taken into account, rather than their status as complete "cultural-artistic" human beings.

From here on it is only a small step to represent the juridical in exchange value terms. Indeed, related to the undocumented and their quest and requests for documents, the juridical is a commodity for which there is a clear market demand. Its products are the various kinds of injustices they encounter along the administrative road. The undocumented, who are all refugees in one way or another, "gain value" for the juridical in that they are considered victims (to be helped or dispelled depending on the way their dossier becomes classified either satisfactory or not) and become "exchange value" in the process of devictimization. As an effect of this participatory market logic, the devictimized, that is, those who obtain the necessary documents to become legal residents, become marketed and "maximized in their autonomy" as immigrant workers. This "need to get a job" logic is part of what participation has come to signify. The question is then: Is this what participation should really be about? Let me recall Adorno:

> The self-evidence of the maxim that work is no disgrace, the guileless absence of all snobbery concerning the ignominy, in the feudal sense, of market relationships, the democracy of the earnings-principle, contribute to the persistence of what is utterly antidemocratic, economic injustice, human degradation. [Moreover], [i]t occurs to nobody that there might be services that are not expressible in terms of exchange value. (2005a, 195)

The reason I quote Adorno here is to point the finger to the "services" or, to put it in my own terminology, "contributions" that remain inexpressible in the dominant and authoritative market vocabulary. As I mentioned earlier, such "contributions" were already announced in the writings of Peggy McIntosh when she referred to the traits and qualities of those who do not belong to the white privileged lifeworld and who remain veiled precisely because of the privileged way "we" address and administrate our lifeworld. Or, on a more general level, in Jacques Rancière's (2010) view, the way he criticizes democracy as a habitat in which any reference to the possibility of dissensus is erased.

Though it might seem that voicing dissensus is precisely what a cultural-artistic contribution is about, Rancière, in fact, is more concerned with (re)creating new access points to the realm of participation. For those thoughts that previously had no part but succeeded in finding such an access point and broke through the logic that provides rules for those that are included in the participatory realm, while at the same time ruling out any other(s), Rancière reserves the name "politics." Not only are the moments when these thoughts become voiced as acts of doing "politics" very rare, a requirement Rancière implicitly puts forward is that these thoughts be voiced in the name of a group. However, in the end these grouped thoughts, which are not to be understood as a representation of social groups but as "forms of inscription of 'the (ac)count of the unaccounted-for'" (Rancière 2001), are merely supplemented to the premises of the logic of participation they cut short on the original task Rancière has taken on himself. This is a task that aims at providing tools of thought to unleash an emancipatory force that has as its quality the ability to break through the logic of participation. Nevertheless, for Rancière, in the end, the logic of participation remains his main point of reference. But even Adorno, in stating that "[p]eace is the state of differentiation without domination, with the differentiated participating in each other" (Adorno 2005b, 247), seems to endorse the perspective of participation. The difference with Rancière is that for Adorno differentiation should be a key aspect of participation, while for the Frenchman the differentiation is to be found outside the logic of participation. For Rancière, peace would be the end result of a "politics" that was able to partake in the logic of participation in which the subject (of grouped thought) is at peace and content with the fact that it has taken part (*prendre*). While the Rancièrean supplement forces the logic of participation to envision the possibility that its premises can become the totality of all possible supplements, which would constitute a Kantian-like perpetual peace extending itself all over the world, Adorno remains more at base. Peace, he asserts, is not about "making the other like itself" (Adorno 2005b, 247), and it is not, to phrase it in the terminology of this volume, about a peace established by laboring with one another *in* the framework of participation, but, rather, it is about a peace between laboring *others*. Adorno is thereby, in my opinion, more concise about the fact that the logic of participation does not have to take precedence in thinking about peace, which can easily be thought to be one of the figures that emerges in the recognition of cultural-artistic contributions. Another such figure is global justice.

GLOBAL JUSTICE

While the requests of the undocumented are formulated at a very local level and are, consequently, processed from the perspective of those who live on the soil these candidate documentees appeal for (permanent) legal residence, from their own perspective these requests have a clear global meaning and reach. In the end theirs is a request to be, after they have obtained the right to legally live on their new foreign soil, permitted to be mobile on a "global" level. For many newly documented, the feat of having received documents signifies that they can, finally, exercise their mobility and travel throughout Europe and the rest of the world (including their home country, which they are now "free" to enter but also "free" to leave to go back to the safe soil that has become their new home ground). However, not only do the difficulties they encounter upon requesting legal residence give voice to the fact that global justice is not easily attainable, they also give voice to the fact that the justice involved in permitting global mobility is still far from being realized. Today, upon becoming immigrant workers, the newly documented can gain access to a particular and very local juridical realm and thus become the participants needed to keep the logic of participation up and running. But before or after receiving documents, the fact remains that their particular cultural-artistic contributions that bear the mark of searching global peace and justice remain negated.

Is global justice then to be equated with the possibility to be mobile on a global level? In fact, that is not the right question to ask. The question today is whether or not the object of global justice, as it requires the realization of being mobile on a global level, is an object that is even possible within the logic of participation.

Taking "culture"—which can easily be replaced with "the logic of participation"—as point of departure, Adorno pointed his finger to the fact that it should be recognized that culture (and, as mentioned above, the ugliness of it) is but a "position within the whole" and that criticism can only then "retain its mobility" (Adorno 1967, 29). This is the point where Adorno suggests that criticism is in need of someone, of some "other" thought than the one that prevails in "culture." To use his words: "Without consciousness transcending the immanence of culture, immanent criticism itself would be inconceivable: the spontaneous movement of the object can be followed only by someone who is not entirely engulfed by it" (Adorno 1967, 29). Not only is the object,[2] be it named peace or global justice, in reach, it also has the quality of being transient and thus in need of someone who can reach and grasp this quality. To put it in the context of my contribution, this someone indeed can be someone who is situated outside the logic of participation, at least he/she needs not to be completely immersed in or intimidated by this logic. In this regard, it is not the experts that co-create the logic of participation with one another that can provide the suitable knowledge to reach peace and justice on a global level, it will be the experts who are confronted with this logic but nevertheless want to labor with others who will guide us toward global justice.

NOTES

1. The center is part of an umbrella organization called CAW De Terp (Antwerp, Belgium) and operates as an independent social welfare organization. Its personnel includes social assistants, social-economy employees, and volunteers who provide assistance to refugees, asylum seekers, undocumented migrants, and people requesting general information concerning legal residence, naturalization, or other information. The research performed in this context encompassed participant observation and in-depth interviews but also assistance in solving several dossiers. It was funded by the EU under the 7th Framework program (acronym: profacity, contract 225511).

2. To be more precise, the object and the way it is configured as referred to here is, while it is always presented as such, never representable in the logic of participation.

BIBLIOGRAPHY

Adorno, Theodor. 1967. *Prisms*. Translated from the German by Samuel and Shierry Weber. Cambridge, MA: The MIT Press.
———. 1984. *Aesthetic Theory*. London: Routledge and Kegan Paul.
———. 2005a. *Minima Moralia: Reflections on a Damaged Life*. New York: Verso.
———. 2005b. *Critical Models*. New York: Columbia University Press.
Benjamin, Walter, and Theodor Adorno. 2000. *The Complete Correspondence 1928–1940*. Cambridge, MA: Harvard University Press.
Buck-Morss, Susan. 1977. *The Origin of Negative Dialectics: Theodor W. Adorno, Walter Benjamin, and the Frankfurt Institute*. New York: The Free Press.
Goethe, Wolfgang. 2010. *Maxims and Reflections*. New York: General Books LLC.
McIntosh, Peggy. 1995. "White Privilege and Male Privilege: A Personal Account of Coming to See Correspondences Through Work in Women's Studies." In *Race, Class, and Gender: Anthology*, second edition, ed. M. L. Andersen and P. H. Collins. Belmont, CA: Wadsworth.
Rancière, Jacques. 1991. *The Ignorant Schoolmaster*. Stanford, CA: Stanford University Press.
———. 2001. "Ten Theses on Politics." *Theory and Event* 5, no. 3: 17–34.
———. 2004. *Disagreement*. Minneapolis: University of Minnesota Press.
———. 2010. *Dissensus: On Politics and Aesthetics*. London: Continuum.
Rancière, Jacques, and Peter Hallward. 2003. "Politics and Aesthetics." Interview. *Angelaki, Journal of the Theoretical Humanities* 8, no. 2: 191–211.

Chapter Four

Trade Unionism and Theories of Global Justice

John Pearson

LIBERAL JUSTICE AND UNION ORGANIZATION

The recent explosion of interest in global justice is both promising and troubling for those with an interest in trade union rights and collective bargaining issues. On the one hand, the theoretical interest in global justice is motivated by concerns that many trade unionists and union supporters share. The concern with deep global inequalities and poverty, interest in issues of fair distribution of goods, resources and the products of social cooperation, and the concern that economic globalization is a potential threat to established conceptions of justice are just some clear and obvious areas of shared concern between global justice advocates and trade unionists.[1] On the other hand, there is potential for tension and conflict between the two approaches. The contemporary interest in global justice issues was initially sparked and has been sustained by the possibility of extending various liberal conceptions of justice beyond the nation-state. However, liberal theories of justice and trade unionism have not traditionally been on particularly friendly terms (Collins 2011). The individualistic emphasis of liberal theories of justice is a source of suspicion among trade unionists—this individualism has been used to attack and undermine collective conceptions of freedom of association and of collective bargaining in particular (Wedderburn 1989).[2] This chapter will discuss how the main prevailing approaches to global justice might understand the role of collective organization, where collective organization is understood as the bundle of rights, institutions, values, and norms that need to be in place for trade unions to function effectively in promoting social justice. The main focus will be on some general concerns that are related to collective organization—most notably, whether the removal of barriers to freedom of association is adequate, or whether institutions at different levels (national, international, and transnational) have strong obligations to actively promote collective organization and collective bargaining. The aim is to provoke debate on the issue of the relationship between global justice and collective organization by suggesting how the different positions in the debate would approach the issue. Since the place of trade unions is undertheorized in the global justice debate, it is worth having an overview of the main positions.[3] However, the chapter also offers some suggestions about how the distinctively republican approach to collective organization might be developed to address some of the problems with the other approaches.

The chapter consists of six sections. The first outlines the models of global justice that will be discussed and identifies some different conceptions of collective organization that might fit with the conceptions of global justice. The next four sections discuss the main theories of justice in relation to collective organization separately. The theories addressed are communitarianism, social liberalism, liberal internationalism, and cosmopolitanism. The final section summarizes and concludes.

MODELS OF GLOBAL JUSTICE AND OF COLLECTIVE BARGAINING

The debate about global justice is an increasingly well-structured and defined subfield of political philosophy. The main positions in the debate are generally well understood, and many of the controversies between the different positions have reached a high level of sophistication. However, because it is not so clear what attitude established theories of global justice would adopt to trade unionism, it seems worthwhile to examine them separately in order to have a better map of the field and hopefully to provoke debate over this important issue. I have tried to identify theorists who are representative of the main positions in the field of global justice. The aim is not so much to provide a review of existing arguments as to try to identify (in many cases, rather speculatively) what position on freedom of association and collective bargaining the different protagonists might adopt if they were pressed to do so. Should those holding the different positions disagree with the positions attributed to them, it is to be hoped that this will provoke them into addressing this issue and clarifying their position.

The main positions in the debate on global justice should be familiar to those with an interest in the field. The positions—communitarianism, social liberalism, liberal internationalism, and cosmopolitanism—will therefore only be outlined very briefly here.

Trade Unionism and Theories of Global Justice Communitarians are some of the strongest opponents of cosmopolitan egalitarianism. Drawing on established communitarian criticisms of liberalism from the domestic level, they argue that cosmopolitan egalitarianism ignores the integrity and legitimacy of different communal cultures. Egalitarian global justice is seen as either impractical (because communities will resist imposition of alien principles of justice) or unattractive (because it ignores other values that a fully rounded theory of justice should acknowledge).[4]

Social liberals object to egalitarian global justice on the grounds that the nation-state is the proper site for egalitarian principles of justice. There is some feature of states that makes them the proper site for principles of egalitarian justice. States are responsible for realizing those principles for their own citizens—obligations of egalitarian justice are not owed by states to individual citizens of other states.[5]

Liberal internationalists hold that there are features of the global economic order that do raise stronger moral obligations than those that hold in situations where no institutional structures exist. However, liberal internationalists deny that these features of the global economic order—be they institutions or other forms of interaction—generate full obligations of egalitarian justice equivalent to what those states owe to their citizens.[6]

Cosmopolitans either argue that there are features of the global economic order that raise full obligations of egalitarian justice, or they argue that the presence or absence of such features is not relevant: human individuals are the correct addressees of justification, and their institutional and other relations are not relevant.[7]

While it is thus possible to identify well-defined positions in the debate on global justice, the relationship between theories of justice and issues of freedom of association and collective bargaining is much less clear. This is an area where the debate is not as well developed. In part, this may stem from a tendency to see liberal conceptions of justice and issues of collective rights as fundamentally opposed. Collective rights—including trade union rights—are often justified in terms of conceptions of social justice that are somewhat alien to the liberal tradition—and discussions of trade unions are somewhat more developed in nonliberal theories of justice.[8] Liberalism is focused on individual rights and freedoms and makes little or no room for collective rights. This is clearly a potential problem for the debate on global justice, which, with some important exceptions, has been dominated by liberal theories of justice. Fortunately, Alan Bogg recently published an enormously important book that puts these discussions in a new perspective (Bogg 2009). Bogg argues that "critical" theories of law that attack liberalism gain much of their apparent force because they exaggerate the unity and homogeneity of the liberal tradition—the idea that liberalism only makes room for individual rights is an unhelpful caricature of that tradition (Bogg 2009, chapter 3). Bogg draws a number of distinctions that can be used to generate a useful taxonomy of approaches to the theory of labor law. This includes a variety of approaches, some of which may allow for greater integration of trade union rights into a liberal perspective than others. We can label the different approaches Bogg identifies in the following ways:

> Market Neoliberalism: This is a position most strongly associated with Friedrich Von Hayek. For Hayek, free markets are essential foundations of liberal freedom. Freedom emerges spontaneously through free markets, so the main role of the liberal state is to protect such markets. Any interference with markets—including interference by trade unions that intervene to set labour standards—will undermine liberal freedom. (Hayek 1960, 1981)

> Natural Rights Neoliberalism: Robert Nozick is the most prominent source of natural rights neoliberalism. For Nozick, all exercises of the power to make contracts between rightful owners of property are legitimate. Trade unions, and even closed shops, are legitimate exercises of contracting powers for Nozick, but states are not entitled to act to encourage them or remove obstacles to their foundation, unless such obstacles themselves violate rights to property and bodily integrity. Nozick also denies that exercises of freedom to contract require any justification in terms of social or community values. (Nozick 1974; Bogg 2009, chapter 3)

These two positions are arguably at the root of the assumption that liberalism neglects trade union rights, yet as Bogg suggests, they are not really representative of a richer liberal tradition. Many of the attacks on liberalism in general only really target neoliberal positions such as Nozick's and Hayek's. Hayek is famously hostile to unions. Although Nozick accepts the right to form unions and even the right to form closed shops, he would not allow for attempts by the state to actively promote unions or to remove obstacles to their formation. However, as Bogg goes on to show, a number of interesting alternative positions have also appeared that can be fitted into a broadly liberal framework:

> Liberal Neutralism: This position accepts the value of communal associations and social forms—a point that distinguishes it from Nozick, who seems indifferent to such associations. However, it is argued that the best way to provide for communal associations, including unions, is to remove obstacles to their formation, and then to allow them to form naturally if individual people wish to support them. This is sometimes described as a "cultural marketplace" view—associations that people value will thrive naturally, those that are not valued will wither away. (Kymlicka 1989; Bogg 2009, chapter 3)[9]

Instrumental-Promotional: On this view, trade unions are important instruments for the promotion of distinctively liberal forms of social justice. John Rawls argued that meaningful freedom depends on access to various primary social goods (Rawls 1971). Stuart White has developed this point and argued that unions are instrumentally necessary for individuals to access these goods. White argues that it is legitimate for a neutral liberal state to promote unions because primary social goods are things that all individuals value, regardless of their other commitments and beliefs. (White 1998; 2001; Bogg 2009, chapter 3)[10]

Republican: On this approach, states should take an active role in promoting collective organization because it helps realize values such as democratic participation and civic virtue. This approach is usually seen as being somewhat at odds with the more neutral liberal tradition, but (as we shall see below) there may be some overlap between such republican approaches and certain forms of liberalism: in particular, Joseph Raz has argued that states should take a more active role in promoting forms of association that promote the essentially liberal value of individual autonomy (Raz 1986, 1995). This might suggest a wider role for such associations, distinguishing it from the narrow focus of the instrumental-promotional approach on securing primary social goods. (Bogg 2009, chapter 3)[11]

In what follows, I want to investigate which of these different approaches to collective organization fits best with the different conceptions of global justice. At one level, the aim is simply to get a better idea of how the different conceptions of global justice would integrate concerns about issues such as freedom of association and collective bargaining—this is worth doing in itself because few authors in the global justice debate have taken up a position on these important issues. However, at a deeper level, I also want to suggest that the development of a distinctively republican approach to freedom of association and collective bargaining is a valuable source of criticism of some of the other positions. My anticipated conclusion is that the republican approach to collective bargaining allows for the extension of republican concerns about political participation and civic virtue beyond the confines of the nation-state, and that this extension can be brought about through freedom of association and collective bargaining.

COMMUNITARIANISM

Communitarian political theorists emphasize the relevance of distinctive local cultures and shared understandings for theories of justice. Typical communitarian arguments include claims that understandings of the subject matter of distributive justice are dependent on the cultural traditions of particular communities and thus cannot be extended across such communities; that liberal individualism is corrosive of the sense of solidarity and common concern necessary to sustain extensive forms of social justice; and that liberal universalism neglects the historical and cultural basis of conceptions of justice (for a useful summary of these arguments see Miller 2000, chapter 7).[12] Communitarianism is generally associated with opposition to extensive forms of egalitarian global justice, and has been highly influential in both academic and public debates. Typically, communitarians have tended to argue that cosmopolitan egalitarianism is both impractical and undesirable: it is impractical because cultural differences make it difficult to apply conceptions of justice across the boundaries of communities, and it is undesirable because it overrides important and valuable local conceptions of justice (Miller 2007, chapters 2 and 3).

Broadly communitarian arguments have had some influence over public debates about labor standards as a global issue. In a discussion of Indian opposition to trade and labor standards linkage in the World Trade Organization,[13] Keven Kolben observes that at least some of the opposition is based on fears that linkage would involve the imposition of alien Western values on Indian society. Kolben cites a Hindu Nationalist source that states the argument in stark terms:

> The reality is that the current manners of conducting our efforts, agriculture, education, research, every jurisdiction is going into the hands of foreigners . . . [The] country will be destroyed. [Such] a mood has developed that whatever commodity, opinion or institution is considered best, is from the West. (Dato-pan Thengri cited in Kolben 2006, 252)

It can be argued that the liberal-neutralist approach to collective organization has a fairly ready answer to communitarian objections of this type. According to this version of the liberal-neutralist approach, the priority is to ensure that workers are not actively prevented from establishing unions or taking part in collective bargaining: liberal neutralists might argue that strong sanctions to compel countries to remove barriers to freedom of association are justified (such as removing laws banning the formation of trade unions), but that countries cannot also be compelled to actively promote collective bargaining. If the cultural traditions of a country militate against workers joining unions, liberal neutralists will not advocate further direct interference. It thus seems possible to argue that a liberal-neutralist approach to international labor standards is compatible with communitarianism: the aim of liberal neutralism is simply to remove obstacles to freedom of association in a given country—once that has been done, the prevailing cultural traditions in the country will determine whether and how union organization will take shape.[14] Indeed, the apparent compatibility between liberal neutrality and communitarianism has led some theorists to develop hybrid liberal-communitarian theories of justice—Will Kymlicka is perhaps the most significant advocate of this type of approach (Kymlicka 1989).[15] One additional extension of this liberal-neutralist version of communitarianism to the labor standards issue is that it might require action at the global level to remove domestic obstacles to freedom of association—there seems no reason in principle for liberal neutralist cosmopolitans to object to such action if it allows for the evolution of associations that emerge spontaneously from the exercise of freedom of association in accordance with local traditions.

Some communitarians, however, might argue that the liberal-neutralist approach is inadequate and thus reject the fusion of liberal neutralism and communitarianism found in the work of thinkers like Kymlicka.[16] One broad communitarian concern is that globalization is undermining the distinct historical and cultural traditions that inform each country's conception of justice. This effect can extend to trade unionism, which is vulnerable to the effects of global economic competition: a familiar objection to economic globalization is that it exerts a "chilling" effect on freedom of association and collective bargaining. Workers and unions may be discouraged from engaging in forms of freedom of association and collective bargaining by the fear that such practices will lead to them being undercut by countries with lower standards—lower labor standards provide advantages such as lower labor costs that can increase countries' competitive advantage (Bagwell and Staiger 1999).[17] Such chilling effects might take two general forms: either legal standards promoting and improving freedom of association and collective bargaining will not be adopted, or existing laws and standards will be weakly enforced. On this communitarian argument, liberal-neutralism leaves too much room for potential competition between countries: fear of competition means that one country's adoption of lower standards can (however unwittingly) discourage others from adopting and implementing the standards that best reflect their own cultural traditions and conceptions of justice. That is to say, simply remaining neutral with regard to all countries' choices regarding collective organization may undermine each country's ability to choose and implement industrial relations structures that match its traditions. This objection to the attempt to fuse liberal neutralism and communitarianism raises a dilemma for communitarians. The traditional response to the threat of competition on labor standards is protectionism: countries withdraw from trade with others by erecting trade barriers and by subsidising their own industries. This seems a tempting approach for those worried about the effect of foreign competition on domestic forms of social justice, including trade union rights. However, such measures are heavily criticized from an economic perspective as being highly inefficient, as well as being unfair to developing countries that may require access to the markets of developed countries in order to make progress on economic development (see James 2012 for a discussion of relevant arguments). Some theorists working in the communitarian tradition, such as David Miller, accept these economic arguments (Miller 2007, chapter

9). The alternative seems to be greater coordination at the global level to ensure that collective bargaining traditions are not undermined—however, communitarians tend to be suspicious of such coordination or to underestimate the need for it. A scheme of compensation or support for countries whose freedom of association and collective bargaining traditions are subject to "chilling" effects seems justifiable from a communitarian point of view, but it also seems to push in the direction of stronger obligations of global justice and cooperation than most communitarians would be prepared to accept.[18]

Even if communitarians can resolve this dilemma, a second criticism of communitarian approaches is that they exhibit a status-quo bias: there is a worry that they tend to take existing cultural traditions at face value. Cultural traditions can involve discrimination and oppression, and these traditions can influence collective organization: the persistence of de facto exclusion of women from trade unions in many countries is a clear example of this (Savage 2000, for example, emphasizes the exclusion of women from trade unions and male working-class culture in general in Western countries). Both the liberal-neutralist and the "compensatory" approaches to communitarianism are vulnerable to this criticism. Liberal-neutralism—as pointed out above—defers to the cultural traditions in a particular country. Once obstacles to freedom of association are removed, neutrality seems to require that there will be no further attempts to promote collective bargaining, even if cultural traditions lead to the de facto exclusion of groups such as women from union membership and collective bargaining. On the "compensatory" approach, workers in countries who can show that they have an established tradition of collective bargaining that has been undermined by globalization might be able to make a case for compensation or support. However, workers in countries that lack such a tradition will not be able to claim that globalization has harmed them by damaging their established structures of freedom of association and collective bargaining—again, the compensatory approach seems directed to what the existing traditions in a given country dictate. If communitarians accept either the liberal-neutralist or compensatory approaches outlined above, they leave themselves vulnerable to the charge of taking existing cultural attitudes to collective bargaining at face value, rather than asking about the origins and effects of those traditions.[19]

Interestingly, some different versions of communitarianism have emerged more recently that can, arguably, avoid the charge of status-quo bias. These approaches are closer to the republican approach mentioned above. Furthermore, as I will argue below, the arguments proponents of these versions of communitarianism advance also make it possible to separate communitarian concerns from their connection to particular nations—this possibility is relevant to the issue of collective organization because it suggests that obligations to promote or protect it extend beyond the national level.

Recent communitarian arguments have shifted the focus from the cultural values particular communities hold to the issue of how the existence of communities is necessary for the fundamentally liberal value of autonomy to have any meaning. Joseph Raz is one of the most prominent exponents of this approach (Raz 1986, 1995): Raz argues that without a network of values, goods, and options, liberal autonomy would have no meaning: there would be no options for the autonomous individual to choose between. Further-more, the values, goods, and options that allow for the exercise of autonomy are themselves socially constituted and require active support from the liberal state. Certain forms of social good are conducive to promoting autonomy—others are not. For Raz, it is a requirement that states support those that are autonomy promoting. This severs the link between existing cultural forms and the value of community: Raz does not advocate respect for all cultural forms, only those that are likely to promote autonomy (Raz 1986, 162). This form of communitarianism can therefore avoid the charge of status-quo bias: the concern is that a given social form supports autonomy, not that it reflects the prevailing status quo or cultural attitudes. All of this is, of course, rele-vant to freedom of association and collective bargaining. Applying Raz's approach to trade union organization, it could be argued that certain forms of freedom of association and collective bargaining are supportive of autonomy and that there is an obligation to promote those forms—trade unionism po-tentially allows for democratic decisions about workplace issues. This is more autonomy promoting than subordination to management decisions. This brings Raz's approach closer to the republican conception of freedom of association and collective bargaining outlined above, because Raz's ap-proach makes the active promotion of particular conceptions of collective bargaining legitimate. Raz's focus on autonomy gives his approach a distinc-tively liberal emphasis.

While Bogg has done some important work to develop and apply Raz's approach to freedom of association and collective bargaining at the domestic level (Bogg 2009, chapter 3), it also seems possible to apply it to the same issues at the transnational level. In principle, Raz's autonomy arguments can be used to generate obligations with regard to collective bargaining that apply at multiple levels—that is, beyond the nation-state. At the domestic level, the possible threat that globalization and economic integration poses to freedom of association and collective bargaining suggests that states are required to cooperate with international institutions that support those rights, precisely in order to support trade union membership as a social structure that promotes autonomy. Similarly, there seems to be no reason why states should ignore the possible effects of their actions on freedom of association and collective bargaining in other countries: there seems to be no reason to confine concern with Raz's particularly social conception of autonomy to the domestic context. Finally, international institutions may also have responsibilities to take account of the possible effects their actions may have on freedom of association and collective bargaining as examples of social practices that promote autonomy.

In summary, the rather crude versions of communitarianism that have influenced public debates on labor standards issues conceal a more interesting and complex set of sources of arguments about labor standards. Some communitarians may argue for a liberal-neutral approach to freedom of association and collective bargaining. Other communitarians may argue that communities have a right to claim support or compensation for the possibly corrosive effects of globalization on their domestic traditions—although dealing with the demands for compensation may push toward greater global cooperation than most communitarians envisage. Finally, Raz's liberal communitarian approach provides a somewhat different perspective: Raz is not so much concerned with existing cultural values and standards as with the role of communities in promoting autonomy. As I argued above, it is also possible on the basis of this approach to weaken the traditional links between community and nations: if autonomy is indeed the fundamental value in Raz's approach, and if social forms such as trade unions are valuable social structures that promote autonomy, there may be a more general duty to promote freedom of association and collective bargaining that both stretches across state boundaries and applies to institutions other than states. Put differently, there seems no inherent reason to draw a strong link between nations and communities if we can show that there are other social sources of autonomy that both exist below the state level and need support across national boundaries: trade unions seem like a good example of such social sources of autonomy.

SOCIAL LIBERALISM

Social liberalism is an approach to global justice that is most closely associated with John Rawls.[20] In the *Law of Peoples* (Rawls 1999), Rawls famously argues that obligations of egalitarian justice are only owed at the domestic level: they apply within the boundaries of entities that resemble nation-states, but not between states or between individual persons at the global level.[21] Rawls's social liberal approach is relevant to issues of freedom of association and collective bargaining at both the domestic and the international levels.

The liberal political and philosophical tradition has often been associated with hostility or indifference to collective rights, including trade union rights.[22] These attitudes are mostly connected to liberalism's focus on individual rights, which are generally assumed to raise conflicts with collective rights. Discussing issues of freedom of association and collective organization, Stuart White has argued that Rawls's liberal domestic theory of justice need not be hostile or indifferent to collective rights relating to trade unions, and in fact can be used to justify an instrumental approach that actively supports the development of collective bargaining institutions (White 1998, 2001). White's argument is that collective bargaining is a distinctive form of freedom of association. Other forms, such as religious or cultural associations, are expressive in character: they enable people to express their distinctive conceptions of the good, and the liberal state properly takes a neutral attitude to them—a liberal state should not promote or favor particular associations that express specific conceptions of the good (White 1998).[23] Trade unions are different from other associations, though: one of their most important functions is to help individuals secure access to basic primary social goods that all individuals—regardless of their expressive beliefs and conceptions of the good—need in order to function as free and equal citizens. As a result, White argues, a liberal state should not adopt a neutral attitude to trade—rather, the state's obligation to promote domestic egalitarianism raises a demand to actively promote the development of collective bargaining as a means to achieving greater equality. White's approach is thus an instrumental-promotional approach to trade union rights (Bogg 2009, chapter 3).

White's approach also has the resources to address liberal objections to the claim that liberal states should adopt an instrumental-promotional approach. There are four main objections to such an approach: that it is unjust, that it is inefficient, that it is ineffective, and that it is overly intrusive. I will discuss these in turn. The injustice claim holds that trade union organization is unfair because unions secure benefits for their members, often at the expense of poorer and weaker groups. However, as Bogg points out (Bogg 2009, chapter 3), White can deflect this objection by stressing that an instrumental-promotional approach requires that trade union organization and collective bargaining should be of the correct kind: unions should be encompassing and authoritative, meaning that they represent the full range of workers' interests and even, as White suggests, represent unemployed people as well. If their representation is encompassing in this way, unions will be less likely merely to defend narrow sectional interests.

A second objection is that unions are inefficient: this objection is rooted in classical and neoliberal attitudes to unions, which hold that they are likely to push wages and employment above levels that markets in equilibrium would sustain—unions are a source of economic inefficiency. White can respond to this argument by drawing on his point that unions do not just have to focus on wages and employment: they can recast themselves as "human capital agencies," taking on responsibilities to train and develop skills that employers tend to neglect because of incentive problems (White 2001). Developing a higher-skilled workforce can lead to greater productivity and competitiveness in the long run. Although the UK is not a particularly good example of this approach, Scandinavian countries in particular seem to have been successful in adopting such an approach. As a further point, unions are again less likely to push for inefficient levels of wages and employment if they are properly encompassing—that is, if they are broadly representative and integrated into negotiating structures (Bogg 2009, chapter 3).

The third objection is that unions are increasingly weak in many societies and are unlikely to be able to achieve the goals of greater equality and social justice from such a position of weakness. White's instrumental approach seems particularly vulnerable to this charge: if unions do not serve the instrumental purposes he claims, his case for their place in a liberal theory of social justice seems dangerously weak. Bogg responds to this objection by again pointing out that the form union organization and bargaining structures take is important (Bogg 2009, chapter 3). For example, bargaining in the UK is decentralized, raising the problem of conflicts between unions and weakening their position. It also has a limited range of subject matter—the legal duty to bargain only covers pay, hours, and holidays. However, such weakness is not inevitable: governments and legislators could take a stronger promotional stance, changing legal structures to encourage encompassing unions with a wider bargaining agenda that addresses broad social justice issues.[24]

A final objection to White's instrumental-promotional approach is the argument that the basic rights the approach secures could also be secured through other means. Hugh Collins has directed a version of this argument against a similar liberal attempt to justify social and economic rights, including trade union rights (Collins 2011). Collins targets Jeremy Waldron's claim that trade union rights can be defended through an argument that unions play a role in helping individuals secure access to basic goods such as food and shelter through employment that is correctly regulated—for example, unions might press for minimum wages that enable people to at least meet their subsistence needs. Collins objects that these basic goods could just as well be secured through direct welfare state provision as through employment regulation and collective bargaining. There are two responses to this. First, unions can also play a role in ensuring that welfare state provision is adequate and effective—they have a strong incentive to do so, since an effective welfare state is in the interests of their members. Second, Collins's conception of the goods that unions aim to secure seems very restricted and falls far short of the conception of social justice at stake in White's argument. Even if it is plausible to suppose that very basic goods would be adequately provided for through a welfare state in the absence of unions, it seems less plausible to argue that more complex social justice issues, such as training, access to education, employment protection, or discrimination, would be adequately addressed in the absence of unions of a sufficiently encompassing and representative form. Collins's conception of social justice thus seems too narrow:

unions have a more obviously important role in addressing the more complex social justice issues referred to.

It thus seems to be possible to construct and defend a plausible case for an instrumental-promotional approach to trade union rights from the perspective of Rawls's social liberal theory of justice. However, as noted, Rawls rejects the claim that obligations to promote social justice extend across international boundaries. Although, on White's argument, a liberal state would be required to adopt an instrumental-promotional approach to freedom of association in order to meet liberal standards of domestic justice, Rawls would reject the claim that there should be any pressure to do so at the international level. Rawls argues that both liberal states and decent nonliberal societies have equal standing in international society. While decent nonliberal societies may be seen as unjust from a liberal perspective, liberal societies must respect them—Rawls prohibits intervention, incentives, and even criticism of decent societies as violations of the equal status of decent societies under the *Law of Peoples* (Rawls 1999). In terms of the specific issues of freedom of association and collective bargaining, Rawls's position on global justice is weaker than the liberal neutralist position. Rawls specifies a limited list of human rights, the violation of which would trigger coercive intervention from other peoples (Rawls 1999). The list includes rights to subsistence, security, and personal property, and some liberty of conscience, but importantly for our discussion, it does not include rights to freedom of association (Rawls 1999). Rawls's truncated list, together with his prohibition on incentives or criticism of decent societies, leads to a position that is even weaker than liberal neutralism. Whereas liberal neutralists would require that states at least remove barriers to freedom of association, so that people can form associations should they wish to, Rawls's approach to human rights is compatible with states maintaining considerable barriers to freedom of association—decent societies do not violate Rawls's minimal list of human rights by maintaining such barriers. As long as such barriers do not violate more basic rights (for example, cases of violence against trade unionists that would violate the right to personal security), Rawls would not even allow intervention to remove the barriers, incentives to remove them, or even criticism of peoples that maintain such barriers. Rawls's approach thus falls short of even the liberal-neutral approach, let alone the more demanding instrumental-promotional one. His approach is compatible with peoples implementing laws that forbid the formation of unions and possibly even with laws that forbid people from gathering to protest about mistreatment by their employers.[25]

Rawls seems to have two main reasons for rejecting obligations on peoples to compel, pressure, or provide incentives for others to improve their domestic freedom of association and collective bargaining structures. The first is a responsibility argument: Rawls holds peoples responsible for the choice to adopt domestic arrangements that promote domestic prosperity and

social justice: following the conclusions of mainstream development economics,[26] Rawls argues that domestic cultural and institutional factors are the
most important in determining a peoples' likelihood of achieving prosperity
and social justice (Rawls 1999; see also Risse 2005 for an argument that also
emphasizes the importance of domestic institutions). He also argues that
peoples are largely responsible for the decision to adopt such structures,
except in cases where extreme disadvantages make this difficult. Rawls's
second objection to stronger action to promote a more active domestic approach to freedom of association is that it would be intolerant: it would be
disrespectful of peoples' standing as free and equal members of the society
of peoples to impose demands to alter their domestic social structures to
include greater freedom of association.

The first of these arguments—the responsibility argument—is not con-
vincing in the case of collective organization. As we have already seen, the
structure of the international economic order is such that it exerts pressure on
domestic industrial relations structures.[27] The fear of competition from countries with lower standards can exert a "chilling" effect on labor standards and
collective bargaining: even if states are not forced to lower standards because
of such competition, they may be discouraged from raising them. It therefore
seems inaccurate to claim that states can be held responsible for choosing to
adopt a particular domestic freedom of association and collective bargaining
regime in conditions of competition that make such choices difficult. Greater
coordination to ensure that states can in fact choose their domestic structures
without fear of competition seems necessary for the domestic responsibility
argument to hold.

Furthermore, if the responsibility argument collapses, it seems to bring
down the toleration argument with it. Liberal toleration seems most appropriate when applied to choices for which agents—either states or individuals—
can be held responsible. The "chilling" argument undermines this claim with
regard to domestic freedom of association and collective bargaining: domestic arrangements with regard to these issues are not simply a matter of choice,
given the pressures that international competition exerts in these areas.
Again, greater coordination to mitigate the effects of competition seems necessary for the claim about domestic responsibility to hold: tolerance does not
seem appropriate in cases where domestic arrangements are a matter of structural economic pressures.

However, we could also push further with the argument. As we have seen,
Rawls also relies on a conception of liberal tolerance of nonliberal, decent
societies to justify his limitations on obligations of intervention at the international level. However, White's instrumental-promotional approach can be
defended as compatible with liberal tolerance. As we have seen, White
stresses a distinction between "expressive" and "instrumental" forms of association: the former are the result of peoples' choices of their conceptions of

the good; the latter serve to help them secure basic goods. White argues that liberal toleration only extends to the former types of association—the latter are not within the scope of toleration because they serve to promote basic forms of social justice (White 1998, 2001). This approach could be extended to international toleration: while the "expressive" social structures of different societies should be tolerated, instrumental associative structures such as trade unions that serve to enable their citizens to secure basic goods are not subject to the same demands. If this argument is sound, it could be argued that it is possible to require states to take a more active role in promoting freedom of association and collective bargaining while still upholding a liberal attitude of tolerance to more "expressive" forms of association found in different cultural contexts.

LIBERAL INTERNATIONALISM

Liberal internationalists occupy a middle position between social liberals and cosmopolitans. For liberal internationalists, social liberals underestimate the moral significance of cross-border interactions in an increasingly interconnected global economy. On the other hand, though, liberal internationalists argue that cosmopolitans exaggerate when they claim that such interactions raise similar obligations to the obligations that hold at the domestic level. The challenge for liberal internationalists is to find a feature of global economic interactions that explains why they raise some kind of obligations of justice, without picking out a feature that also exists at the global level, which would push in the direction of stronger cosmopolitan obligations.

A. J. Julius has defended an interesting version of the liberal internationalist approach (Julius 2006). I shall argue below that Julius's approach seems at first sight to fit employer-employee relationships quite well and is thus relevant to the broad issues of collective organization. Julius criticizes Thomas Nagel's argument that obligations of justice only apply to institutions that coercively impose rules in the name of their members (Nagel 2005), but he also criticizes the cosmopolitan response to Nagel. On the one hand, Nagel's argument seems false, as cosmopolitans have argued: states coerce outsiders as well as their own citizens—most notably through preventing immigrants from entering (Abizadeh 2007). On the other, the cosmopolitan coercion argument does not tell us much about the distinctive effects of contemporary economic globalization. The coercion argument based on immigration only focuses on a historical form of coercion that stretches back to the "first time a guard's arrow stopped an alien intruder" (Julius 2006, 187). For Julius, the feature of global interactions that raises demands for justification is that they involve different parties directing the wills of others: institutional structures are structures through which people can direct others to serve their purposes. Julius adopts a Kantian position with regard to such structures, arguing:

> The thing to notice is that you shouldn't use other people by directing their action to your benefit unless you can show that the resulting sequence of actions and results is something they themselves have reason to want to come about. (Julius 2006, 188)

Julius goes on to distinguish the domestic from the global level by stressing the different levels of density of interaction at the two levels. People direct the wills of others by reshaping the networks in which they are involved in order to advance their own interests: it is this relationship of reshaping and direction of wills that raises demands for justification. The distinction between the domestic and the global levels is that the domestic level is closed and complete: in a closed and complete network, everyone bears the reshaping relation only to other members of the group, and every member bears it to every other member. Julius then goes on to argue that it is only in such closed and complete networks that demands of egalitarian justification (Julius specifies Rawls's difference principle) apply. However, other, looser networks do exist at the global level. In such looser networks, a person's action will not exclusively affect other members—it may also have spillover effects on outsiders. On the other hand, the projects a person pursues will not affect the actions of every other person. The effects on outsiders will raise demands for justification from those outsiders, but those demands do not need to be given a full egalitarian response.

At first sight, this approach seems appealing from the perspective of collective organization: in the concern with direction of others' wills, Julius seems to have identified a feature of cross-border interactions that maps neatly onto the relationships between workers and employers. Such relationships are not coercive—they would be condemned as slavery or forced labor if they were. Yet it seems intuitively implausible to claim—as Nagel does—that the relationship between an employer and an employee raises no moral requirements stronger than those that would apply even in the absence of an ongoing institutional relationship. Direction of will seems to fit well with the employer-employee relationship, showing that such relationships, while not coercive, nevertheless involve a form of interaction that raises demands for justification. A further reason for the appeal of the direction of will approach is that the distinction between closed-complete and open networks seems to capture the way employer-employee relationships stretch across national borders: it seems plausible to suggest that an employer can be based in one country and employ some people in another country, without entering into a closed-complete network with all the citizens of the host country.

Despite these attractions, Julius's liberal internationalist approach raises a couple of puzzles when we apply it to the issue of collective organization. The two puzzles are closely interconnected: first, it can be argued that Julius needs to be clearer about exactly why closed-complete networks in particular raise obligations of egalitarian justification. Second, it is not clear if he thinks those who are not now in closed-complete relationships are under any obligation to enter into such relationships.

There are two obvious answers to the first puzzle: either egalitarian justification is owed because the participants cannot agree on the shares of the outcome of their interaction, or it is owed because the closed-complete network puts the participants in a relationship of equality to one another. The first suggestion is not compelling, though, because it does not distinguish between closed-complete and other networks. After all, disagreement about the relative shares of interactions is just as likely to be a feature of networks that are not closed or complete—even an isolated one-off transaction such as the purchase of a used bicycle is likely to raise such disputes. A more promising argument would look at the structure of closed-complete relationships and ask about how they change the position of their members. One argument relates to the dependency of the members of the group. I may be dependent on my share of the outcome of a network of cooperation—most people depend on their wages in order to live a minimally decent life. A network could be defined as closed-complete if each member is dependent on the network to a similar degree: in this case, each member's ability to direct the network is limited because of their dependency. They cannot, for example, realistically threaten to withdraw from the network. This would suggest a relationship of equality of power between the members of the network—each is in a roughly equal relationship of dependency on it and thus has roughly equal power to direct the wills of their fellow members. Of course, one does not need to be an industrial relations expert to realize that employer-employee relationships are not generally like this: in most cases, employers are in a better position to threaten to withdraw from the relationship because they can easily find other workers—they are not dependent in the way workers are. In sectors where capital is highly mobile, the power of employers is still greater—in some sectors, threats to relocate to other countries are very powerful. Employer-employee relationships seem like a particular form of partially closed, partially complete network in which one party is more able than the others to withdraw from the relationship.

This brings us to the second puzzle: are those currently in partially complete, partially closed networks under any obligation to enter into closed-complete relationships with those they interact with? In the case of employer-employee relationships, the answer would seem to be yes: the dependency of the employees on the employers in most such relationships suggests that it is necessary to try to equalize the power relationship between them. Indeed, this is the point of many standard industrial relations tools such as legal obligations to bargain and rights to strike. The point of these tools is to compensate for the different levels of dependency between employers and employees by reducing the employer's ability to threaten to walk away from the relationship and by rebalancing the power between employers and employees.

The upshot of all this is that a plausible interpretation of the liberal internationalist position is that the nature of employee-employer relationships is such that they generate an obligation to enter into full collective bargaining structures that cut across national boundaries. The vulnerability and dependency of workers puts them in an unequal relationship with employers, leaving them vulnerable to employers' unequal ability to direct their wills, and collective organization provides a means to rebalance this inequality. However, liberal internationalists like Julius might add that the scope of obligations of justice is still limited compared to the case of the fully closed and complete network that is the state. In the (idealized) case of an isolated state, the network is closed with regard to all aspects of its members' lives—each person would be equally dependent on all the others for a wide range of socially produced goods. The scope of goods relevant to work relationships is more limited—it could be restricted to issues such as pay, holidays, and pensions, for example.

The general point here is that the liberal internationalist approach could be developed to endorse stronger cross-border collective bargaining structures, but only with regard to a more limited set of issues than those that would be relevant in fully closed and complete relationships. The ground for this is that employment relationships put workers in relationships of dependency on employers that are not closed or complete, but that raise obligations to enter into closed-complete relationships, at least with regard to the narrow range of issues that are directly relevant to work relationships, such as pay and pension provisions.

It may be possible to push the liberal internationalist argument beyond this limited approach to the scope of transnational collective organization, though. The approach to collective organization outlined above fits best with the instrumental-promotional approach to collective bargaining referred to in our taxonomy. However, it could be objected that the instrumental-promotional approach is too limited to succeed, even on its own terms. There are two concerns. The first is that not all workers are likely to be equally dependent on an employer. Background differences in wealth, access to social security provision, and so on will alter the level of dependency, with such differences becoming more pronounced as we cross national boundaries. The second is that limiting the scope of bargaining may reduce workers' opportunities to develop the relevant skills necessary to bargain effectively. In both cases, the problems push us toward a more civic conception of collective bargaining. In the first case, the differences between different types of workers may require either a greater degree of civic virtue or arrangements such as closed shops and strong obligations to abide by decisions such as the decision to go on strike. Such adaptations may be necessary to compensate for differences between workers that would undermine their equal status in the bargaining relationship. In the second case, the need for broader opportunities to develop civic virtues and bargaining skills may push toward demands for a broader bargaining agenda, providing workers with more opportunities to bargain and exercise civic virtue. The general point is that cross-border collective bargaining may push toward a republican approach in which greater intervention to promote collective bargaining of the right kind is required.

In summary, work relationships are a dense form of institutional relationship that cut across national borders, and thus seem to be a good example of the kind of structures that for liberal internationalists raise obligations of justice that cut across state boundaries. However, the relationships of dependency between employers and employees involve relationships of power that, as argued above, raise stronger demands for justification than those Julius envisages. It was argued that employer-employee relationships raise an obligation to enter into relationships equivalent to closed-complete networks in order to neutralize the inequalities of power between workers and employers. If this argument is correct, Julius's liberal internationalist position puts him on a path to rather dense structures of collective organization and collective bargaining, since these are necessary to ensure that worker-employer relationships sufficiently resemble closed-complete networks. Indeed, as pointed out at the end of this section, the requirements for collective bargaining may even push in a republican direction, because the level of civic virtue necessary for transnational collective bargaining to be effective is high. This could require strong structures to ensure workers bargain as equals and a wide bargaining agenda in order to give them sufficient opportunities to develop civic virtues.

COSMOPOLITANISM

Two common features of cosmopolitan theories of global justice are direct concern with the moral standing of individuals and prioritarian concern with the global poor.[28] With regard to the first feature, for most cosmopolitans, individual persons are the fundamental unit of moral concern when attempting to justify the global economic order. Egalitarian justifications are owed to all individuals, not just to fellow members of a state. The standard cosmopolitan argument for this position is that the features that raise obligations of justice within the borders of a state are also present at the global level, so the global economic order raises similar demands for justification (Abizadeh 2007). With regard to the second point, many cosmopolitans focus on the position of the global poor in particular—following Rawls and other prioritarians, they argue that egalitarian justifications should be focused on a particular concern for the worst off in a group among which comparisons are to be made (Kapstein 2004).

It could be argued that the "individualist" and "prioritarian" features of cosmopolitanism are in considerable tension when we consider them in relation to issues of freedom of association and collective bargaining. On the one hand, if the global economic order is indeed sufficiently analogous to the nation-state context, it would seem that cosmopolitans might simply expand the same arguments about freedom of association and collective bargaining from the domestic level to the global level. Given the Rawlsian-liberal inspiration behind many cosmopolitan theories, this would imply that they might adopt an instrumental-promotional attitude to freedom of association and collective bargaining, expanding such an approach to the transnational level.[29] On the other hand, though, the cosmopolitan concern with the position of the worst off raises a potential conflict here: cosmopolitans might raise several worries with regard to the possibility of transnational collective bargaining. First, given the severity of global poverty, it could be argued that a focus on freedom of association and collective bargaining seems misguided. Freedom of association and collective bargaining seem less important than more fundamental concerns such as access to the means of subsistence and basic security. Second, it could be argued that involving the global poor in structures of collective bargaining will do little to help their situation. In an analogy with a domestic left-liberal criticism of collective bargaining, it could be argued that the outcomes of collective bargaining will reflect the existing endowments of those involved (Bogg 2009, chapter 3). Poor, unskilled, developing-country workers have relatively little bargaining power against either employers or better-off workers, and these natural endowments of bargaining power will be reflected in the outcomes of collective bargaining. A third concern is that collective organization simply won't reach the very worst off people in developing countries. A major concern here is that many of the poorest people in developing countries work in the informal sector—an economic sector that falls outside the scope of established collective bargaining structures. As a result, poor people will not be included in collective bargaining structures, and their interests will be inadequately represented.

A further criticism is that concerns relating to freedom of association and collective bargaining are somewhat secondary to more urgent issues such as the problems of desperate poverty and hunger that people in developing countries face. It could be argued that these issues should have priority over concerns about collective bargaining and freedom of association in any theory that gives priority to the position of the worst off.

It is possible for those who advocate advancing freedom of association and collective bargaining at the global level to address these concerns, though. With regard to the first issue, as Bogg points out, any instrumental-promotional approach to collective bargaining will need to be sensitive to the purposes it is intended to serve (Bogg 2009, chapter 3). It is possible to distinguish between different types of collective bargaining—decentralized bargaining in particular seems likely to favor the interests of already privileged groups, whereas more centralized bargaining structures are less likely to do this. The underlying point is that it is possible to shape the nature and outcomes of bargaining through legislative choices about the most appropriate bargaining structures. This argument—which Bogg stresses in the domestic context—could carry over to the global level as well: if we want collective bargaining to address the interests of the poorest and worst off, we need to make important choices about the appropriate levels and structures of bargaining. This might, for example, involve trying to centralize global-level collective bargaining as much as possible or trying to form regional blocs in bargaining structures so that the interests of the poorest countries carry greater weight. Again, the underlying point is that it is possible to choose between different structures, and that it may be possible to learn from what has been most effective in the domestic context (e.g., centralized bargaining over decentralized bargaining) in advancing the interests of the worst-off groups.

With regard to the second issue, Jeremy Waldron provides a useful response to the apparent dilemma between urgent issues of desperate poverty and other issues such as freedom of association and collective bargaining.[30] Rights such as freedom of association and collective bargaining can be justified in terms of promotion of human agency: such rights enable people to take collective control over their working lives and other social concerns. As Waldron points out, though, such rights will have little meaning if people are too poor and desperate even to act as responsible agents: "If we truly respect human agency as an end in itself, we must follow that end where it leads and, in the circumstances of human life, that may well require us to attend to the needs of persons whose ability to function as agents is imperilled by poverty or diseases or by the fear of those predicaments" (Waldron, quoted in Collins 2011, 152). The key point here is that attending to urgent issues of poverty is compatible with advancing freedom of association and collective bargaining, precisely because freedom from extreme poverty is a necessary condition for the kind of agency that freedom of association and collective bargaining aim to advance.

The third objection suggests that freedom of association and collective bargaining would not actually reach the very worst off in developing countries: on this view, trade unions serve to advance the interests of groups who take part in formal employment, and neglect the interests of outsiders. However, this argument seems based on a rather narrow conception of the scope of collective bargaining. In fact, cosmopolitan political theorists have made some arguments that might well expand the scope of concerns of collective bargaining. For example, Arash Abizadeh has stressed that Rawls's claim that considerations of justice apply only to schemes of social cooperation is implausible and needs to be reformulated (Abizadeh 2007). Put briefly, if Rawls argues that a scheme of social cooperation is a model of fairness, it would be absurd to claim that considerations of fairness only apply to schemes of social cooperation: considerations of justice would only apply to schemes that are already fair and would thus lose any critical bite. It makes more sense to identify forms of interaction that raise an instrumental demand for structures of fairness. As Abizadeh points out, Rawls himself identifies such schemes in his reply to Robert Nozick: as Rawls argues, unregulated schemes of economic exchange will lead to unfairness over time as the various exchanges accumulate and generate inequalities among the participants. Simple, unregulated economic exchange raises demands for institutional structures to ensure fairness over time. This point can be extended to the problem of the informal sector and collective bargaining: while workers in the informal sector are not able to participate in collective bargaining, their role as economic actors strongly suggests that they should be able to. Rather than arguing that traditional collective bargaining structures neglect the interests of informal sector workers, we should find ways to include them on the grounds that they are economic actors with similar interests to other workers.

It thus seems possible for advocates of an instrumental-promotional approach to collective bargaining to address some of the main concerns that conventional cosmopolitans might raise in response to the advocacy of collective bargaining as a way to address issues of global justice. It would be an overstatement to claim that cosmopolitans will inevitably endorse the instrumental-promotional approach to collective bargaining. However, the parallels cosmopolitans draw between the domestic and the global levels, coupled with the important work of theorists like White in embedding collective bargaining in a Rawlsian framework of global justice, suggest that cosmopolitans need to investigate this option and, if they reject it, provide some more robust reasons than those outlined above for doing so.

The previous paragraph suggests that there is an interesting internal debate to be had between liberal cosmopolitans and theorists like White, who propose an instrumental-promotional approach to freedom of association and collective bargaining at the domestic level. There is also a possible external criticism of White's instrumental-promotional approach, though. Republican political theorists will again object that the instrumental-promotional approach to collective bargaining will be unlikely to succeed in the absence of stronger action to develop civic virtues necessary for effective collective bargaining. A purely instrumental attitude to collective bargaining may not be enough to sustain appropriate participation in often demanding bargaining processes. Such arguments usually lead to something of an impasse: a corollary to these republican claims about civic virtue and participation is that the appropriate place for the development of civic virtues is the nation-state.[31] If the nation-state is the appropriate site for developing civic virtue, this potentially confines the scope of the most robust forms of democratic participation within those boundaries, since the fellow-feelings and sense of common cause will be restricted to those who share a national identity.

However, the discussion of republicanism and communitarianism above suggests that freedom of association and collective bargaining themselves provide a potential way to avoid this impasse. Trade unions are institutions that provide possible sites for the development of civic virtues that are not inevitably confined to the nation-state.[32] While it may be true that many unions often do remain trapped in a nationally focused approach, it is not inevitable that this should be the case—unions do engage in activities that show signs of transnational solidarity and could be encouraged in this tendency. Decisions about the scope of collective bargaining units and the range of subject matter to be addressed though bargaining could serve to alter the national focus of collective bargaining. For example, it might be possible to define the scope of collective bargaining units in terms of sectors that extend across national boundaries. It would also be possible to legitimize solidarity action across national boundaries—such action often faces severe legal obstacles. Policy decisions like these could provide an environment in which the civic virtues that are associated with collective bargaining are less strictly confined to national contexts.

A second point is that the republican approach discussed above (which draws on Bogg's interpretation of Raz) potentially helps address a further normative objection to extending collective bargaining in the ways suggested. One objection to doing this is that extending collective bargaining in the ways suggested would conflict with liberal respect for values such as national self-determination—a value that cosmopolitans generally make at least some room for.[33] Requiring states to adopt a civic republican approach to collective bargaining would undermine their legitimate choice as to which kind of collective bargaining regime to adopt. On the civic republican approach Bogg adopts, such an argument loses much of its force: before deciding whether a given regime of collective bargaining is indeed legitimate, we have to examine the social practices on which it is founded. If it turns out that these practices generally serve to undermine autonomy, we are not bound to respect those practices as legitimate. Put differently, the civic approach suggests that we are not bound to mirror social practices with regard to collective bargaining and should take a critical attitude to the legitimacy of the practices based on whether or not they promote autonomy.

CONCLUSION

This chapter has discussed how different approaches to global justice might understand collective organization by trade unions. I will summarize the communitarian, social liberal, liberal internationalist, and cosmopolitan approaches before offering some final conclusions. Some communitarian approaches might see collective organization as simply one form of communal value among others—we should remove obstacles to collective organization, but not actively promote it. This is an approach that fits quite well with liberal-neutralist forms of communitarianism such as Will Kymlicka's approach. Other communitarians might argue for action to compensate for the corrosive effect of globalization on collective organization, although again, such compensation would only be required if its collective organization is shown to be part of a country's established traditions. Yet another alternative is to argue for the active promotion of collective organization as a social form that realizes the value of autonomy: this is a position that Alan Bogg has developed on the basis of the work of Joseph Raz.

John Rawls's version of social liberalism famously adopted a limited list of human rights. As we saw above, because Rawls did not include freedom of association in his list, his approach seems compatible with the existence of considerable barriers to collective organization. This position is based on the claim that states are responsible for maintaining their own domestic structures of justice, so any obstacles to collective organization are their own responsibility. This claim can be criticized though: it is not clear in an integrated global economy that states really are free to choose how to deal with collective action. This suggests a need for greater coordination to ensure states are in fact able to make domestic choices in this area. As a further point, it was also argued that requiring states to set up stronger collective organization structures might not be a violation of liberal tolerance among different societies: because collective organization is instrumental and not expressive in purpose, requiring collective organization does not involve violating the liberal tolerance of different states' cultural traditions. On this view, social liberalism would in fact be compatible with an instrumental-promotional approach to collective bargaining—although this takes us a long way from Rawls's limited set of human rights obligations.

Liberal internationalists acknowledge the existence of cross-border relationships distinct from those that hold within states. Such relationships raise obligations of justice, but of a different kind than those that hold between states and their citizens. Examining Julius's argument, I suggested that employer-employee relationships are a distinctive example of this kind of relationship. There are power imbalances between employers and employees that create obligations to enter into denser institutional networks than currently exist: in practice, this would mean transnational collective bargaining and collective organization structures. Liberal internationalists might argue that the subject matter of such bargaining should be limited to matters directly relevant to the particular work relationship. From a republican position, however, it could be argued that the relationship needs to be denser: in order to succeed, transnational collective bargaining needs both a broad agenda and a strong structure. The liberal internationalist position thus seems to be gradually pushed toward increasingly dense institutional structures at the transnational level.

Finally, cosmopolitans might express some doubts about the urgency of issues of collective organization in the face of extreme poverty. I attempted to address the main concerns that cosmopolitans might raise by arguing first that it might be possible to adapt transnational collective organization so that it is attentive to the needs of the poor; second, that many of the concerns that cosmopolitans raise about extreme poverty are also relevant to individuals' ability to participate meaningfully in collective organization; and third, that the concern about including poor people in collective organization can be addressed if we conceive of the basis of rights to collective organization in terms of a broader conception of economic activity that would take in the informal sector.

Throughout these discussions, an underlying concern has been whether any of the liberal conceptions of collective organization outlined above are adequate to sustain genuinely meaningful and effective forms of such organization. This is a republican objection: republicans are likely to object that the generally instrumental liberal approach to collective bargaining is unlikely to be adequate to sustain the civic virtues necessary for effective collective bargaining. This is potentially problematic because civic virtue is usually associated with nation-states in the republican tradition: if civic virtue is so confined, it will be difficult to extend it across national borders. However, a promising suggestion is to further develop the republican conception of collective organization referred to above. On this conception, trade unions and collective organization are institutional structures in which civic virtues can in fact be learned independently of the national context. The republican conception of collective organization and Joseph Raz's distinctive conception of communitarianism both seem like valuable sources that can be used to develop this argument. If, as was also pointed out above, more effective collective organization by workers is necessary to make any progress toward global justice, and if civic virtues are necessary to sustain such collective action, it will be vital to develop this distinctive version of republicanism.

NOTES

1. Other issues of common concern would include the worry that globalization is undermining established forms of democratic representation; the possibilities and problems of

stronger transnational regulatory structures; and issues relating to the justice of international migration. Political philosophers with an interest in global justice have only relatively recently begun to address more specific labor-related issues. Examples include Meyer (2002); Young (2006); Brock (2009), and James (2012).

2. Wedderburn documents the Thatcher regime's use of Hayek's political theory to justify politically motivated attacks on trade unions in the UK.

3. The discussion about whether labor rights are also human rights is a major topic in labor law. See especially Alston (2005). Here again, the perceived individualistic nature of human rights has led to conflict with labor rights and labor standards advocates—the tension between human rights and labor rights is emphasized in Kolben (2009). One of the few discussions of this issue from a political theorist is Risse (2009).

4. Many early communitarians were also explicit opponents of liberalism. MacIntyre and Sandel are obvious examples. More recently, there has been a convergence between liberals and communitarians. Communitarians have developed more liberal versions of the communitarian approach (for example Kymlicka and Miller), while some liberals have modified their theories to take account of communitarian arguments (most significantly Rawls). For discussion of these convergences, see Miller (2000) and Swift and Mulhall (1996).

5. Prominent advocates of social liberal positions include Rawls (1999), Nagel (2005), and Risse (2005).

6. The liberal internationalist position has only relatively recently begun to receive detailed discussion, and it is sometimes hard to situate particular authors as liberal internationalists given its intermediate position. Theorists who have adopted positions that might be classified as liberal internationalist include Julius (2006), James (2012), Cohen and Sabel (2005), and Sangiovanni (2007).

7. As Sangiovanni (2007) points out, it is possible to distinguish between relational and nonrelational versions of cosmopolitanism. Thomas Pogge's work is an example of a relational view because Pogge argues that various forms of global interconnectedness raise obligations of justice that would not exist in the absence of such connections (Pogge 1989, 2002). Simon Caney is critical of this view, arguing for a nonrelational position in which obligations of justice are owed to people simply in virtue of their humanity (Caney 2004).

8. Philip Pettit addresses such issues briefly (1997). The most detailed recent treatments of work-related issues from political philosophers have come from those working in the republican tradition: see Shapiro (1999) and Sandel (1998).

9. Bogg (2009, 93ff).

10. Bogg (2009, 101ff).

11. Bogg (2009, 107ff).

12. Prominent communitarian positions include Walzer (1983), Sandel (1998), MacIntyre (1988), and Miller (1995). Of these, Miller (2007) has developed the most fully elaborated version of a communitarian-inspired approach to global justice, although he increasingly distances himself from a sharp cosmopolitan-communitarian divide.

13. Linkage involves the requirement that market liberalization should be made conditional on countries ensuring that they implement at least minimal labor standards such as the International Labour Organisation's Core Labour Standards. For an important recent linkage proposal see Barry and Reddy (2006).

14. Removing obstacles to freedom of association is of course a complicated and controversial process. On one view, freedom of association is just another civil and political right along with property rights—once such minimal rights are in place, the cultural marketplace can operate freely. However, on a stronger view, we also need to ask whether particular groups are placed at a disadvantage in the cultural marketplace due to inequalities of power or resources. On this view, state intervention may be needed to address such disadvantages as they occur over time. Both White and Kymlicka endorse this stronger, "power-adjusted" conception of freedom of association.

15. Kymlicka endorses a "power-adjusted" approach to freedom of association—see the previous note.

16. Michael Sandel, for example, is a prominent critic of liberal neutralism and has discussed trade union rights in the United States in this context, although he does not extend his discussion to the transnational level. See Sandel (1998) and Bogg (2012).

17. Bagwell and Staiger and Barry and Reddy stress that the "chilling" hypothesis is more plausible than the "race to the bottom" hypothesis that has informed much debate over issues such as labor standards. The main difference is that whereas the race to the bottom hypothesis holds that countries will actually lower labor standards, the chilling hypothesis holds that they will be discouraged from either raising standards or from enforcing existing standards (Bagwell and Staiger 1999; Barry and Reddy 2006).

18. It is of course possible that those who, like Kymlicka and White, adopt a power-adjusted conception of liberal neutrality might see such a scheme as a form of power adjustment.

19. Bogg stresses a number of arguments about preference formation to suggest that supposedly democratic decisions about trade union representation are not legitimate. For example, he notes the way the "endowment effect"—the fact people often prefer to keep goods already owned rather than exchange them for unknown goods of a higher value—can be applied to trade union representation: workers are more likely to support unionisation once they have been union members (Bogg 2009, chapter 3).

20. Charles Beitz applied the label "social liberalism" to identify Rawls's domestic theory of liberal justice and to distinguish it from the cosmopolitan version (Beitz 1999).

21. Discussing Rawls's *Law of Peoples* in a broader context is made somewhat complicated because of the distinctive vocabulary Rawls uses. "Peoples" correspond roughly to nation-states that meet certain standards of legitimacy and include both liberal democratic and "decent hierarchical" societies.

22. This hostility is especially closely associated with the specifically *libertarian* branch of liberalism and within that tradition the work of Hayek in particular, as Bogg (2009, chapter 3) stresses. However, liberal interpretations of freedom of association more generally are often seen to be hostile to union rights. The liberal and human rights prohibition of "closed shops" is a clear example. See White (1998) for discussion.

23. This is a clear contrast with Raz, who argues that states have a duty to promote the liberal value of autonomy.

24. Bogg stresses Charles Sabel and Joel Rogers's "artifactual" approach to labor law, which holds that legal norms can serve to shape social practices, so that it is circular to assume that legal norms should simply reflect social practices (Bogg 2009, chapter 3).

25. Rawls stipulates that "decent hierarchical" societies should implement systems of consultation between their governments and their citizens, but it is not clear if Rawls would include rights to protest in such consultation systems (Rawls 1999).

26. Risse (2005) makes the link between global justice and mainstream development theory more explicit, stressing that domestic institutions contribute to a country's prosperity, but also that it is difficult for outsiders to actively intervene to construct such institutions. From this, Risse concludes that obligations of global justice are limited.

27. See the above discussion of Bagwell and Staiger and the "chilling" phenomenon.

28. Refer to Pogge, Kapstein, etc.

29. That is, if the analogies between the domestic and the global levels hold, the arguments White makes for trade unions as a feature of domestic liberal theories of justice should also extend to the global level.

30. See the discussion of Waldron in Collins (2011).

31. An argument David Miller has stressed throughout his work on global justice (Miller 1995, 2000, 2007).

32. Miller (2000) suggested that citizenship virtues learned in one context could carry over to others. Although Miller suggests this is an objection to global justice, it is not clear why the position is an objection to principles of global justice. In fact, it seems more appropriate to see Miller's argument as a practical point about how best to achieve global justice.

33. Kok Chor Tan's *Justice without Borders* is an important discussion of the issue of how far cosmopolitans should make room for national self-determination.

BIBLIOGRAPHY

Abizadeh, Arash. 2007. "Co-operation, Pervasive Impact and Coercion: On the Scope (not Site) of Distributive Justice." *Philosophy and Public Affairs* 35, no. 4: 318–358.

Alston, Philip, ed. 2005. *Labour Rights as Human Rights*. Oxford: Oxford University Press.

Bagwell, Kyle, and Robert Staiger. 1999. "The Simple Economics of Labour Standards and the GATT." In *Social Dimensions of US Trade Policy*, ed. Alan Deardorff and Robert Stern. Ann Arbor: University of Michigan Press.

Barry, Christian, and Sanjay Reddy. 2006. "International Trade and Labour Standards: A Proposal for Linkage." *Cornell International Law Journal* 39, no 4: 546–635.

Beitz, Charles. 1999. "Social and Cosmopolitan Liberalism." *International Affairs* 75, no 3: 515–529.

Bogg, Alan. 2009. *The Democratic Aspects of Trade Union Recognition*. Hart.

Brock, Gillian. 2009. *Global Justice: A Cosmopolitan Account*. Oxford: Oxford University Press.

Caney, Simon. 2004. *Justice Beyond Borders: A Global Political Theory*. Oxford: Oxford University Press.

Cohen, Joshua, and Charles Sabel. 2005. "Global Democracy?" *NYU Journal of International Law and Politics* 37, no. 4: 763–797.

Collins, Hugh. 2011. "Theories of Rights as Justifications for Labour Law." In *The Idea of Labour Law*, ed. Guy Davidov and Brian Langille. Oxford: Oxford University Press.

Hayek, Friedrich von. 1960. *The Constitution of Liberty*. London: Routledge.

———. 1981. *1980's Unemployment and the Unions*. London: IEA.

James, Aaron. 2012. *Fairness in Practice*. Oxford: Oxford University Press.

Julius, A. J. 2006. "Nagel's Atlas." *Philosophy and Public Affairs* 34, no 2: 176–192.

Kapstein, Ethan. 2004. "Models of International Economic Justice." *Ethics and International Affairs* 18, no. 2: 79–92.

Kolben, Kevin. 2006. "The New Politics of Labour: India's Defeat of the Workers' Rights Clause." *Indiana Journal of Global Legal Studies* 13, no. 4: 225–259.

———. 2009. "Labour Rights as Human Rights?" *Virginia Journal of International Law* 50: 449–484.

Kymlicka, Will. 1989. *Liberalism, Community and Culture* . Oxford: Oxford University Press.

MacIntyre, Alasdair. 1988. *Whose Justice, Which Rationality?* Indiana: University of Notre Dame Press.

Mayer, Robert. 2002. "A Walzerian Theory of Exploitation." *Polity* 34: 337–354.

———. 2007. "Sweatshops, Exploitation and Moral Responsibility." *Journal of Social Philosophy* 38, no. 4: 605–619.

Miller, David. 1995. *On Nationality*. Oxford: Oxford University Press.

———. 2000. *Citizenship and National Identity*. Cambridge: Polity Press.

———. 2001. "Distributing Responsibilities." *Journal of Political Philosophy* 9: 453–471.

———. 2007. *National Responsibility and Global Justice*. Oxford: Oxford University Press.

Nagel, Thomas. 2005. "The Problem of Global Justice." *Philosophy and Public Affairs* 33, no. 2: 113–147.

Nozick, Robert. 1974. *Anarchy, State and Utopia*. Oxford: Blackwell.

Pettit, Philip. 1997. *Republicanism: A Theory of Freedom and Government*. Clarendon Press.

Pogge, Thomas. 1989. *Realizing Rawls*. London: Cornell University Press.

———. 2002. *World Poverty and Human Rights*. Cambridge: Polity.

Rawls, John. 1971. *A Theory of Justice*. Cambridge, MA: Harvard University Press.

———. 1993. *Political Liberalism*. New York: Columbia University Press.

———. 1999. *The Law of Peoples*. Cambridge, MA: Harvard University Press.

Raz, Joseph. 1986. *The Morality of Freedom*. Oxford: Oxford University Press.

———. 1995. *Ethics in the Public Domain*. Oxford: Clarendon Press.

Risse, Mathias. 2005. "What Do We Owe the Global Poor?" *Journal of Ethics* 9, no. 1–2: 81–117.

———. 2009. "A Right to Work? A Right to Leisure? Labour Rights as Human Rights." *Journal of the Law and Ethics of Human Rights* 3, no. 1: 1–41.

Sandel, Michael. 1998. *Liberalism and the Limits of Justice*. Cambridge: Cambridge University Press.

Sangiovanni, Andrea. 2007. "Global Justice, Reciprocity, and the State." *Philosophy and Public Affairs* 35, Issue 1: 3–39.

Savage, Michael. 2000. *Class Analysis and Social Transformation*. Buckingham: Open University Press.

Shapiro, Ian. 1999. *Democratic Justice*. New Haven: Yale University Press.

Swift, Adam, and Stephen Mulhall. 1996. *Liberals and Communitarians*. Oxford: Blackwell.

Tan, Kok Chor. 2004. *Justice without Borders*. Cambridge: Cambridge University Press.

Walzer, Michael. 1983. *Spheres of Justice: A Defence of Pluralism and Equality*. Oxford: Blackwell.

Wedderburn, Bill. 1989. "Freedom of Association and Philosophies of Labour Law." *Industrial Law Journal* 18, no. 1: 1–38.

White, Stuart. 1998. "Trade Unionism in a Liberal State." In *Freedom of Association*, ed. Amy Gutmann. Princeton: Princeton University Press.

———. 2001. "The Ambiguities of the Third Way." In *New Labour: The Progressive Future?*, ed. S. White. Basingstoke: Palgrave.

Young, Iris. 2006. "Responsibility and Global Justice: A Social Connection Model." In *Justice and Global Politics*, ed. Ellen Frankel Paul, Fred Miller, and Jeffrey Paul. Cambridge: Cambridge University Press.

Chapter Five

The Collapse of State Socialism in the "Soviet Bloc" and Global Labor Migration

József Böröcz

According to data collected by national censuses in the UN member states and published by the United Nations (UNPD 2009), the proportion of the foreign-born[1] among the world's population[2] has increased from approximately 2.5 percent to 3 percent between 1960 and 2005, and the average size of the foreign-born population in each of the world's states has grown from 8.1 percent to 11.7 percent during the same period.[3] A small but steadily growing proportion of the world's labor force crosses state boundaries in order to participate in the exploitation process in states with which they have no citizenship relation.

Cross-border labor migration revolves around a set of often seemingly minuscule, but in their implications, sharply consequential distinctions within the category of labor, regarding the legal "status" of the worker. Most consequential of all is the distinction between "citizen labor" and "noncitizen labor." The significance of citizenship lies in the fact that its absence (with respect to the site of labor) exposes labor to the possibility, indeed great likelihood, that the conditions under which its participation in the production process occurs are more oppressive, more abusive, and overall, more exploitative, than what labor that has the protections embodied in citizenship is exposed to. Of course, the formal equality encoded in citizenship conferred by the modern capitalist state "rarely leads to equality in practice" (Castles and Miller 2009, 44),[4] but few observers would dispute that, all other things equal, noncitizen status involves greater levels and often more violent denials of rights.

The process of the worldwide, organized displacement of labor across borders began during the colonial period of capitalism (it was clearly detectable by the mid-nineteenth century) (Mckeown 2004, 155–189) as an integral part of colonial policy, and an emerging global practice, by the west European colonizing states. Today, it would be very difficult to find a capitalist state in which noncitizen labor is not employed. Levels of the presence of noncitizens in the labor force of course do vary,[5] and that variation has important political-economic and geopolitical implications.

If somebody were to learn about the phenomenon of global labor migration exclusively from the mainstream sociological literature on migration in English, one would get the impression that it is a process that takes place primarily in the United States and the former colonizer states of western Europe.[6]

Viewed from the rest of the world, that US- and EU-centric focus is in fact quite invalid: As figure 5.1 indicates, in the United States, the population share of the foreign-born had not exceeded the world average until the late 1990s.[7] The overall presence of the foreign-born in the European Union has not even reached[8] the world mean in such terms during the entire period of 1960 to 2005.

Scholarly work on the global political economy of the cross-border displacement of labor assumes, almost without any exception, that the geographical displacement of labor takes place as part, and an important function, of a system that privileges the appropriation of the labor of others by codifying legally, justifying morally, and enforcing through legitimate violence, the social relation of *private property*. The idea of global labor migration is both historically and conceptually tied to capitalism.

Meanwhile, a significant feature of our world since 1917 has been that the basic rule of private property has been dominant, in the strict sense of the word, only within certain geopolitical limits: for three to four generations, we have had a global capitalism that has had, embedded in it, a geopolitically delimited bloc of states whose internal logic has been partly, and in rather inconsistent ways—and, yet, quite unmistakably—at odds, often in conflict, with the overall logic of the system. This "anomaly" involved one-fourth to one-third of the world's population (Maddison 2001, 2003), and about 10 to 20 percent of the gross world product during the last two generations, depending on the period of observation. Even after the collapse of the Soviet "bloc," over one-fifth of humankind continues to live as citizens of explicitly and avowedly state-socialist states, commanding approximately 13 to 15 percent of the economic output of humankind (and growing rapidly) (ibid.).

With a group of state socialist societies having just exited state socialism, their recent experience raises a number of interesting, yet little-discussed, questions regarding global labor migration. Of those, I will touch upon a few, focusing on some of the ways in which the collapse of state socialism in

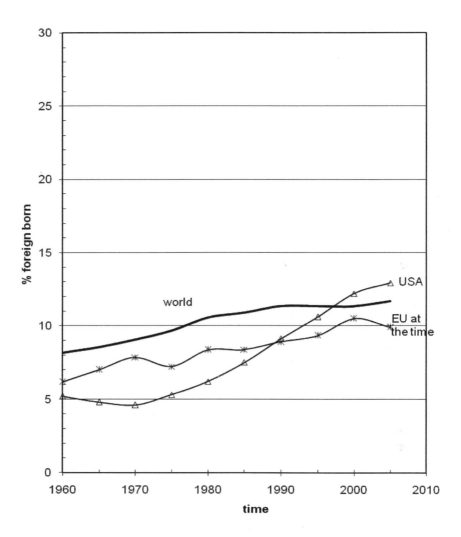

Figure 5.1.   Percentage of Population Foreign-Born: World, EU, and USA (un-weighted means), 1960–2005. *Source: Computed from Maddison, The World Economy, online dataset.*

eastern Europe and northern Eurasia is relevant for discussions of global labor migration. For this, first, let me outline some important aspects of labor under state socialism.

THE COLLAPSE OF STATE SOCIALISM AND GLOBAL LABOR MIGRATION

The end of the sociopolitical and socioeconomic exception of state socialism involved the elimination (or, as it was explicitly discussed in the case of the GDR, the "unwinding" or "de-development") of the features that made it an anomaly in the world capitalist system, and taking over the resource endowments of these societies, hitherto partly secluded from access by global capital. With the removal of the obstacles hitherto posed by the socialist bloc, the world's labor force, available without much interference by its own state, was enlarged by approximately 7.9 percent of the world's population. The geopolitical significance of this transformation was magnified by the fact that it happened on the very border of one of the cores of global accumulation, the European Union.

The first measure in the "unwinding" of state socialism involved the removal of the constitutional-legal conditions that provided for the guarantee for full employment (the right and obligation to work). Parallel with that, the property-owner role of the state was eliminated in record time. Given the endemic shortages of domestic capital in private hands (that could be used for purchasing such assets), two groups of would-be owners stepped forward: foreign multinational corporations (through foreign direct investment schemes, or FDI), and small groups of powerful domestic political elites that had managed to convert their position in the state socialist hierarchy at the point of the collapse into property ownership. With the removal of the barriers to the entry of foreign capital at the borders of the erstwhile bloc, the FDI-technique predominated, by and large, in the east-central European and Baltic states; the conversion of political position was characteristic of the privatization of the now-defunct Soviet state's assets, especially in Russia, Ukraine, and the Central Asian republics of the former USSR. The speed and the fierceness of the privatization drive was such that it swept away even such forms of property—as, for example, cooperatives—that had represented a property form that was, technically, only tolerated, and certainly not directly owned, by the socialist state. In fact, in some instances, the post-state-socialist legal transformation explicitly forbade alternative forms of property (e.g., cooperatives).

As a result of the wholesale privatization of the former socialist states' assets, virtually the entire labor force of the former Soviet bloc lost what was, in effect, protected, legally guaranteed employment by the state. In most cases, this involved the explicit and deeply humiliating experience of outright layoffs. A fraction of this labor force was rehired by the new owners—under radically different conditions: salaries were reduced, collective contracts were scrapped, and previously more or less assured avenues of promotion and job security were eliminated. Under the guise of "protecting the workplace from political interference," formal and informal bans on trade unions have become a norm. At about the same time, the specifically state-socialist safeguards against such actions were removed from the legal systems. As the post-state-socialist states became reluctant to enforce even the remaining, more lax labor laws, labor had nowhere to turn for protection. In virtually the entire post-state-socialist bloc, this has resulted in reductions in the size of the labor force, forcing very significant proportions of formerly employed into unemployment.

The privatization of the formerly state-owned enterprises and other forms of property was a transformation of enormous magnitude, resulting in the transfer of 85 percent to 95 percent of the assets of these societies in the course of a remarkably short—in many cases two-to-five-year—period sometime in the early 1990s. Because of the debt burdens carried over from the last period of state socialism, much of the privatization revenues was used for debt relief, making this transaction strikingly similar to the debt-equity swaps that had devastated a number of Latin American economies.

Because of the sudden loss of one of their main income sources (their productive assets) and the preferential (tax-free) arrangements provided to the new, private owners, almost without exception the post-state-socialist states have been facing tremendous fiscal deficits. Such deficits, coupled with the neoliberal ideological hegemony under which the transformation took place, had resulted in the removal of most of the redistributive functions of the post-state-socialist state, leaving the task of the reproduction of labor power to society at large. This caused tremendous increases in the costs of child rearing and moved gender relations in the family back by a good two generations. In this sense, the societies of the former Soviet bloc have begun to show a striking resemblance to Latin America during much of the twentieth century: a group of geographically contiguous, densely interconnected peripheral and semiperipheral societies with states that leave a considerable part of the task of the reproduction of labor to society, generating and maintaining enormous social inequalities.

Drops in the quality, in the quantitative availability, and ultimately the removal, of social welfare provisions was made even more severe by the fact that the years following the collapse of state socialism saw precipitous drops in the economic performance of all formerly state socialist states. Figures 5.3, 5.4, and 5.5 give a visual representation of the process, by depicting changes in per capita GDP by the Soviet bloc states between 1960 and 2001.[9]

The drops began well before the actual collapse of state socialism and accelerated precipitously afterward, with the destruction of the COMECON (the state socialist trading bloc). As it is clearly visible, most hard hit were those smaller former republics of the USSR that had been denied European Union membership, and the poorer former federal states (Macedonia and Serbia-Montenegro) of war-torn Yugoslavia. The societies of the former So-

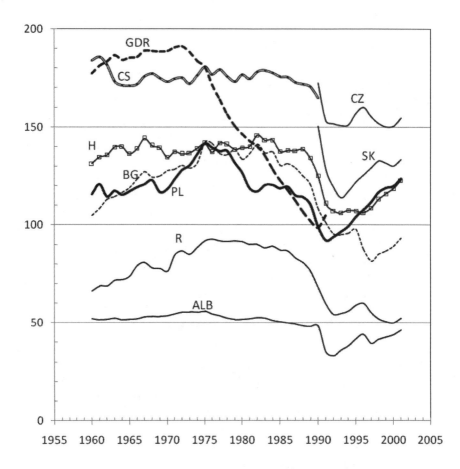

Figure 5.2. Economic Performance before and after the Collapse, Erstwhile State Socialist East-Central Europe, GDP/cap as % of World Mean, 1950–2008. *Source: Computed from Maddison, The World Economy, online dataset.*

viet bloc experienced drops in living standards to the tune of 25 percent to 75 percent, signaling a regionwide economic collapse unprecedented in peace times.[10]

The first, and most striking, result of the undoing of state socialism is the *precipitous destruction of the peaceful, predictable and stable conditions under which state-socialist labor had existed* until the collapse. This involved the unfolding of a number of parallel transformations:

• Because of the removal of the constitutionally guaranteed right to work, and because of the overall restructuring of the ownership structure of the formerly state-socialist economies, the work environment has lost a num-

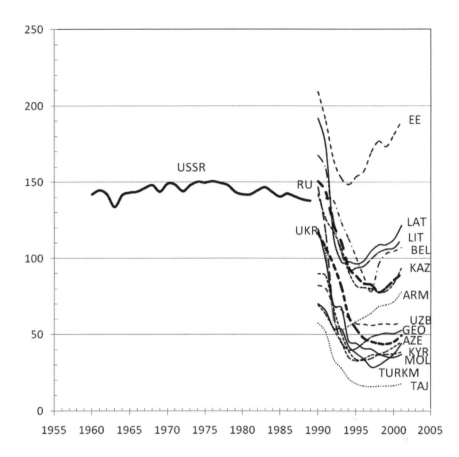

Figure 5.3.   Economic Performance before and after the Collapse, Erstwhile USSR, GDP/cap as % of World Mean, 1950–2008. *Source: Computed from Maddison, The World Economy, online dataset.*

ber of guarantees, safeguards, and protective measures. Work had become clearly and significantly more *precarious* (that is, "uncertain, unpredictable and risky from the perspective of the worker" [Kalleberg 2008/2009, 2]) for all employees, and especially the working class, all over the former Soviet bloc. Large groups of workers have exited from the labor force and have given up hopes for full employment. The precarization of work created powerful pressures for making labor more mobile geographically, including cross-border employment.

• The removal of such basic institutions as collective contracts and access to unions, coupled with the general precarity of post-state-socialist work and the collapse of the post-state-socialist economies, has put a tremendous

Figure 5.4. Economic Performance before and after the Collapse of State Socialism, Erstwhile Yugoslavia, GDP/cap as % of the World Mean. *Source: Computed from Maddison, The World Economy, online dataset.*

downward pressure on wages. The crisis of the post-state-socialist state budgets has reduced the nonmonetary aspects of labor's remuneration.

• The end of all restrictions on travel abroad made various forms of labor migration a possible option for a large number of workers from the post-state-socialist bloc.

The empirical question that all these factors together raise is this: If the conditions of post-state-socialist labor are indeed so deeply disadvantaged, and if opportunities of exit are so clearly available, is labor from the former state-socialist states flooding the labor markets of the European Union, the United States and other wealthy economies?

The answer needs to be a subtle and differentiated one. First of all, except for the three Baltic states (which had gained membership in the EU in 2004, along with five former socialist states in east-central Europe), citizens of the former USSR have, in effect, been excluded from access to the territory of both the EU and the United States. In this regard, the default visa status of most citizens of the successor states of the erstwhile USSR went from feared adversary to something vaguely reminiscent of that of the "Global South." The visa regulations and foreigner-policing activities of the EU and the United States jointly assure that, except for the highly skilled, the managerial elites and academics, and a trickle of flows on the basis of family reunification, organized crime is the only effective mechanism that moves citizens of the non-EU-member successor states of the former USSR to them. For a sizeable portion of the former Soviet labor that is present in the EU and the United States, their very presence itself the result of having become crime victims (e.g., sex workers who are victims of cross-border trafficking).

Both the European Union and the United States significantly tightened their visa issuance policies at the point where it was realistic to expect the appearance of east European labor migrants on their doorsteps. That this was not simply a reaction to the 9-11 crisis as indicated, for instance, by the fact that, after the attainment of "full" EU membership by eight of the former Soviet bloc states, a vast majority of the European Union's states refused to grant the right to free movement for employment (a basic EU citizenship right and the most ambitious purpose of the EU as a contiguous "single market") to such newcomers for an additional seven years.[11] Acting in concert with the EU, the United States had refused to extend the "no-visa" entry permits to citizens of the former state-socialist members of the European Union until 2009 (i.e., for a period of approximately five years) even for tourist travel, a decision based explicitly on the expectation that former state-socialist labor would enter the United States as "tourists" and overstay their visas. The power of the European Union's delaying tactics in accepting east European labor is indicated, for example, in the ways in which the border police force of Germany, the European Union's largest and most powerful member state, has been restructured, after Germany ceased to have any borders with a non-Schengen state, to involve immigration-policing activities throughout the territory of the Federal Republic. Civilians—such as taxi drivers—are routinely enlisted as potential informers, being asked to report "suspicious foreigners" to this police force (Euskirchen, Lebuhn, and Ray 2007, 6).

Lack of language skills, nonfamiliarity with local contexts and especially workplace customs, expectations of discrimination, and absence of the all-important, effective informal social networks[12] in the higher-remuneration states were the main additional reasons for the widely noted, initial reluctance of the citizens of the now "fully" EU member former state-socialist states to initiate sizeable labor flows westward. These factors do, however, have a tendency to wane over time, and recent evidence suggests that the presence of labor from eastern Europe is increasing in Britain, and there is a similar growth in the presence of Romanian citizens, especially of reasonably highly skilled labor (such as nurses and professionals in similar caregiving professions) in the rapidly aging societies of Spain, Portugal, Italy, and France (i.e., in the contexts where the local language, being neo-Latin like their mother tongue, poses less of a challenge to speakers of Romanian). The construction and tourism industries also provide opportunities for east Europeans to find employment in western Europe.

A possible reason why the presence of east European labor in western Europe and North America is not much greater than what it is today may have to do with the fact that, from the perspective of big capital in western Europe and in the United States, there is relatively little specific need for it. Given the very high levels of foreign direct investment in most post-state-socialist economies,[13] the valorization of east-central European labor by west European and North American capital is already taking place on a large scale, without requiring the physical movement of the labor force to western Europe or North America.[14] Arguably, the FDI schemes that have dominated the economic transformation process in east-central Europe after the collapse could be understood—as they have been seen, and hence vehemently opposed, by the various west European trade unions, for instance—as ways in which greater degrees of access to east-central European labor can be achieved by west European capital. That it is possible to achieve this result without relying on the socially sensitive, politically complicated, and, clearly, economically more expensive option of inducing labor migration is a key component of the strategies of major multinational corporations based in western Europe or the United States, operating in the former-state-socialist context. In this sense, foreign direct investment and undocumented labor migration are complementary, and in some ways interchangeable, techniques in core capital's pursuit of surplus margins.

Meanwhile, a well-documented effect of the penetration of the domestic structures of peripheral and semiperipheral societies by institutions (such as capital, markets, consumption ideologies, lifestyles, etc.) of the global core is the emergence of a willingness on the part of these poorer societies to access income-earning and life-conduct opportunities in the core. As a result, in short, while FDI tends to diminish the specific demand for erstwhile state-socialist labor in the core, the very integration of these societies into western European circuits of capital produces an ever-increasing proclivity to migration. This effect is further enhanced by the European Union's official discourse regarding labor migration, a language that puts forth "free movement of persons" as one of the "Four Pillars" of the "European common market."[15]

The presence of east European labor in western Europe and the United States has, hitherto, remained relatively insignificant—*from the perspective of the host societies*. The situation is completely different if we view it from the perspective of the migrant-emitting societies. For more than a decade, one of the new social problems in rural Albania is the near-complete absence of men due to labor migration, mainly to Italy and Greece. Although there has been considerable variance in the temporal and spatial patterns through which east European and post-Soviet societies have turned to international migration as an income-earning strategy—from the Hungarian medical professionals serving as weekend on-call doctors in the British National Health System or the Polish lower-middle-class and working-class women who use their weekend to do one or two twelve-hour shifts as cleaning persons in Berlin, through the tens of thousands of young east Europeans serving part time or full time in bars, cafes, and restaurants in western Europe, to the women and men working as service providers in the gray market of sex work and porn production—there is some empirical evidence suggesting that almost all of the erstwhile state socialist societies have experienced marked increases in their migrant remittance dependence over the decades since the regime change (Böröcz 2012b). The tension between the two facts—the relative insignificance of the presence of east European labor in western Europe and the United States and the, by comparison, enormous significance of that same migration process for most societies in the post-state-socialist context—constitutes a great, and intensifying, tension in the politics of "east-west" migration today.

Finally, there are two geopolitical aspects to the post-state-socialist transformations that have significant implications for cross-border labor migration. First, the collapse of state socialism also implied the disintegration of the region's three federal states. The breakups happened, as it is well known, by political fiat (and with none to very little political violence) in Czechoslovakia and the USSR, whereas the secessions by Slovenia and Croatia, leading to the eventual division of Yugoslavia, involved no less than five civil and international wars. Because changes in rights, principles and practices regarding citizenship lie at the heart of these transformations, they have exerted very significant effects on labor, especially the issue of the relationship between citizen and noncitizen labor.

Plainly put, the breakup of the erstwhile socialist federal states created noncitizen labor pools of significant size in the smaller successor states by administrative fiat. Nonlocal citizens of these suddenly defunct federal socialist states found themselves, literally from one day to another, in the position of noncitizen labor. The situation of post-federal, post-state-socialist noncitizen labor is in some ways the exact opposite of east European labor migrants in western Europe: they have extremely close familiarity with the local conditions, they have, as a rule, excellent language skills, their work

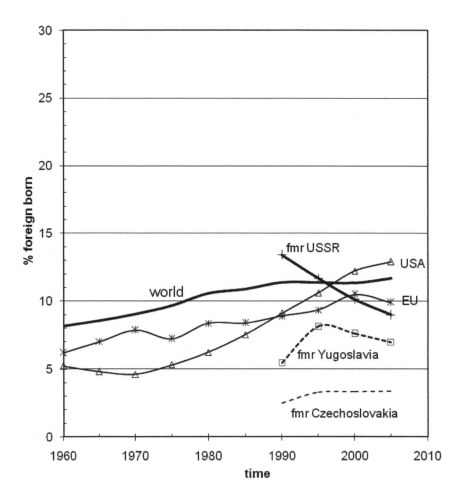

Figure 5.5. Percent of Population Foreign-Born: World, EU, United States, the Former USSR, Former Yugoslavia, and Former Czechoslovakia (unweighted means), Select Years, 1960–2005. *Source: Computed from United Nations, World Migrant Stock, http://esa.un.org.*

skills and habits are directly compatible with the local customs, and they have extended informal networks, sometimes going back several generations. What changes, by virtue of the breakups, is "just" one little formality: that of citizenship. Given the skills, the familiarity, and the network endowments of this noncitizen labor, the removal of a general citizenship rights creates a "perfect" structural condition for the transformation of these fellow citizens into (predominantly undocumented) "migrants."

Figure 5.5 presents the aggregate average percentages of the "foreign-born"—that is, citizens of states other than the successor states—in these societies. It is clear that the fifteen successor states of the USSR, and to a somewhat lesser extent the five now-independent republics of Yugoslavia, became instantaneously significant "players" in the field of cross-border labor migration just by virtue of drawing a large number of new borderlines among themselves. On average, the successor states of the Soviet Union had a "foreign-born" population of 13.4 percent at the time of the end of the USSR, a magnitude that is approximately 2 percent higher than the world average (and about 4.1 percent higher than both the United States and the European Union at the time).

Aggregate averages do hide important variation. To disentangle this, figure 5.6 presents the rates of the foreign-born in the fifteen successor states of the former USSR. The highest percentage of "foreign-born" lives in two small and relatively wealthy former republics, Latvia, Estonia, followed by Kazakhstan, Armenia, Kyrgyzstan, Ukraine, Moldova, and Belarus. Except for Ukraine and Russia, all the other successor states have seen a decrease over time in the proportion of the "foreign-born," and those mentioned so far, except for Armenia, have had levels of "foreign-born" populations that were higher than the world average during the first fifteen years after the dissolution of the USSR. Russia, the largest, most diverse and most powerful successor state of the former USSR, has maintained a stable level of the presence of the "foreign-born," around 7.5 percent to 8 percent (this is the level where the proportion of the foreign-born stood in the United States in the mid-1980s).

In spite of Yugoslavia's much smaller size, figure 5.7 suggests a variation among its successor states similar to that of the USSR. Croatia and Slovenia, the two wealthiest republics (which initiated Yugoslavia's protracted dissolution crisis by declaring secession), show levels of the presence of foreign-born populations comparable to the world mean. (In fact, Croatia's figures are consistently above the world average.) On the other extreme, the numbers of foreign-born among the residents of war-torn Bosnia-Herzegovina are negligible.

One thing in common among the cases of Latvia, Estonia, Slovenia, and Croatia is their membership in the European Union. This brings us to the second geopolitical issue, the effects of selective European Union membership on migration patterns in the post-state-socialist part of the world. Frankly, the breakup of the three federal states had already had much to do with the emergence of the European Union as a unified, expanding supra-state entity on their borders, and the strong implicit, and vague explicit promises of EU membership made to the wealthier federal republics by key west European states.

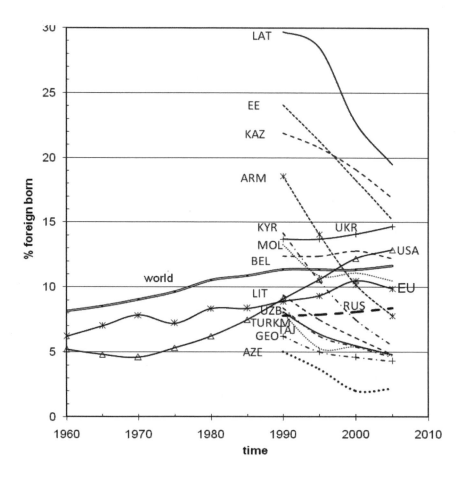

Figure 5.6. Percent of Population Foreign-Born: World, EU, United States, and the Successor States of the Erstwhile USSR (unweighted means), Select Years, 1960–2005. *Source: Computed from United Nations, World Migrant Stock, http:// esa/un/org.*

The fact that EU membership happened first for eight, and then an additional two, and then one more, former socialist state (with several more waiting "in line") has made their labor markets quite attractive to citizens of the poorer members of the former socialist bloc, as well as to citizens of various parts of the third world. Joining various international refugee agreements was also a criterion for full EU membership, opening, at least in theory, the possibility that third-country nationals could claim political asylum in the new EU member states as well.

And yet, again, the expected sudden increases in inbound flows of third-country migrants (i.e., people from outside the EU) have, so far, failed to

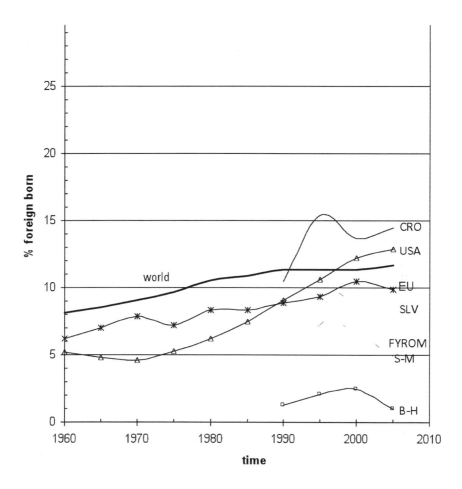

Figure 5.7. Percent of Population Foreign-Born: World, EU, United States, and the Successor States of Erstwhile Yugoslavia (unweighted means), Select Years, 1960–2005. *Source: Computed from United Nations, World Migrant Stock http:// esa.un.org.*

materialize. Of the eight current, former state-socialist member states of the Schengen system (the European Union's common visa and immigration mechanism), Hungary is a good example to look at, for two main reasons. First, it was widely considered to be a market frontrunner during the last two decades of state socialism and the post-socialist transformation, fast adjusting to the requirements of EU membership and neoliberal adjustment in general, attracting much more than its share of the foreign direct investment after the collapse of state socialism. Second, at the time of the transformation, it was among the more well-to-do states of the former socialist bloc.

Given those conditions, one would expect high levels of foreign-born populations in Hungary approximately two decades after the transformation.
Yet, with the proportion of the foreign-born around 3 percent (the figure
for 2005 is 3.1 percent), Hungary shows a strikingly low level of exposure to
foreign labor migration. If we take into account the fact that a vast majority
of the foreign-born are ethnic Magyars (co-ethnics of the majority group in
Hungary) from neighboring, and poorer, Romania, it is very clear that Hungary somehow has remained almost completely clear of global-transnational
labor migrant flows.

What explains the well-nigh complete absence of a foreign labor force in
Hungary, then? One piece of evidence comes from the pioneering work of
Hungarian historical sociologist Attila Melegh and his colleagues, who have
found strong evidence for a combined class and race bias in the visa practices
of the Hungarian consulates abroad (Illés and Melegh 2009). This is most
surprising, as the highly foreign-owned Hungarian economy is known to
have had severe local labor shortages, and the by now two-generations-long
demographic crisis of exceptionally low birthrates has created severe imbalances in the state's much-reduced social security and welfare budgets. In
other words, it would be very much in the interest of the Hungarian state to
encourage and manage labor immigration. Meanwhile, public sentiments run
high against "foreigners"[16] in a country that has almost no foreign-born
population and, of those few that are there, the majority are co-ethnics from a
neighboring state. In Hungarian visa practices, we find a way in which the
post-state-socialist crisis of identity reinforces the structural class and race
exclusion of the EU's Schengen system.

CONCLUSION

The collapse of state socialism in the Soviet bloc was part and parcel to a
worldwide general neoliberal ideological hegemony: the perceived "end" to a
system was conceived, and the direction of the political transformation was
partly inspired, by reference to neoliberal ideology, and the collapse of the
labor-protective systems of state socialism have made all alternative thinking
within, or beyond, free-market capitalism more difficult. In this sense, the
collapse of state socialism made life harder for labor all over the world.

Clearly, state socialism was rife with endemic problems, tensions, conflicts, and structural imbalances. It was also a system that was unable to
sustain itself in eastern Europe and northern Eurasia and collapsed under its
own weight.

The highly skilled labor force of the former Soviet bloc, suddenly made
unprotected, precarious, and de-valued, has become an easily accessible resource for west European and North American capital. Given the xenophobic

political consensus in western Europe and the power of foreign direct investment, coupled with selective and restricted admission to the EU, there emerged a model for the reintegration of these societies in the world economy that has, for the first two decades after the post-state-socialist transformation, limited the substantive presence of former socialist labor in western Europe.

Meanwhile, the new member states of the EU have used their accession to the Schengen visa system to preserve their exceptionally low exposure to foreign labor, in spite of the pressing structural economic and demographic imperatives that would prompt the opposite. In those economies that have allowed the presence of foreign labor, for example, the largest and economically most powerful successor states of the USSR, the engagement of noncitizen labor takes place through institutional arrangements that are strikingly reminiscent to the undocumented labor migration directed to western Europe and North America, with strikingly similar structures of transnationalism and remittance dependence on part of the labor-emitting societies. What makes the post-Soviet situation particularly bitter is, of course, the fact that today's "foreign labor" is yesterday's fellow citizens.

NOTES

1. While conceptually perhaps not a perfect measure of the extent of labor migration per se, and almost certainly vulnerable to systematic underreporting, proportion of the foreign-born is an adequate indicator for our purposes simply because of its availability due to censuses. (More sharply focussed, survey-based measures are far from being available for the entire world.)

2. "International Migrants as Proportion of the Population," *World Migrant Stock*.

3. Given the notorious underreporting of the foreign-born in national censuses (on which the UN data are based) and the fact that labor market participation rates for noncitizen labor can be significantly higher than the proportion of the foreign-born, those figures can be considered to be lower-bound, conservative estimates.

4. For a description of the ways in which various nonmainstream social movements have challenged the stubborn forms of discrimination even after citizenship is acquired, see Monisha Das Gupta, *Unruly Immigrants. Rights, Activism, and Transnational South Asian Politics in the United States*. Durham, NC: Duke University Press, 2006.

5. The coefficient of variation of the UNPD data quoted above ranges between 1.4 to 1.6 standard deviations/mean for the forty-five-year period covered, with a decreasing tendency. Computed from data pertaining to the proportion of the foreign born in *World Migrant Stock*.

6. Based on this, there often emerges the neo-Malthusian argument that these societies are at, or near, some kind of a point of saturation by foreign labor.

7. By 2005—the latest observation point in the *World Migrant Stock* data—12.9 percent of the population of the United States was foreign-born; this is 1.2 percent higher than the world average for that year.

8. The EU came closest to the world average in 2000: At that point, the foreign-born constituted 10.5 percent of its population, or .8 percent below the world mean.

9. The economic performance figures have been computed from the online data supplement to Angus Maddison, *The World Economy: A Millennial Perspective*, Paris, OECD, 2001, and *The World Economy: Historical Statistics*, Paris, OECD, 2003.

10. For a more detailed analysis of the economic trajectories of post-state-socialist societies, see József Böröcz, "Notes on the Geopolitical Economy of Post-State-Socialism," 103–124, in

Nina Bandelj and Dorothy J. Solinger (eds.), *Socialism Vanquished, Socialism Challenged: Eastern Europe and China, 1989–2009*, Oxford: Oxford University Press, 2012.

11. "At their Luxembourg meeting in 1991 the Council of Europe ministers responsible for migration issues were confronted with a new and largely uncharted situation. Suddenly, it seemed, there was likely to be mass migration from the East, towards the lotus lands of Western Europe." John Salt, "Current Trends in International Migration in Europe," *Council of Europe / Conseil de l'Europe*, CDMG (2005) 2, January 2005, 3.

12. As an implicit indication of the power of informal networks, it is noticeable that among labor migrant groups present in Germany, for instance, citizens of what used to be Yugoslavia—that is, the only state that had allowed large-scale labor migration to western Europe during the socialist period—constitute one of the largest groups, second only to citizens of Turkey.

13. See, for example, Nina Bandelj, "The Global Economy as Instituted Process: The Case of Central and Eastern Europe," *American Sociological Review*, 74: 128–149.

14. See also Thomas Straubhaar, "East-West Migration: Will It Be a Problem?" *INTERECONOMICS* (July–August 2001): 167–170.

15. See, for example, http://europa.eu/rapid/press-release_MEMO-13-384_en.htm as of July 19, 2013.

16. See Pál Nyíri, "Xenophobia in Hungary: A Regional Comparison, Systemic Sources, and Possible Solutions," CEU Center for Policy Studies, Working Paper Series, 2003, http://pdc.ceu.hu/archive/00002079/01/eve_xenophobia_polpap.pdf as of 8 September 2009, and Jon E. Fox, "From National Inclusion to Economic Exclusion: Ethnic Hungarian Labor Migration to Hungary," *Nations and Nationalism* 13, no. 1 (2007): 77–96.

BIBLIOGRAPHY

Bandelj, Nina. 2009. "The Global Economy as Instituted Process: The Case of Central and Eastern Europe." *American Sociological Review* 74: 128–149.

Böröcz, József. 2009. "Geopolitics of Property Relations: State Socialism under Global Capitalism." In *The European Union and Global Social Change: A Critical Geopolitical-Economic Analysis*. New York: Routledge.

———. 2012a. "Notes on the Geopolitical Economy of Post-State-Socialism." In *Socialism Vanquished, Socialism Challenged: Eastern Europe and China, 1989–2009*, ed. Nina Bandelj and Dorothy J. Solinger. Oxford: Oxford University Press.

———. 2012b. "Regimes of Remittance Dependency: Global Structures and Trajectories of the Former Soviet Bloc." Presented at the Launching Conference of SEEMIG, a research project entitled "Managing Migration and Its Effects in South East Europe: Transnational Actions towards Evidence Based Strategies," (SEEMIG-SEE/C/0006/4.1/X) realized from a research grant provided by the South East Europe Transnational Cooperation Programme, Institute of Informatics and Statistics of the Faculty of Natural Sciences of the Comenius University in Bratislava, Slovakia, September 19, 2012.

Castles, Stephen, and Mark J. Miller. 2009. *The Age of Migration: International Population Movements in the Modern World*, fourth edition. New York: The Guilford Press.

Das Gupta, Monisha. 2006. *Unruly Immigrants: Rights, Activism, and Transnational South Asian Politics in the United States*. Durham, NC: Duke University Press.

Euskirchen, Markus, Henrik Lebuhn, and Gene Ray. 2007. "From Borderline to Borderland: The Changing Border Regime, Transnational Labor and Migration Struggles in Europe." Paper presented at the International Seminar Cambio del Siglo, Universidad Autónoma Metropolitana (UAM-X), México D.F., May 22–24.

Fox, Jon. E. 2007. "From National Inclusion to Economic Exclusion: Ethnic Hungarian Labor Migration to Hungary." *Nations and Nationalism* 13, no. 1: 77–96.

Illés, Sándor, and Attila Melegh. 2009. "Hungary in the Schengen System: Bastion or Gateway? Quantitative and Qualitative Analysis of the Schengen-Based Visa System and Visa Issuance Practice in Hungary." Hungarian Europe Society. Available at http://

www.europatarsasag.hu/20070811tol_fajlok_itt/2009juni/Vizum_internet_a5.pdf. Accessed September 8, 2009.

Kalleberg, Arne. 2009. "Precarious Work, Insecure Workers: Employment Relations in Transition," 2008 Presidential Address of the American Sociological Association. *American Sociological Review* 74, no. 1 (February): 1–22.

Maddison, Angus. 2001. *The World Economy: A Millennial Perspective*. Paris: OECD.

———. 2003. *The World Economy: Historical Statistics*. Paris: OECD.

Mckeown, Adam. 2004. "Global Migration, 1846–1940." *Journal of World History* 15 (June 2004): 155–189.

Nyíri, Pál. 2003. "Xenophobia in Hungary: A Regional Comparison. Systemic Sources and Possible Solutions." CEU Center for Policy Studies, Working Paper Series. Available at http://pdc.ceu.hu/archive/00002079/01/eve_xenophobia_polpap.pdf. Accessed September 8, 2009.

Salt, John. 2005. "Current Trends in International Migration in Europe." *Council of Europe/ Conseil de l'Europe*, CDMG, 2. January .

Straubhaar, Thomas. 2001. "East-West Migration: Will It Be a Problem?" *INTERECONOMICS* (July–August): 167–170.

United Nations Population Division (UNPD). 2009. *World Migrant Stock. The 2005 Revision.* Population database, http://esa.un.org/migration/index.asp?panel=1. Accessed August 10, 2009.

Chapter Six

Labor Migration and Justice

An Analysis of the Labor Migration Policy of the European Union

Patrick Loobuyck

Labor migration is an important part of globalization and the capitalistic world system. The formal and informal labor market is increasingly international, and this is true for the high- and for low-skilled workforce. In 2010, there were 214 million migrants in the world. The majority of people leaving their home countries are migrating for work. Migrant workers (those who migrate for employment) and their families account for about 90% of total international migrants, but also the migrants with other migration motives (e.g., refugees or marriage migrants) are often economically active in their guest country.[1] The contribution of these migrant workers to the world economy is undeniable, and for several countries it is a structural part of their economic system. The global financial and economic crisis creates another context for labor migration today, but labor migration will not disappear.[2] The question is no longer are we in favor or against labor migration. The challenge now is to develop an (international) policy to manage labor migration in a fair and just way.

THE IDEAL SITUATION: TRIPLE WIN

Labor migration is not a bad phenomenon if some important conditions are fulfilled. A labor migration policy must fight the unjust and bad consequences for migrant-sending and migrant-receiving countries as well as for the migrants themselves. Therefore, labor migration needs at least a juridical and institutional context in which the rights and the welfare of the migrants and their families are adequately protected. Migrants cannot be used merely as tools. Protection of migrant rights is central to realizing development benefits of migration for all parties.[3] In ideal circumstances, we can speak of a *triple-win* outcome for home countries, host countries, and (the family) of the migrants themselves. Labor migration has several potential opportunities: migrants can improve their economic position and quality of life; host countries can attract the labor forces they need; and the home countries can take advantage from the remittances, the knowledge, and skills of returning migrants, and a potential decrease of the unemployment rate.

The fact that a country takes its own (economical) interests into consideration to develop a labor migration policy is not bad in itself. A market-driven labor migration policy is not necessarily illegitimate or immoral as long as the interests of the countries of origin and the rights and welfare of the immigrants are taken in account as well. Labor migration is not a right but a favor, and as such it is different from humanitarian and family migration. That is the reason why economical and demographical needs can play a legitimate role in labor migration programs, while this is not (or at least to a lesser extent) the case for programs on humanitarian migration. Moreover, a labor migration policy may not disturb or hinder the humanitarian duties concerning migration. It would be illegitimate for a state to use its labor migration programs as an excuse to diminish their humanitarian part of migration (family migration, asylum, the acceptance of refugees by resettlement programs, and in some cases also the regularization of undocumented migrants).

THE REAL SITUATION

Unfortunately, we do not live in an ideal world, and often labor migration has bad consequences for the different countries involved or for the (families of) the migrants. Labor migration can increase the unemployment rate in the host countries, and it can create unfair competition or distort the labor market in the host countries, especially when migrants are used for flexible or informal employment, working long hours for low wages. A good labor migration policy tries to avoid these negative consequences and tries to attain the opposite. Several examples, now and in the past, demonstrate how controlled labor migration can improve the labor market, and the influx of migrants is not necessarily at the expense of existing employees.[4]

For the home countries the problem of the so-called brain drain can arise. It is possible that rich countries use labor migration programs to drain poorer ones of their best-qualified and most useful people. Especially some African development countries are confronted with this phenomenon. The ILO (International Labor Organization) estimates that development countries lose

10 to 30% of their professional skilled labor force by labor migration toward richer countries, and the IOM (International Organization for Migration) mentions that Ethiopia lost 75% of its skilled workforce between 1980 and 1991. This phenomenon has to be taken seriously, and until today the policy responses to the international movement of skilled labor have been too weak.[5] However, not every high-skilled migrant who leaves his home country toward a richer or more developed country is part of a brain drain. It depends on the particular situation in the home country and the potential positive effects of migration for that country. First, sustained migratory flows may be associated with a large flow of remittances; and second, migrants may return home after having acquired a set of productive skills. The latter means that an initial brain drain can turn into brain circulation, which gives interesting opportunities for the country of origin. Even if the migrants themselves do not return, they can use their knowledge to develop and support economical initiatives in the country of origin. As such, they can build a bridge between the host and the home country and enhance the opportunities for (transnational) entrepreneurship.[6] A famous example is the link between Silicon Valley in the United States and the development of the software industry in and around Bangalore in India.[7]

Also the remittances are often seen as a positive effect for the countries of origin.[8] A study of the International Fund for Agricultural Development (IFAD) and the Inter-American Development Bank (IDB) shows that migrants working in industrialized countries sent more than US$300 billion to developing nations in 2006 (including the informal flows).[9] This is much more than the almost US$104 billion that, according to the Organization for Economic Co-operation and Development, donor nations provided in aid to developing countries that year. Remittances are generated by some 150 million migrants who send money home regularly, typically between US$100 and US$300 at a time. In Africa and Asia, the continents with the biggest population that lives on less than US$2 a day, several countries are dependent on this inflow of remittances. IFAD discovered that the remittances are mostly used for basic necessities such as food, clothing, and medicine. Between 10% and 20% is saved. However, too often these savings are hidden, rather than put to work in financial institutions, constituting a major missed opportunity for local economic development. An important aim of policy could be to channel this money so that it is used more for investment and contributes more to prosperity in rural areas.[10]

Next to the brain drain, there are other characteristics of the real (non-ideal) world with negative consequences on labor migration. Because many industrialized countries maintain a rather restrictive (labor) migration policy, several people use facilitators or smugglers to enter the country of destination—in a legal or an illegal way. The migration conditions for some people are really bad, and illegal migration leads often to exploitation, the violation of human and labor rights, and forced employment, often in the informal, unprotected, and unregulated economy or in the sex industry.

Labor migrants are also more vulnerable to discrimination, especially in times of economic downturns. Too many (temporary) migrants all over the world have to work under their level, in poor working conditions and for low wages. They are seen as exploitable and expendable, a source of cheap, docile, and flexible labor. Much of their employment is precarious, and they are overrepresented in the so-called 3D jobs (dirty, dangerous, and degrading work) because these jobs are refused by the local employees of the host society. These (often informal) jobs can be found in several sectors such as agriculture, construction, and cleaning. The main actors who are responsible for this situation are not in the first place the migrants but the employers, and there is inefficient control by the government.

To protect labor migrants, the General Assembly of the UN accepted on 18 December 1990 the migrant workers convention (into force since 1 July 2003). This *International Convention on the Protection of the Rights of All Migrant Workers and Members of Their Families* provides a set of binding international standards to address the treatment, welfare, and human rights of both documented and undocumented migrants, as well as the obligations and responsibilities on the part of sending and receiving states. In October 2009 there were forty-two ratifications and fifteen signatories. However, the Western industrialized countries are absent.[11] In 1994 the European Commission urged the member states to examine if ratification would be possible, but until today this call is still unanswered.

Finally, there is also the problem of forced migration. Most labor migrants are motivated by the desire for higher wages and better opportunities, but some are really forced to leave their home country on account of famine and poverty, natural disasters and environmental degradation, and violent conflict or persecution. Many economic migrants have few options to remain in their countries of origin. If labor migration is the result of these coercive circumstances, it is a bad thing. To cope with this problem, we need policies to address the root causes of migration, such as economic development in poor countries.[12]

THE INTRA-EUROPEAN LABOR MIGRATION POLICY AFTER EU ENLARGEMENT

In several documents, the EU acknowledges that immigration is a reality and there are no reasons to believe that immigration flows will decrease. The total number of non-nationals (people who are not citizens of their country of residence) living on the territory of an EU member state on 1 January 2010 was 32.5 million persons, representing 6.5% of the EU-27 population. According to Eurostat, there have been between 1.5 and 2 million net arrivals each year in the EU since 2002. During 2009, about 3 million people immigrated into one of the EU member states. In 2009 20.2 million third-country nationals were resident in the EU—this is 4% of the total EU population. In an open Europe without internal borders a common immigration policy for Europe becomes necessary, because in such a context no member state can manage immigration on its own. [13]

Next to the labor migration from third-countries into the EU, there is also labor migration between the member states. In 2010 more than one-third (a total of 12.3 million persons) of all non-nationals living in the EU-27 were citizens of another EU member state. Since the enlargement of the EU through the accession of twelve new member states since 2004, this migration was several times a point of discussion. We will first focus on this internal labor migration, and secondly, we will discuss the EU labor migration policy toward newcomers of third-countries.

TRANSITIONAL RESTRICTIONS

On 1 May 2004, ten new member states joined the EU. Only Sweden, Ireland, and the United Kingdom opened their labor markets. The other old member states feared social and economic problems as a result of the free movement of the new European citizens. Therefore they negotiated a transitional period of seven years (2y + 3y + 2y) wherein they can implement restrictive arrangements on the free movement of employees of the new member states. [14] In May 2006, Spain, Portugal, Greece, Italy, and Finland removed these arrangements. The other countries opened only a part of their labor market. In Belgium, for instance, citizens of the new European member states were easily welcome in the bottleneck jobs. In November 2008 the European Commission published a report to show the positive effects of the enlargement. [15] In the report, the commission has called upon member states to consider whether they need to continue applying restrictions on the free movement of EU-8 workers in light of the situation of their labor markets, notwithstanding their rights set out in the Treaties of Accession concerning transitional arrangements. Except Germany and Austria, all the other member states removed the transitional arrangements before May 2009. [16] Member states that still apply restrictions may maintain them after 30 April 2009 in the event of a serious disturbance of the labor market or a threat thereof and after notifying the commission before May 2009.

With the accession of Romania and Bulgaria on January 2007, only two countries of the old EU-15 (Finland and Sweden) opened their labor market. The ten new member states of 2007 were more open: only Malta and Hungary did not open their labor markets for Romanians and Bulgarians. After two years also Greece, Spain, Portugal (January 2009), Denmark, and Hungary (May 2009) opened their borders, the other ten member states continued their transitional arrangements. Only in the event of a serious disturbance of the labor market or a threat thereof, member states can get the permission of the commission to keep some restrictions after 2012. At the end of 2011, the Belgian, French, Dutch, and German governments extended the transitional restrictions for two years. In 2014 all the borders have to be open.

We can expect that in the near future the discussion concerning labor migration will be focused on the migration from third-countries. Only when the accession of Turkey comes in the picture, the debate of free movement of EU employees will be reopened.

THE ARGUMENTS

In defense of the transitional arrangements, it has been argued that free movement of employees would be detrimental to the new member states because of the brain drain and shortage of labor in specific sectors and professions. The commission mentions some reports that indicate that emigration has contributed to labor shortages in some countries, for example, the Baltic States and Poland. This was mostly the case in specific sectors as construction and health care. However, in many countries labor shortages have been aggravated by factors other than emigration, such as economic growth, low labor market participation, and low internal mobility.[17] A country such as Poland used migration from Russia, Belarus, and Ukraine, but also from China and India, to fill the gaps in the labor market. The number of immigrants in Poland doubled in a short time after 2004.

Furthermore, the differences in the skill mix between emigrants and the sending countries' labor forces seem to be relatively moderate, thus suggesting that the overall brain drain may be limited.[18] Moreover, we can expect that this phenomenon is at an end now. The improved economic conditions in the new member states have reduced the incentives for high-skilled citizens of the new member states to work abroad. Moreover the ageing of the population in these new member states makes it necessary that more people stay and work in the domestic labor market. And finally, much of the migration from the new member states was temporary. In the UK, more than 50% of recent migrants have already returned to their countries of origin. And returning workers tend to bring back new skills that are valuable for their home country's economy. A sizable outflow of workers also led to substantial remittances from abroad (about 5.5% of GDP in Bulgaria and Romania and 1.5% of GDP in Poland) that support the domestic economy.[19]

The most decisive argument against the free movement of labor from the new member states was the disturbance of the labor market in the host countries. Trade unions, for instance, supported the introduction of a transitional period before permitting the free movement of labor. They argued that a large influx of new migrants will make it more difficult for existing foreign workers to integrate into society, that the larger labor reserve will depress wage levels, and that the risk of social dumping will be increased.[20]

According to the commission, these were not the right expectations.[21] Indeed, migration has in some cases created pressure on the provision of education, housing, and health care services at the local level, and some of these migration flows have generated some disturbing effects in segments of the labor market, for instance in the UK. However, it is estimated that the recent level of intra-EU labor mobility adds about 0.3% to the GDP of the EU as a whole in the medium term. So the overall effect of post-enlargement intra-EU mobility is positive. Furthermore, evidence at hand suggests that this EU migration has not led to major labor market disturbances in those member states with the biggest inflows. There seems to be only little impact of this post-enlargement labor mobility on wages and employment of local workers. Workers from the new member states have helped to meet higher demand for labor and reduce bottlenecks (e.g., in the construction and services sectors) and have thus made a significant contribution to sustained economic growth in the receiving countries. Moreover, labor migrants were not an extra burden for the welfare state. Data for the UK show that only a very small number of EU-8 nationals claim tax-funded benefits or housing support. Most of this migration appears to be temporary. One of the negative points mentioned by the commission is that migrants from the new member states tend to work more in low-skilled jobs (one-third of migrants compared to 10% of resident workers), although they have relatively high qualifications (40% of migrants fall into the high-skilled category compared to 25% of the workforce in the old member states).

RESTRICTIVE BUT SOCIAL MEASURES?

While it has been argued that restrictions on free movement of labor from the new members states were social measures to protect their own labor market and employees, there is evidence that the contrary is true. Despite the restrictive measures, labor migration happened, but quite often in an illegal or semilegal way. Migration to the old member states was attractive for the citizens of the new member states because the wages are much higher; employers in the old member states were happy with newcomers from the new member states because they can use them in a flexible and cheap way for jobs that are refused by the local employees.

The European Commission launched the hypothesis that the closure of the borders pushed the migration in semilegal and illegal circuits with bad consequences for everyone: abuses, false and unfair competition, a weak protection of the migrants, fake statutes, illegal work, and no social contributions for the government. At a meeting of a so-called High Level Group on Free Movement of Persons, with representatives of member states and the European and the national social partners on 16 September 2005, it was acknowledged that the restrictions may have encouraged EU-8 nationals to look for other ways to perform economic activity in EU-15 member states. This has been reflected in an exceptionally high influx of posted workers or workers claiming to be self-employed. The social partners strongly emphasized that erosion of labor standards and social dumping by immigration should be avoided. However, they also "pointed out that restrictions on legal work actually lead to a proliferation of undocumented work, bogus 'self-employed' work, and fictitious service provision and sub-contracting. Lacunae in enforcement of existing Community legislation and in particular of the posted workers directive were also reported."[22] The overriding majority of the social partners, except for those representing trade unions in a few countries, stated that they were in favor of a lifting of the restrictions in order to avoid negative collateral consequences of maintaining restrictions in place. They argued that only when the restrictions are lifted, it is possible to create a level playing field.

In January 2006, the Dutch Minister of Social Affairs estimated that there were between twenty-six thousand and thirty-six thousand illegal workers from the new EU-8 member states at work in the Netherlands.[23] And reports indicate that the incidence of illegal employment of EU-8 citizens working without permit decreased after the Netherlands decided to open its labor market in 2007.[24] Also in Belgium, there is an increasing number of migrants from East European countries who are legally here but work in illegal circumstance. Part of this group has been called "investment migrants":[25] they come temporarily to work hard and to earn a lot of money (at least in their eyes) in a short term, but they do not have the intention to stay longer than necessary. After getting some money, they go home. And sometimes this scenario is repeated several times.

One of the "semi" illegal ways to immigrate and to work in the old member states is working as a bogus self-employer. The transitional measures did not forbid the free movement of services within the EU. Since May 2004 it was possible for self-employers and companies to accept orders in the old member states. They have to accept the minimal core of labor and employment law of the host country, but the social contributions and taxes can be paid in the country of origin, where these taxes are much less than in the old member states. This creates false competition. Moreover, it is possible that business companies from the old member states make a joint venture in the new member states to accept work in the old member states. In these situations, efficient control and inspection become very difficult. Especially because of this unfair competition, several employers' associations argued against the restrictive transitional measures.

A CASE STUDY: BELGIUM

At the end of 2005, UNIZO, the union of independent Flemish entrepreneurs in Belgium, wrote:

> Despite we do not have exact proves and figures, we can say that a substantial part of the self-employed people from abroad work in sub-contract for a Belgian company. They work always for the same employer, do not have their own material, do not make price-offers, do not speak Dutch so they cannot recruit their own costumers. They do not work for the common prices and are bogus self-employed workers who are in unfair competition with the Flemish companies with Flemish employees paying their social contribution in Belgium.[26]

Evidence at hand shows that the analysis of UNIZO is right. In May 2006, the transitional measures are being eased in Belgium. The governments made lists of bottleneck jobs. In Flanders this list contains 112 professions. For these jobs, employers can easily engage citizens of the new EU member states. In 2007, 26,734 and in 2008, 34,285 permits were given for bottleneck jobs in Belgium (most of them in Flanders: 25,243 in 2007, 32,522 in 2008). Mainly people from Poland made use of it. In 2009, 15,257 and in 2010, still 11,437 work permits were given, only for Romanian and Bulgarian workers in bottleneck jobs—for the other new EU citizens did not need work permits anymore.[27] The government hoped that this opening for bottleneck jobs (together with the start of LIMOSA[28] and a more efficient social and labor inspection) would help to decrease the amount of (semi) illegal work, for instance in construction.

At first sight the bottleneck measure was a success, and government representatives quoted the high number of work permits for bottleneck jobs in the parliament and the media. However, if we look more closely at the facts and figures, it is not sure if the government succeeded with its ambition to decrease the amount of (semi) illegal work. In Flanders, most of the work permits were given for seasonal work in agriculture (17,400 in 2007; 21,500 in 2008; 10,600 in 2009; and 8,000 in 2010). In construction the use of these work permits is very low: 1,195 bricklayers and 435 stucco workers in 2008.[29] This is much less than the Confederation of Construction expected. The figures suggest that many people still use the other semilegal or illegal way of (bogus) posted workers and (bogus) self-employers, because we know that in 2008, many more Polish people were at work in construction in Flanders and Brussels.

We could also expect that the number of self-employers from the new EU member states would decrease after the bottleneck measure of 2006. However, the contrary is true. The amount of self-employers from the new member states increased after the enlargement of 2004, but it grew most of all after 2006. The number of self-employers from the new member states in 2006 was already doubled in 2008 (most of them are from Poland, Romania, and to a lesser extent from Bulgaria). The amount of Romanian self-employers in Belgium increased from 7,337 in 2009 to 12,096 in 2011.[30] This evolution suggests that many people still use and prefer this way of labor migration above paid labor in charge of a Belgian employer. However, more than 40% of the self-employed Bulgarians and Romanians in 2012 do not have any income after three years of "self-employed activity." This shows that the status of self-employment is used for other reasons.

All of this is not really surprising. The restrictive measures "obliged" the Belgian employers to find "creative" solutions to employ citizens from the new member states. And the same is true for the new EU citizens since labor migration toward the old member states was very attractive for them. When the borders go open now, people do not change their actions because the creative solutions, used in the last years, seem efficient, cheap and easy.

In conclusion, we could say that the Belgian transitional restrictive arrangements were less social than was expected, for instance by trade unions. The arrangements "created" illegal activities and did not protect the interests of the local and the migrant employees, and they did not protect a fair competition of the labor market. In terms of justice, it seems that opting immediately for open borders in May 2004 was not necessarily worse than the option for restrictive transitional measures.

LABOR MIGRATION FROM THIRD-COUNTRIES

Many West European countries started with guest worker programs after WWII. During the 1940s and 1950s, Belgium, for instance, entered into bilateral agreements with Italy, Spain, and Greece; and in 1964 with Morocco and Turkey. Because of the oil crisis, several countries implemented a so-called migration stop around 1974. It does not mean that migration did not happen anymore, only economic migration from third-countries was no longer possible. Family migration, asylum, and EU migration became the most significant patterns of immigration.

This migration stop eroded during the last decennia. All kinds of exceptional measures and categories are introduced to facilitate labor migration, especially for high-skilled professionals and for seasonal workers in agriculture. In Belgium, for instance, work permits are easily issued by the Flemish region for special categories of non-EU employees, like highly educated persons, managerial staff, special technicians, and academics. More than 7,600 such a permits have been given in 2008; 6,364 in 2009; and 6,751 in 2010, mostly for highly educated persons and managerial staff from India, Japan, and the United States.[31]

Also, on the European level there were initiatives. On the Tampere European Council, 15–16 October 1999, the European countries agreed on a number of policy priorities on asylum and migration. Concerning labor migration, we read:

> The European Council acknowledges the need for approximation of national legislations on the conditions for admission and residence of third country nationals, based on a shared assessment of the economic and demographic developments within the Union, as well as the situation in the countries of origin. It requests to this end rapid decisions by the Council, on the basis of proposals by the Commission. These decisions should take into account not only the reception capacity of each member state, but also their historical and cultural links with the countries of origin.[32]

The commission acknowledged several times that from the demographic and economic perspective the EU needs a proactive economic migration policy.[33] The demographic developments show that all EU countries experience declining fertility or have stagnating fertility below replacement level.[34] On average women in Europe give birth to 1.5 children. As a result, positive net migration will be the only population growth factor. However, it will not be possible in the long run to counterbalance the negative natural change. These demographic developments are not without consequences for the welfare state and the labor market. At current labor participation rates and in the absence of migration (zero migration variant), Western and Central Europe's labor force would decline by twenty-three million during the period 2005–2025 and by another forty-three million during the period 2025–2050. Moreover, the share of people aged sixty-five years or over in the total population of the EU is projected to increase from 17.1% in 2008 to 30% in 2060. And whereas in 2008 there are four persons of working age (fifteen to sixty-four years old) for every person aged sixty-five years or over; in 2060 the ratio is expected to be two to one.[35] The commission has also mentioned the potential importance of labor immigration as a means of achieving the goals of the Lisbon agenda, namely, to fulfil the target of full employment and to make the EU the most competitive economy in the world. Furthermore, the commission warns that the EU must increase its attractiveness for high-skilled professionals if the EU doesn't want to lose the global battle for talent and knowledge from the United States, Canada, and Australia.

In 2001 the commission launched a proposal for a council directive about the several aspects of labor migration.[36] This proposal did not succeed[37] and was revoked in 2005.[38] Afterward, the issue of labor migration has been divided in several parts, and meanwhile three different directives have been accepted: in 2005 a directive to facilitate the immigration of scientific researchers from third-countries[39] and in 2009 a directive against illegal employment[40] and the so-called blue-card directive.[41] The centerpiece of the directive against illegal employment is a general prohibition on the employment of third-country nationals who do not have the right to be resident in the EU, accompanied by appropriate sanctions against employers who infringe that prohibition. Moreover, the member states should ensure effective and adequate inspections on their territory.

In order to make the EU more attractive to highly qualified workers from around the world and sustain its competitiveness and economic growth, the blue-card directive is intended to facilitate the admission of such workers and their families (within six months) by establishing a fast-track admission procedure and by granting them equal social and economic rights as nationals of the host member state in a number of areas. The standard period of validity of the EU Blue Card is between one and four years, but the card can be renewed. After eighteen months an EU Blue Card holder and his family may move to another member state for the purpose of highly qualified employment. This European initiative is without prejudice to the competence of the member states to maintain or to introduce new national residence permits for any purpose of employment. The third-country nationals concerned should have the possibility to apply for an EU Blue Card or for a national residence permit. Only the United Kingdom, Ireland, and Denmark are not participating in the adoption of this directive.

MIGRATION, DEVELOPMENT, PARTNERSHIPS

That the EU wants to elaborate a market- and demography-driven labor migration policy is not necessarily a bad evolution. At least some essential conditions should be fulfilled. The social protection and the rights of the immigrants should be guaranteed, unfair competition and semi- and illegal practices should be avoided and the labor migration should be organized in a way that neither the host society nor the country of origin is worse off because of this migration. Where it is possible, it should be organized in a way that the host country and especially the country of origin are better of with the labor migration.

The European texts show that the EU clearly has the intention (at least on paper) to fulfill these conditions. The Tampere conclusions mentioned already the need for "a comprehensive approach to migration addressing political, human rights and development issues in countries and regions of origin and transit. . . . Partnership with third countries concerned will also be a key element for the success of such a policy, with a view to promoting co-development" (§11). In search of a common immigration policy, the terms "solidarity and immigration" are explicitly used together,[42] and "maximising the development impact of migration and mobility" is an important pillar in *The Global Approach to Migration and Mobility* of the commission.[43] Moreover, this *Global Approach* text is accompanied by a commission staff working paper on migration and development.[44] The Blue Card directive (§22) insists on "ethical recruitment policies": "Member States should refrain from pursuing active recruitment in developing countries in sectors suffering from a lack of personnel." The member states should develop mechanisms and measures "that would minimise negative and maximise positive impacts of highly skilled immigration on developing countries in order to turn 'brain drain' into 'brain gain.'" Moreover, "[s]pecific reporting provisions should be provided for to monitor the implementation of this Directive, with a view to identifying and possibly counteracting its possible impacts in terms of 'brain drain' in developing countries and in order to avoid 'brain waste'" (§24).

The commission is also in favor of integrating migration issues into the Union's development cooperation, other external policies, and the fight against illegal migration and brain drain. Since the 1990s migration plays an increasingly important role in establishing multilateral and bilateral agreements with migrant-sending countries, especially in Africa, Asia, and Latin America. These agreements aim at fostering "an improved migration management" "through cooperation, capacity building and dialogue between the countries involved."[45]

More recently, the European Commission launched the idea of mobility partnerships between the EU and third countries to establish more solidarity.[46] Such partnership can be negotiated by the EC with third countries "that have committed themselves to cooperating actively with the EU on management of migration flows, including by fighting against illegal migration, and that are interested in securing better access to EU territory for their citizens."[47] Next to the commitments expected from the third countries (reducing the incentives for irregular migration, readmitting its own nationals, improving the security of travel documents against fraud, combating illegal migration, migrant smuggling and human trafficking, promoting productive employment, decent work, and improving the economic and social framework conditions), there are also the commitments given by the EC and member states participating in such package (e.g., improving the opportunities for legal migration for nationals of the third country, helping third countries to manage legal migration flows, helping to address the risk of brain drain and to promote circular migration or return migration). In 2012 there were mobility partnerships with Armenia (2011), Georgia (2009), the Republic of Moldova and Cape Verde (2008). Negotiations are going on with Ghana, and negotiations are planned with Egypt, Morocco, and Tunisia.

The communication of the commission also insists on circular migration because it "will help EU Member States address their labor needs while exploiting potential positive impacts of migration on development and responding to the needs of countries of origin in terms of skill transfers and of mitigating the impact of brain drain."[48] The directives for high-skilled labor migrants and for scientific researchers facilitate already this kind of circular migration, and the same will be true for the coming directive for seasonal workers.[49] Insisting on circular migration is not a priori a bad option. However, we must take into account that temporary migration is always accompanied by possibly (legal and illegal) permanent settlement and discriminatory practices to prevent (unskilled) migrants from settling. On this issue, the history of migration is an interesting but hard taskmaster.[50]

BETWEEN INTENTION AND IMPLEMENTATION ...

The intentions of the EU concerning migration are in line with the minimal principle of justice that migration should not make anyone worse off. The challenge for the future is the implementation of these intentions in concrete and effective policy measures. This is not an easy task. Firstly, there is always a gap between idealistic intentions and textual formulations on the one hand, and the implementation in the concrete world on the other hand. It is, for instance, not easy to translate the intention to be aware of negative consequences of brain drain into effective policies. And the same is true for the battle against the exploitation of (especially low-skilled, temporary) migrants and against smugglers. Also the intention to address the social-economic root causes of forced migration needs a much more well-organized and energetic international policy of fair trade and redistribution. Secondly, there is also a different perception of migration between the European Union and the member states. For the latter migration is often seen as a security threat, while the "Eurocrats" in Brussels seem to be much more sympathetic toward migration, migrant rights and the link with international development.[51] The Eurocrats do not face the pressure of the public opinion in the way that national governments do. The electoral pressure in the member states, especially there where extreme right, anti-immigrant parties are successful, is a possible hindrance for the implementation of the European intentions. If the European migration project will succeed, it is dependent on many concrete elements. The goodwill of the member states is undeniably one of them.

NOTES

1. International Labour Organization (ILO). 2010. *International Labour Migration: A Rights-Based Approach*. ILO, Geneva; UN, *International Migration Report 2009: A Global Assessment*. United Nations, ST/ESA/SER.A/316. For earlier facts and figures see Stalker, Peter. 1994. *The Work of Strangers: A Survey of International Labour Migration*. ILO, Geneva; Stalker, Peter. 2000. *Workers without Frontiers: The Impact of Globalization on International Migration*, ILO, Geneva.

2. For the impact of the crisis on labor migration and migrant workers: Koehler, Jobst, Laczko, Frank, Aghazarm, Christine, and Schad, Julia. 2012. *Study on Migration and the Economic Crisis in the European Union: Implications for Policy, Research and Publications Division*, International Organization for Migration/Independent Network of Labor Migration and Integration Experts; Awad, Ibrahim. 2009. *The Global Economic Crisis and Migrant Workers: Impact and Response*. ILO, Geneva.

3. ILO. 2010. *International Labour Migration: A Rights-Based Approach*. ILO, Geneva; Directive 2011/98/EU of the European Parliament and of the Council of 13 December 2011 on a single application procedure for a single permit for third-country nationals to reside and work in the territory of a Member State and on a common set of rights for third-country workers legally residing in a Member State.

4. Borjas, George. 1995. "The Economic Benefits from Immigration." *Journal of Economic Perspectives* 2: 3–22; Borjas, George. 1999. *Heaven's Door: Immigration Policy and the American Economy*. Princeton University Press, Princeton; Tribalat, Michèle. 1991. *Cent ans d'immigration, étrangers d'hier, français d'aujourd'hui*. Paris: PUF, 195–256.

5. Wickramasekara, Piyasiri. 2003. *Policy Responses to Skilled Migration: Retention, Return and Circulation*. ILO, Geneva; Whelan, Anna. 2004. "Effectiveness of Strategies for Discouraging Brain Drain." *Bulletin of the World Health Organization* 82, 8: 619–621; Stark, Oded. 2004. "Rethinking the Brain Drain." *World Development* 32, no. 1: 15–23.

6. Saxenian, AnnaLee. 2002. "Brain Circulation: How High Skill Immigration Makes Everyone Better Off." *The Brooking Review* 20, no. 1: 28–31; Teferra, Damtew. 2005. "Brain Circulation: Unparalleled Opportunities, Underlying Challenges, and Outmoded Presumptions." *Journal of Studies in International Education* 9, no. 3: 229–250.

7. Saxenian, AnnaLee. 2000. "The Bangalore Boom: From Brain Drain to Brain Circulation." In *Bridging the Digital Divide: Lessons from India*, ed. Kenniston, Kenneth, and Kumar, Deepak. Bangalore: National Institute of Advanced Study.

8. For discussion: Ghosh, Bimal. 2006. *Migrants' Remittances, and Development: Myths, Rethoric and Realities*. IOM/The Hague Process on Refugees and Migration; De Haas, Hein. 2005. "International Migration, Remittances and Development: Myths and Fact." *Third World Quarterly* 26, no. 8: 1269–1284.

9. IFAD. 2007. *Sending Money Home: Worldwide Remittance Flows to Developing Countries*. Washington, DC.

10. For an in-depth assessment of the contributions that migration is making to receiving and sending countries: OECD. 2007. *Gaining from Migration: Towards a New Mobility System*.

11. Vanheule, Dirk. 2009. "The International Convention on the Protection of the Rights of All Migrant Workers and Members of Their Families." *International Human Rights Law in a Global Context*. Bilbao: University of Deusto; Pecoud, Antoine, and De Guchteneire, Paul. 2006. "Migration, Human Rights and the United Nations: An Investigation into the Obstacles to the UN Convention on Migrant Workers' Rights." *Windsor Yearbook of Access to Justice*, 241–266; Vucetic, Srdjan. 2007. "Democracies and International Human Rights: Why Is There No Place for Migrant Workers?" *International Journal of Human Rights*, 403–428; MacDonald, Euan, and Cholewinski, Ryszard. 2007. "The Migrant Workers Convention in Europe. Obstacles to the Ratification of the International Convention on the Protection of the Rights of All Migrant Workers and Members of Their Families: EU/EEA Perspectives." *Etudes UNESCO sur les migrations*, Paris, UNESCO. For the effects of ratification for Belgium see Vanheule, Dirk, Foblets, Marie-Claire, Loones, S., and Bouckaert, Steven. 2005. "The Signifi-

cance of the UN Migrant Workers' Convention of 18 December 1990 in the Event of Ratification by Belgium." *European Journal of Migration and Law* 6, no. 4: 285–321.

12. Thorburn, Joanne. 1996. "Root Causes Approaches to Forced Migration: Part of a Comprehensive Strategy? A European Perspective." *Journal of Refugee Studies* 9, no. 2: 119–35.

13. Presidency Conclusions, Tampere European Council 15 and 16 October 1999: §10ff.; COM. 2008. 359 final, June 17, 2008: Communication from the Commission to the European Parliament, the Council, the European Economic and Social Committee and the Committee of the Regions: A Common Immigration Policy for Europe: Principles, Actions and Tools; COM. 2011. 743 final, November 18, 2011: Communication from the Commission to the European Parliament, the Council, the European Economic and Social Committee and the Committee of the Regions: The Global Approach to Migration and Mobility.

14. These restrictive transitional arrangements were not applied toward the new member states Cyprus and Malta.

15. COM. 2008. 765 final, November 18, 2008: Communication from the Commission to the European Parliament, the Council, the European Economic and Social Committee and the Committee of the Regions: The Impact of Free Movement of Workers in the Context of EU Enlargement—Report on the First Phase (1 January 2007–31 December 2008) of the Transitional Arrangements Set Out in the 2005 Accession Treaty and as Requested According to the Transitional Arrangement Set Out in the 2003 Accession Treaty.

16. May 2007: the Netherlands; November 2007: Luxemburg; July 2008: France; May 2009: Belgium and Denmark.

17. COM, 2008, 765.

18. COM, 2008, 765.

19. COM, 2009, 79 final, February 20, 2009. Communication from the Commission to the European Parliament, the Council, the European Economic and Social Committee, the Committee of the Regions and the European Central Bank: Five Years of an Enlarged EU—Economic Achievements and Challenges; SEC, 2009, 177.

20. De Baene, Jean-Marie. 2009. "Labor Migration: A Gulf Dividing the Socialist Trade Union Leadership and the Rank and File?" *Belgian Society and Politics* 2009: 122–124.

21. COM, 2008, 765; COM, 2009, 79 final; Directorate-General for Economic and Financial Affairs. 2009. *Five Years of an Enlarged EU—Economic Achievements and Challenges.*

22. COM, 2006, 48 final, February 8, 2006: Communication from the Commission to the Council, the European Parliament, the European Economic and Social Committee and the Committee of the Regions: Report on the Functioning of the Transitional Arrangements Set Out in the 2003 Accession Treaty (1 May 2004–30 April 2006).

23. *Naleving van de Wet arbeid vreemdelingen: een eerste onderzoek onder werkgevers in opdracht van het ministerie uitgevoerd door het bureau Regioplan Beleidsonderzoek.* December 2005.

24. COM, 2008, 765.

25. Van Meeteren, Masja, Van San, Marion, and Engbersen, Godfried. 2008. *Zonder Papieren. Over de positie van irreguliere migranten en de rol van het vreemdelingenbeleid in België.* Leuven: Acco.

26. UNIZO-standpunt. 2005. *Vrij verkeer van werknemers in de EU: knelpunten wegwerken en sociale dumping vermijden.* 8 December.

27. Vlaams Subsidieagentschap voor Werk en Sociale Economie. Dienst Migratie en Arbeidsbemiddeling. *Jaarverslag 2010. Arbeidsvergunningen en arbeidskaarten in Vlaanderen,* Brussel.

28. A governmental databank for migrant self-employers.

29. Vlaams Subsidieagentschap voor Werk en Sociale Economie. Dienst Migratie en Arbeidsbemiddeling. *Jaarverslag 2008. Arbeidsvergunningen en arbeidskaarten in Vlaanderen,* Brussel.

30. *Jaarverslag 2011.* Rijksinstituut voor de Sociale Verzekeringen der Zelfstandigen.

31. Vlaams Subsidieagentschap voor Werk en Sociale Economie. Dienst Migratie en Arbeidsbemiddeling. *Jaarverslag 2010. Arbeidsvergunningen en arbeidskaarten in Vlaanderen.* Brussel.

32. Presidency Conclusions, Tampere European Council. 15 and 16 October 1999, §20.

33. See for instance COM, 2004, 811 final, January 11, 2005: Green Paper on an EU Approach to Managing Economic Migration, European Commission, Brussels.

34. Eurostat's Population Projections, EUROPOP2008 Convergence Scenario 2008–2060.

35. Münz, Rainer. 2009. "Demographic Change, Labour Force Development and Migration in Europe: Current Situation, Future Outlook and Policy Recommendation." In *Labour Migration and Its Development Potential in the Age of Mobility*, 15–16 October 2009, Malmö, Sweden, Round table theme 1: Labour immigration, SE2009.EU.

36. COM, 2001, 386 final, July 11, 2001: Proposal for a Council Directive on the Conditions of Entry and Residence of Third-Country Nationals for the Purpose of Paid Employment and Self-Employed Economic Activities.

37. For an analysis of this failure: Luedtke, Adam. 2011. "Uncovering European Union Immigration Legislation: Policy Dynamics and Outcomes." *International Migration* 49, no. 2: 1–2, 14ff.

38. COM, 2005, 462 final, September 27, 2005: Communication from the Commission to the Council and the European Parliament: Outcome of the Screening of Legislative Proposals Pending before the Legislator.

39. Council Directive 2005/71/EC of 12 October 2005 on a specific procedure for admitting third-country nationals for the purposes of scientific research.

40. Council Directive 2009/52/EC of 18 June 2009 providing for minimum standards on sanctions and measures against employers of illegally staying third-country nationals.

41. Council Directive 2009/50/EC of 25 May 2009 on the conditions of entry and residence of third-country nationals for the purposes of highly qualified employment.

42. COM, 2008, 359.

43. COM, 2011, 743 final, November 18, 2011: Communication from the Commission to the European Parliament, the Council, the European Economic and Social Committee and the Committee of the Regions: The Global Approach to Migration and Mobility.

44. SEC (2011) 1353 def. November 18, 2011.

45. Adepoju, Aderanti, Van Noorloos, Femke, and Zoomers, Annelies. 2010. "Europe's Migration Agreements with Migrant-Sending Countries in the Global South: A Critical Review." *International Migration* 48, no. 3: 42–75.

46. COM, 2007, 248 final, May 16, 2007: Communication from the Commission to the European Parliament, the Council, the European Economic and Social Committee and the Committee of the Regions on Circular Migration and Mobility Partnerships between the European Union and Third Countries; COM, 2008, 359 final.

47. COM, 2007, 248.

48. COM, 2007, 248.

49. COM, 2010, 379 final, July 13, 2010: Proposal for a Directive of the European Parliament and of the Council on the Conditions of Entry and Residence of Third-Country Nationals for the Purposes of Seasonal Employment.

50. For discussion see Doomernik Jeroen. 2013. "Does Circular Migration Lead to 'Guest Worker' Outcomes?" *International Migration* 51, no. 1: 24–39; Castels, Stefan. 2006. "Guest Workers in Europe: A Resurrection?" *International Migration Review* 40, no. 4: 741–766; Rush, Martin. 2006. "The Potential of Temporary Migration Programs in Future International Migration Policy." *International Labor Review* 145: 7–36; Rush, Martin, and Martin, Philip. 2008. "Numbers vs. Rights: Trade-Offs and Guest Worker Programs." *International Migration Review* 42: 7–36; Chang, Howard F. 2008. "Guest Workers and Justice in a Second-Best World." *University of Dayton Law Review* 34: 3–14; Attas, Daniel. 2000. "The Case of Guest Workers. Exploitation, Citizenship and Economic Rights." *Res Publica* 6: 73–92; Carens, Joseph. 2008. "Live-in Domestics, Seasonal Workers, and Others Hard to Locate on the Map of Democracy." *Journal of Political Philosophy* 16: 371–496; Ottonelli, Valeria, and Torresi, Tiziana. 2012. "Inclusivist Egalitarian Liberalism and Temporary Migration: A Dilemma." *Journal of Political Philosophy* 20, no. 2: 202–224.

51. Luedtke, Adam. 2011. "Uncovering European Union Immigration Legislation: Policy Dynamics and Outcomes." *International Migration* 49, no. 2: 1–27; Luedtke, Adam. 2005. "European Integration, Public Opinion and Immigration Policy: Testing the Impact of National

Identity." *European Union Politics* 6, 1: 93–112; Lahav, Gallya. 2004. *Immigration and Politics in the New Europe: Reinventing Borders*. Cambridge: Cambridge University Press.

Chapter Seven

Justice for the "Other" Caregivers

Addressing the Epistemic Dimension of Injustice

Zahra Meghani

In recent years it has been argued that in liberal democracies there should be public democratic deliberations to determine what constitutes fair treatment of undocumented workers. Those deliberations could lead to the formulation of policies and laws that would justly treat that population. This chapter argues that that approach may not result in liberal democracies where the majority of the citizens subscribe to a "vision"-distorting kind of nationalism. That form of nationalism does not recognize that undocumented workers are the moral equals of citizens in the substantive sense; it is only nominally committed to respecting their equality. The case is made in this chapter that this distorted "vision" problem must be resolved if undocumented workers are to be treated fairly. The treatment of undocumented direct care workers (DCWs) in the United States is used to motivate and instantiate the central argument of this chapter.

The chapter begins by identifying the key characteristics of the female undocumented DCW population. It is followed by a brief account of the political, economic, and social factors that shape their decision to work in the United States. After that, it is argued that this group of workers, along with the larger population of undocumented workers, qualifies as oppressed. Then, Seyla Benhabib's approach for addressing the problem of the unjust treatment of noncitizen residents in liberal democracies is discussed. The argument is made that her strategy may not be effective in liberal democracies where the majority of the citizens are committed to a "vision"-distorting type of nationalism. In the final section of the chapter, a possible, partial solution to that epistemic problem is outlined. It could be a crucial step in ensuring that undocumented workers, including female undocumented DCWs, are treated as the full moral equals of citizens.

THE WORK CONDITIONS OF FEMALE UNDOCUMENTED DIRECT CARE WORKERS (DCWS)

Undocumented direct care workers (DCWs)[1] constitute approximately 4% of the DCW population as a whole.[2] Persons from Mexico and Central America make up 33% of that group, and people from the Caribbean and Africa constitute 18% and 20%, respectively (Martin et al. 2009, 27). In other words, the largest percentage of female undocumented DCWs in the United States are from Mexico, Central America, the Caribbean, and Africa. In general, there is not much data about undocumented DCWs because, presumably, like any other undocumented population, its members are reluctant to identify themselves, fearing arrest, imprisonment, and deportation. However, by drawing on the general profile of DCWs, some assumptions may be justifiably made about undocumented DCWs. Below, a brief outline of the work conditions of DCWs is provided.

In the United States, in 2008, an estimated three million DCWs provided care to elderly or disabled Americans (PHI 2011). In coming years, their numbers are supposed to increase considerably in response to the graying of the US population (Seavey 2010–2011). The services they perform tend to range from administering medication to checking vital signs to bathing to feeding to assisting with dressing to attending to their charges' bodily functions. The vast majority of DCWs work in homes or community-based settings (PHI 2011). An estimated 90% of DCWs are women (PHI 2011), and a significant number of them are minorities (PHI 2011). Compensation for direct care services is relatively meager. For instance, in 2009, the median hourly wage in the United States was $15.95, but DCWs earned only $10.58 (PHI 2011, 3). Many DCWs, especially home health aides, who tend to be women, do not get retirement benefits (Leutz 2009, 6). Employers usually do not provide them with health insurance coverage (PHI March 2011) or sick leave (Nursing Home Community Coalition of New York 2003; U.S. DHHS HRSA 2004a, 2004b; Case, Himmelstein, and Woolhandler 2002; Lipson and Regan 2004; Kaye et al. 2006; Dawson 2007; USA GAO 2001; Smith and Baughman 2007). This is especially troubling because DCWs are often injured while caring for their patients. Job satisfaction amongst DCWs is low; they feel disrespected by society and their supervisors (Bowers, Esmond, and Jacobsen 2003).

From this profile of DCWs, the following conclusions may be drawn about the subpopulations of undocumented DCWs:

1. It is likely that the vast majority of undocumented DCWs are women.
2. Given that the institutions that employ DCWs require that potential employees provide an official identification document, it is probable that the majority of undocumented DCWs work in noninstitutional, community-based, or home settings.
3. It may be assumed that the wages they earn are below the US median hourly wage. In fact, it may very well be the case that their median hourly wages are lower than those of their American counterparts. As they are undocumented, they are not in a strong position to negotiate fair market wages for their work.
4. It is very probable that undocumented DCWs do not have retirement benefits.
5. Although they may suffer injuries while providing care to their charges, it is unlikely that they have health insurance[3] or sick leave.

The presence in the United States of female undocumented DCWs from poorer countries should be understood in light of the flow of human labor from the south to the north. Some of the key factors responsible for this tide of workers are the neoliberal policies and programs of the IMF and the WB and the free trade agreements of the WTO (Kirk and Okazawa-Rey 1998; Chang 2000; Parreñas 2003; Sassen 2002, 2003; Espinoza 2003; Ehrenreich and Hochschild 2003). The policies, programs, and treaties of these transnational financial and trade organizations are primarily shaped by the wealthy nations that dominate these entities. In both the WB and the IMF, the United States has the largest share of voting power amongst member nations (Schrecker and Labonte 2007, 286). That gives it the power to significantly shape the structural adjustment programs (SAPs)[4] that those financial entities impose on borrowing nations in the global South. SAPs have required that debtor countries in Asia, Latin America, and the Caribbean eliminate price control on basic goods and utilities; substantially cut government spending on health care, education, childcare, and social welfare; and significantly limit government subsidies for food, fuel, and public transportation (Kirk and Okazawa-Rey 1998). These changes have hit hardest the poor of those countries, making it more difficult for them to survive in their nation of origin.[5]

The international free trade agreements negotiated under the auspices of the WTO[6] have also made it difficult for many of the poor in the global South to eke out an existence in their home nation. While wealthy countries like the United States and certain EU states have compelled poorer nations to end subsidies to their farmers, they have continued to provide assistance to their own farmers, including large-scale agribusiness farms. That has enabled them to flood the international market, including poorer countries, with underpriced farm products. As a result, small-scale farmers in poor nations have lost their livelihood, and some of them have sought work in richer nations. For instance, the billions in subsidies the United States provides to its farmers have allowed them to sell underpriced corn in Mexico. As a consequence, thousands of small-scale corn farmers in Mexico have been run out of business (Weiner 2002).

The effect of SAPs and free trade agreements has been to increase the flow of human labor from poorer nations to richer ones. Many from the global south who have sought work in wealthy liberal democracies have only been able to find employment as undocumented workers. That is because those nations permit very few foreigners to work within their territories. In the United States, undocumented workers are usually employed in the farming, construction, and manufacturing industry. A percentage of undocumented persons have found employment in the service industry. Presumably, a female subset of that group from Mexico, Central America, the Caribbean, and Africa is employed as DCWs in the United States.

UNDOCUMENTED WORKERS IN THE UNITED STATES: AN OPPRESSED POPULATION

In the United States, female undocumented DCWs are subject to multiple kinds of injustices. It is because of who they are and what they do that they are systematically discriminated against and exploited, as well as rendered more vulnerable to crime than many other populations. In 2007, Colorado, Maine, Minnesota, Mississippi, and Utah enacted legislation disqualifying undocumented workers, including undocumented DCWs, from receiving unemployment insurance benefits, even though those workers have paid and continue to pay state and federal taxes as well as unemployment insurance premiums (Colorado HB 1286; Maine LD 1015; Minnesota SB 0167; Mississippi SB 2448; Utah SB 103). Colorado, Idaho, Indiana, and Texas have passed laws requiring anyone applying for benefits to provide documentation about their residency status (Colorado HB 1314; Idaho SB 1157; Indiana SB 504; Texas SB 589). That effectively renders undocumented workers ineligible for public benefits, regardless of how desperately they might need them. Thus, these laws ensure that along with the larger population of undocumented workers, undocumented DCWs are unable to receive public benefits. With the passage of the 1996 Personal Responsibility and Work Opportunity Reconciliation, undocumented persons were divested of the right to Medicaid coverage (Medicaid is a federal and state fund program that provides funds for medical care for certain groups of the poor). So, unlike their counterparts who are US citizens, undocumented DCWs are ineligible to receive that benefit even though they may meet the poverty criteria for Medicaid. The state of Minnesota has enacted legislation that disqualifies undocumented persons, including undocumented DCWs, from receiving general medical care that is funded by the federal or the state government (Minnesota HB 1078). In 2007, Nevada and Oregon passed laws barring undocumented workers from receiving workers' compensation in the event of accident, injury, or death (Nevada AB 496; Oregon HB 2244 and SB 202). Thus, undocumented DCWs who are injured in the course of their employment cannot receive workers' compensation. This is particularly troubling because DCWs have one of the higher rates of work-related injuries among various professions (Newcomer and Scherzer 2006; Pennington, Scott, and Magilvy 2003). These federal and state laws denying medical benefits and workers' compensation to undocumented persons have a gendered, classist, nationalist, racist effect on the undocumented DCW population because the majority of that group comprises foreign women of color living in or at the edge of poverty.

Other state laws and policies also have this kind of differentiated impact. They create more and worse hardships and risks for female undocumented persons than for their American counterparts. Florida, Indiana, Kansas, Louisiana, and North Dakota have effected legislation that require noncitizens to provide documentation of their legal status in the United States in order to obtain a driver's license (Florida SB 2114; Indiana SB 463; Kansas SB 9; Louisiana HB 766; North Dakota SB 2112). Thus, undocumented workers cannot acquire a driver's license in those states. Many DCWs (including, presumably, female undocumented DCWs) live in urban areas and work in suburban home settings (Salter and Vilner 2006, 5). As female undocumented DCWs tend to work in home settings, the lack of a driver's license is a serious hardship for these women. They have to rely on a patchy public transportation system that service American suburbs. Alternatively, they can "choose" to drive without a valid driver's license or they can work at places that are within walking distance. While this drastically limits the employment prospects of undocumented DCWs, female undocumented DCWs face additional risks if they have to walk through crime-ridden parts of cities to get to or get home from work. Without a driver's license, the ability of undocumented workers, including female undocumented DCWs, to go to a grocery store, post office, or doctor's office is also severely curtailed. As a driver's license is usually the form of identification used to open a bank account, undocumented workers cannot use banks. Thus, they have to resort to check-cashing facilities, which exploit their customers by charging them very high fees. Moreover, the lack of access to a banking facility also means that many undocumented workers carry their earnings on them. That marks them out as targets for criminals, who view them as "walking ATMs" and who know they won't report the crime out of a fear of deportation (Medina 2007). This is one more risk faced by female undocumented workers, including those who are DCWs.

These policies and legislative enactments—at the state and federal levels—normalize and put the government's imprimatur on the discriminatory treatment and exploitation of the entire class of undocumented workers. Moreover, some of these policies and laws put female undocumented DCWs at additional risk of being victims of crime. However, the population of undocumented workers tends to have no recourse available to it because it is convention in most democracies to bar noncitizen residents (including undocumented workers) from participating in political processes, even about matters that profoundly affect their existence.[7] Historically, in most countries, democracy has meant, and continues to mean, the rule of the citizens, by the citizens, for the citizens. The well-being of undocumented workers is left to citizens, who attend to it when and how they see fit. These democracies seem to be only ostensibly committed to respecting undocumented workers as the moral equals of citizens.

Given that undocumented workers as human beings have the same moral status as the citizens of liberal democracies where they have found work, the denial of political voice to them by those countries reduces them to a dominated population. For instance, in the United States, a relationship of domination exists between American citizens and undocumented workers. A particular group, say group b, qualifies as dominated if another group, say group c, is able to arbitrarily define the possible courses of action open to members of group b (including the conditions under which members of group b may act) without any regard for the interests and opinions of b; group b, however, is not socially situated to set any constraints on group c (Young 2000, 32, 258–259). American citizens have the power to make crucial decisions about the life possibilities of undocumented workers living in the United States; the latter group has no reciprocal power over the former.

While a population may be dominated, it does not necessarily mean that the dominant population will necessarily exploit it or discriminate against it. However, in the United States, female undocumented DCWs (along with the larger set of undocumented workers) are subject to a variety of injustices as evidenced by the laws and policies discussed above. They are an oppressed group. An oppressed population is one whose members (by virtue of their group membership) are the subject of institutional constraints that inhibit their self-development, even though they are the moral equals of others who do not face such barriers (Young 2000, 31). The United States' political and legal institutions do not allow undocumented workers to have political agency, thus they bar their efforts to engage in self-determination. Citizens of the United States do not face those institutional constraints.

A straightforward solution to the oppression of female undocumented DCWs and the larger population of undocumented workers would be changes in policies and laws that discriminate against them, permit their exploitation, or expose them to risks that other populations do not have to face.[8] However, this strategy might not be successful in all liberal democracies where undocumented workers are oppressed. For instance, in nations where the majority of the citizens oppose policy and legal reforms that would result in undocumented workers being treated as the full moral equals of citizens, elected officials may not be willing to make those changes. But if the government does carry out those reforms, the segment of the citizenry that opposes them may continue with practices that exploit and discriminate against undocumented workers. They could do so in ways that are under the radar of the law. For instance, in the United States the enfranchisement of women and African Americans did not mean and still has not meant the end of exploitation of and discrimination against those populations (although those groups fare much better now than they did previously). The persisting wage differential between the genders and white and African Americans has been extensively documented by the US Department of Labor. That is because the underlying causal factors, that is, sexism and racism, still exist and continue to act in complicated ways with each other and other forms of oppression. Legal and policy measures, whilst absolutely crucial in addressing problems of injustice, have limited ability to change deeply ingrained oppressive ideological commitments. Thus, in order to effectively address the oppression of any group, much more than policy and legal changes is required.

Recently it has been proposed that in liberal democracies there should be public democratic deliberation about what constitutes the just treatment of noncitizens who are asylum seekers, refugees, and (documented and undocumented) resident aliens (Benhabib 2004). Ideally, the dialogue would lead to changes that would ensure that those populations of noncitizen residents are treated as the moral equals of citizens and afforded political agency. The next section evaluates that approach with respect to undocumented workers, including female undocumented DCWs.

BENHABIB'S DELIBERATIVE DEMOCRACY APPROACH AND THE DISTORTED "VISION" PROBLEM

Seyla Benhabib has made a notable attempt to address the issue of the mistreatment of asylum seekers, refugees, and (documented and undocumented) resident aliens in liberal democracies. As the solution to that problem, she does not advocate the end of the state system (2004, 2). Rather, evoking the moral equality of all persons, she has argued for the disaggregation of political rights from citizenship status and the affording of political voice to noncitizen residents. The disaggregation of political rights from citizenship status is not to occur by fiat, without the consent of citizens. Otherwise the fundamental principle that underlies the democratic state—the right of citizens to engage in self-determination—would be violated. The separation of political rights from citizenship status is to be the product of sustained democratic deliberations between citizens and noncitizens about the rights of noncitizens. The democratic iterations Benhabib espouses involve "public argumentation, deliberation, and learning through which universalist claims are contested and contextualized, invoked and revoked, throughout legal and political institutions as well as in the public sphere of liberal democracies" (Benhabib 2004, 19). A key merit of the democratic iterations approach is that it entails public reasoning in two senses. First, the public directly and collaboratively engages in a reasoning exercise aimed at addressing the question at hand. Second, the efforts to address a particular issue, in this case, the fair treatment of noncitizens, is public, that is, open and transparent. The public nature of the democratic iterations also means that they have binding power. The decisions reached by that process cannot be rejected by the public because it has made them.

Benhabib's proposal for addressing the problem of the unjust treatment of asylum seekers, refugees, and resident aliens in liberal democracies is commendable. It does not impose on the citizens of liberal democracies any laws or policies that they find unacceptable even as it attempts to ensure that the moral equality of asylum seekers, refugees, and (documented and undocumented) resident aliens is recognized. This chapter limits itself to assessing the possibility of the success of that approach with respect to justice for undocumented workers, including female undocumented DCWs.[9] This chapter argues that Benhabib's approach may not work in certain liberal democracies. Specifically, it might not be effective in nations where undocumented workers are treated unfairly *because* the dominant segment of the citizenry subscribes to a form of nationalism that distorts their moral "vision." They believe that their right to engage in self-determination as a democratic polity gives them the right to treat undocumented workers as they consider appropriate.

The kind of nationalism that motivates the citizenry of any nation to support policies and laws that discriminate and exploit undocumented workers is akin to other forms of oppression such as sexism, racism, and ethnocentrism. These ideologies of these forms of oppression justify the domination, exploitation, marginalization, objectification, or subjection to violence of particular groups on the basis of arbitrary biological traits or social characteristics supposedly unique to those populations.[10] These ideologies characterize those groups as bearing certain traits that mark them as "different." The "difference" is not construed as a value neutral variant of what an oppressive ideology deems to be the norm; rather, it is marked as inferior or deficient relative to the norm. These ideologies distort the "vision" of the oppressed as well as those who benefit from the injustice.[11] Insofar as those who receive unwarranted advantages by virtue of their sex, race, class, ethnicity, or nationality unreflectively take to be their interests and opinions what the ideology defines them to be, in a very important sense they harm themselves (and others). It does not allow them to live a life of integrity. Their lives are based on a fiction about their capacities and merits; they do not have incentive to exert themselves to realize their potential. Mill, for instance, has argued that the experience of living in a patriarchy has a deeply corrupting influence on the character of males:

> [H]ow early the notion of his inherent superiority to a girl arises in his mind; how it grows with his growth and strengthens with his strength . . . how sublime and sultan-like a sense of superiority he feels, above all, over the woman he honors by admitting her to the partnership of life. Is it imagined that all this does not pervert the whole manner of existence of the man, both as an individual and as a social being? . . . The self-worship of the monarch, or of the feudal superior, is matched by the self-worship of the male. . . . [They] are inspired with pride that values itself upon accidental advantage, not of its own achieving. (Mill 1911, 178–179)

Similarly, in liberal democracies where a powerful segment of the citizenry subscribes to a form of nationalism that contends that citizens' right to engage in self-definition gives them the right to treat undocumented workers as they consider appropriate, the moral "vision" of those citizens is damaged. That kind of nationalism fosters the illusion that citizens are more than the equals of undocumented workers such that a mere accident of birth gives them the right to deny or limit the latter opportunities for engaging in self-determination and self-development. Citizens are casts in the role of persons worthy and responsible enough to shoulder the "burden" of monitoring and controlling undocumented workers. Thus, as evidenced by the earlier discussion of policies and federal and state laws, (many) citizens of the United States have no compunction about asking their legislators to create exploitive laws and policies. They also have no scruples about discriminating against undocumented workers, going so far as to deny them basic goods and services. Moreover, many law and policy makers have no reservations about devising such laws and policies.

A POSSIBLE PARTIAL SOLUTION TO THE DISTORTED "VISION" PROBLEM

This essay proposes an alternative to Benhabib's strategy for addressing the problem of the unfair treatment of undocumented workers in liberal democracies. It builds on and modifies the approach advocated by her. While there should be public democratic deliberations about what constitutes just treatment of undocumented workers, the process should be tailored so that place of prominence is given in the public discussions to analyses and critiques of nationalism (and its complicated interaction with other systems of oppression) that have been developed by oppressed groups (which are committed to the equality of all).[12] As the experience of oppressed groups tends to be the complicated product of interplay between different forms of oppression, it is crucial that those connections are identified. For instance, the exploitation and discrimination that female undocumented DCWs are subject to is the product of a complex interaction between multiple forms of oppression, including the kind of nationalism discussed here: sexism, racism, neoliberalism, and classism. While "decoding" oppressive ideologies is not easy, oppressed groups have more reasons to "see" through them and formulate critiques of them than those who are privileged by them. The former's socially disadvantaged position makes it more probable that unlike those who benefit from the oppression, they will do two things. First, they will question the account of reality provided by the oppressive ideology, and second, they will subject them to critical scrutiny. For that reason, the critical analyses of the dominant oppressive paradigms developed by such groups should be used to begin deliberations and dialogues about justice for particular groups.

The critique developed by the oppressed is not "natural." In other words, it is not the case that any and all members of an oppressed group possess those critical insights by the mere fact of their group membership. The critical analysis "must be struggled for and represents an achievement which requires both science to see beneath the surface of the social relations in which all are forced to participate, and the education which can only grow from the struggle to change those relations" (Hartsock 2004, 37). But this does not mean that the critiques of systems of oppression formulated by oppressed groups should be accepted unquestioningly. Rather, they should be considered *valuable starting points* for discussions about ending injustice.[13]

The insightful analyses of racism and sexism developed by civil rights and feminist groups[14] are fine examples of such critiques.[15] It is of considerable importance that those who have unquestioningly accepted an oppressive ideology's account of reality—be they persons who belong to the group(s) privileged by the system of oppression or those who are oppressed—engage with such analyses because they challenge the culturally pervasive oppressive value and belief system as well as the practices based on it. That could be a significant step in dismantling systems of oppression.

Thus, during democratic iterations about the unjust treatment of undocumented workers, particular attention would have to be afforded to critical analyses of the relationship between (the form of) nationalism (that is oppressive of undocumented workers) and other types of oppression developed by oppressed groups that are committed to the moral equality of all. Different such groups may have formulated different critiques of that form of oppression and its interaction with other kinds of oppression, such as sexism and racism. For instance, some may have focused on the interaction between that kind of nationalism and sexism, and others may have considered the interplay between that type of nationalism, classism, and racism, and so on. It is crucial that those analyses are not pushed to the side or ignored in the deliberations about justice for undocumented workers, including female undocumented DCWs.

This approach presupposes a principled commitment on the part of the populace to hearing voices from the margins that espouse equality. That in turn assumes that the public understands that oppression tends to have a distorting effect on one's moral "vision." That recognition is contingent on the awareness that oppressive ideologies can shape social reality.[16] As the participants in the public democratic deliberations about the just treatment of undocumented workers might not be aware of that, there would have to be educational sessions about the workings of such ideologies. Those sessions would have to precede the public dialogue and deliberations.

It would also have to be impressed on the participants that they have a moral responsibility to understand how such ideologies function. The accounts they provide of social reality are not perfect, that is, complete and smooth. They always contain gaps, inconsistencies, and incoherencies in their "picture" of the world.[17] Given that one has the ability to "see" those imperfections and cracks *and* one does see them, one should (in conjunction with others),[18] at the very least, question the ideologies that categorize some groups as deficient or inferior.[19] The obligation exists because there are profound implications for those that are deemed inferior or deficient. For instance, patriarchal ideologies categorize women as inferior to men in terms of physical strength or intelligence, but given that there are numerous cracks, gaps, or inconsistencies in that "picture" of social reality, men and women who subscribe to such beliefs have a responsibility, at the very minimum, to question them.[20] They are morally obligated to do so because the categorization of women as deficient or inferior has serious implications for women's well-being.[21] Those who subscribe to the form of nationalism that does not consider undocumented workers the full moral equals of citizens have a similar obligation. The evidence belying the characterization of undocumented workers from poorer countries as inferior free loaders is ubiquitous. So, those who do not even question (the form of) nationalism (that is oppressive of undocumented workers) are choosing to be ignorant.[22] That is morally inexcusable because it has profound consequences for undocumented workers.[23]

The version of public democratic deliberations developed here could lead to fundamental, meaningful policy and legal reform that recognizes that undocumented workers, including female undocumented DCWs, are the moral equals of citizens in the substantive sense. Their oppression could no longer be condoned. They would have to be afforded political voice at the very least about matters that affect their well-being, such as terms of entry and exit into the country where they have found employment, guarantee of at least a living wage, health insurance coverage, sick leave, and retirement benefits.[24] No longer could decisions about such matters be made unilaterally by citizens, some of who may subscribe to a moral "vision" distorting form of nationalism.

Political voice for undocumented workers would also mean that particular groups of undocumented workers, such as female undocumented DCWs, would be able to object to policies and laws that compromised their well-being. For instance, they could argue that legislative measures like Nevada's AB 496 and Oregon's HB 2244 and SB 202, which deny undocumented workers compensation in the event of an employment-related injury, have a pernicious gendered, racist, classist effect on them as a group. As discussed earlier, undocumented DCWs are primarily women of color who live in or at the borderlands of poverty, and the rate of occupational injury is higher in their profession than in other lines of work. Those undocumented DCWs, along with other populations of undocumented workers, would also be in the position to advocate for their particular needs and interests. Their representatives would be able to draw on those groups of workers' lived experience. This is important because they might not be as well served by someone who means well and who speaks on their behalf but is unfamiliar with the hardships they confront.

CONCLUSION

With a population that is graying, the United States has come to rely on female undocumented DCWs. The case has been made that these women, along with other groups of undocumented workers, confront multiple kinds of injustices that have the imprimatur of the state. Recently, it has been proposed that the problem of the unfair treatment of undocumented workers in liberal democracies could be resolved by means of public democratic deliberations about the issue. It has been argued that that approach may not be successful because it does not take into account the hold that a "vision" distorting form of nationalism may have on the citizenry in those countries. This chapter proposes an alternative approach that entails tailored public democratic deliberation, which aims to address the "vision" distortion caused by that form of nationalism and other oppressive paradigms. That would be a critical step if undocumented workers, including female undocumented DCWs, are to be treated fairly.

NOTES

1. This section of the chapter draws on Meghani and Eckenwiler (2009).
2. It is estimated that amongst DCWs, 20% were born outside the United States. Within that population of DCWs, approximately 21% are undocumented persons (Martin et al. 2009, 27).
3. This may be deduced from the fact that DCWs who work in home settings tend not to have health insurance coverage (PHI March 2011).
4. In the wake of criticisms of SAPs, the WB and the IMF have recently claimed that their focus is on poverty reduction. Thus, they no longer use the term "structural adjustment" to describe their reform measures. But this change in terminology does not mark an ideological shift; the transnational financial institutions continue to require of poor debtor nations that they implement neoliberal reforms (Schrecker and Labonte 2007). Thus, "SAPs" is used in this paper to denote such policies and programs.
5. It is unclear whether the employment opportunities created by SAPs for poor women are adequate compensation for the state assistance that poor women and their children lose because of SAPs. The employment opportunities created by SAPs usually take the form of jobs in the factories of multinational corporations that have a poor record of respecting human rights of workers, abiding by local environmental and safety standards and paying local living wages (see Kirk and Okazawa-Rey 1998; Enloe 1998; Arnold and Bowie 2005).
6. Corrupt political regime, civil wars, and preexisting poverty have also played a significant role in worsening the life prospects of the poor in these nations.
7. There are some communities that allow noncitizens some voice in local political matters.
8. That, of course, does not mean that all undocumented workers are subject to the same injustices, regardless of factors such as sex, race, nationality, ethnicity, age, and profession. There are considerable differences in their experience of oppression depending on their group membership. For instance, female undocumented DCWs (as women undocumented workers from the global South engaged in care work) confront injustices that are the product of complicated interaction between a variety of factors, including xenophobia, nativism, sexism (including a devaluing of care work), racism (the vast majority of female undocumented DCWs are women of color), and classism.
9. It lies beyond its scope to consider the question whether it can ensure fair treatment for asylum seekers, refugees, and documented resident aliens in liberal democracies.
10. The term "ideology" is a contested one. It is used here loosely to denote the complex of beliefs, attitudes, and values that create and maintain particular kinds of social relations amongst groups.
11. These ideologies may also affect the "vision" of groups that are third parties in the sense they are neither the oppressed nor the beneficiaries of the oppression. For instance, a particular racist ideology might construe group r to be superior to group q, whilst being silent about those who belong to group t. However, members of group t might subscribe to that racist worldview and treat group q as inferior to them.
12. Analyses developed by oppressed groups that consider some humans inferior to others because of their sex, race, ethnicities, nationality, or some other arbitrary social or biological trait would not receive a place of prominence.
13. This point is adapted from Harding's work (1996, 1998) on reshaping scientific inquiry.
14. The concerns of the two groups have crucial overlaps.
15. It is worth noting that the civil rights groups that included whites and supporters of the feminist agenda were not just women. The point here is that critical analyses of oppression can be formulated by those who benefit from it, but it is more likely that the oppressed will develop them because of their experience of injustice.
16. This is not to suggest that humans are helpless in the face of such ideologies. They do have some agency, and some persons have more than others depending on their social circumstance, but the point here is that these are fairly powerful forces that structure human existence.
17. This argument is an adaptation of and builds on Filice's work (1990, 402).
18. Knowledge-building exercises are always communal endeavors (Nelson 1993).

19. The work of critically analyzing oppressive ideologies has to be a communal epistemic endeavor. Physiologically speaking, humans need other humans to make sense of the world (Nelson 1993).

20. Ideally, it would lead them to reject patriarchy.

21. This case is not equivalent to that of someone who recognizes the falsity of the claims made by a patriarchal ideology but continues to act in accordance with it because either it is to his (or her) advantage to do so or he (or she) fails to care about those affected by his (or her) actions. In either case, his (or her) actions are not morally excusable.

22. The only way someone could have remained unaware of that evidence is if he or she was not part of a human community that would have allowed him or her to realize that within any group there are significant variations in people's character and behavior, *and* did not have any interaction with the "Other," *and* was not exposed to any research, novels, or news that called into question claims about the supposed inferiority of the "Other."

23. That case is different from that of those who know the characterization of undocumented workers as lazy, inferior parasites to be false but who continue to behave as if it were true because it is to their advantage to do so or they fail to care about the harm to that population by their action. Neither stance is morally acceptable.

24. This argument presupposes that limited political voice does not entail citizenship. This chapter does not attempt to argue for citizenship for undocumented workers because that task lies beyond its modest scope. However, it might be possible to make that argument using the thesis developed in this chapter.

BIBLIOGRAPHY

Arnold, D. G., and N. E. Bowie. 2005. "Sweatshops and Respects for Persons." In *Contemporary Issues in Business Ethics*, ed. J. R. DesJardins and J. J. McCall. Belmont: Thomsons/Wadsworth.

Benhabib, S. 2004. *The Rights of Others: Aliens, Residents and Citizens*. Cambridge, MA: Cambridge University Press.

Bowers, Barbara J., Sarah Esmond, and Nora Jacobsen. 2003. "Turnover Reinterpreted: CNAs Talk about Why They Leave." *Journal of Gerontological Nursing* 29, no. 3: 36–43.

Case, Brady G. S., David U. Himmelstein, and Steffie Woolhandler. 2002. "No Care for the Caregivers: Declining Health Insurance Coverage for Health Care Personnel and Their Children 1988–1998." *American Journal of Public Health* 92, no. 3: 404–408.

Chang, G. 2000. *Disposable Domestics: Immigrant Workers in the Global Economy*. Cambridge, MA: South End Press.

Colorado, House Bill 1286. 2007. Retrieved September 8, 2007, from http://www.leg.state.co.us/.

Colorado, House Bill 1314. 2007. Retrieved September 8, 2007, from http://www.leg.state.co.us/.

Dawson, Steven. 2007. "PHI: Quality Care through Quality Jobs." Paper presented at the meeting of the Committee on the Future Healthcare Workforce for Older Americans, San Francisco, CA, June 28.

Delaware, House Bill 116, chapter 125. 144th General Assembly. 2007. Retrieved September 8, 2007, from http://www.legis.state.de.us/.

Ehrenreich, Barbara, and Arlie Russell Hochschild, eds. 2003. *Global Woman: Nannies, Maids, and Sex Workers in the New Economy*. New York: Metropolitan Books.

Enloe, C. 1998. "The Globetrotting Sneaker." In *Women's Lives: Multicultural Perspectives*, ed. G. Kirk and M. Okazawa-Rey. Mountain View: Mayfield.

Espinoza, R. 2003. "Migration Trends: Maps and Chart." In *Global Woman: Nannies, Maids, and Sex Workers in the New Economy*, ed. B. Ehrenreich and A. R. Hochschild. New York: Metropolitan Books.

Filice, C. 1990. "On the Obligation to Keep Informed about Distant Atrocities." *Human Rights Quarterly* 12, no. 3, 397–414.

Florida, House Bill 7181, Chapter 162/Senate Bill 2032. 2007. Retrieved September 8, 2007, from http://www.myfloridahouse.gov.

Florida, Senate Bill 2114, chapter 147. 2007. Retrieved September 8, 2007, from http://www.flsenate.gov/.

Harding, S. 1996. "Rethinking Standpoint Epistemology: What Is 'Strong Objectivity?'" In *Feminism and Science*, ed. E. F. Keller and H. Longino. Oxford, UK: Oxford University Press.

———. 1998. *Is Science Multicultural? Postcolonialism, Feminism, and Epistemologies.* Bloomington: Indiana University Press.

Hartsock, N. 2004. "The Feminist Standpoint: Developing the Grounds for a Specifically Feminist Historical Materialism." In *The Feminist Standpoint Theory Reader: Intellectual and Political Controversies*, ed. S. Harding. New York: Routledge.

Holding, R. 2007. "Voting Block." *Time* 169, no. 17, 60–61.

Idaho, Senate Bill 1157, Fifty-Ninth Legislature 2007. Retrieved September 8, 2007, from http://search.state.id.us/.

Indiana, Senate Bill 463, Act 184, 115th General Assembly. 2007. Retrieved September 8, 2007, from http://www.in.gov/.

Indiana, Senate Bill 504, 115th General Assembly. 2007. Retrieved September 8, 2007, from http://www.in.gov/.

Institute of Medicine (IOM). 2008. *Retooling for an Aging America: Building the Health Care Workforce.* National Academy of Sciences, http://www.nap.edu/catalog/12089.html.

International Labor Organization. 2004. *Towards a Fair Deal for Migrant Workers in the Global Economy.* Geneva: International Labour Office.

International Monetary Fund (IMF). 2008. *About the IMF: IMF Members' Quotas and Voting Power, and IMF Board of Governors.* Washington, DC: IMF. Retrieved October 29, 2009, from http://www.imf.org/.

Kansas, Senate Bill 9. 2007. Retrieved September 8, 2007, from http://www.kslegislature.org/bills/2008/9.pdf.

Kaye, Stephen H., Susan Chapman, Robert J. Newcomer, and Charlene Harrington. 2006. "The Personal Assistance Workforce: Trends in Supply and Demand." *Health Affairs* 25, no. 4: 1113–1120.

Kirk, G., and M. Okazawa-Rey, eds. 1998. "Living in a Global Economy." In *Women's Lives: Multicultural Perspectives*. Mountain View: Mayfield.

Leutz, W. N. 2009. "Immigration and the Elderly: Foreign-Born Workers in Long-Term Care." Retrieved January 12, 2012, from http://www.fosterquan.com.

Lipson, Debra, and Carol Regan. 2004. *Health Insurance Coverage for Direct Care Workers: Riding Out the Storm.* Washington, DC: Better Jobs Better Care.

Louisiana, House Bill 766. 2007. Retrieved September 8, 2007, from http://www.legis.state.la.us/.

Maine, LD 1015, 123rd Maine Senate. 2007. Retrieved September 8, 2007, from http://www.mainelegislature.org/.

Martin, S., B. L. Lowell, E. M. Gozdziak, M. Bump, and M. E. Breeding. 2009. "The Role of Migrant Care Workers in Aging Societies: Report on Research Findings in the United States." Institute for the Study of International Migration, Georgetown University. Available at: http://isim.georgetown.edu/.

Medina, Jennifer. 2007. "New Haven welcomes a booming population of immigrants, legal or not." *New York Times*, March 5th. Available at: http://www.nytimes.com/2007/03/05/nyregion/05haven.html?pagewanted=all/.

Meghani, Zahra and Eckenwiler, Lisa. 2009. "Care for the Caregivers?: Transnational Justice and Undocumented Non-Citizen Care Workers." *International Journal of Feminist Approaches to Bioethics*, 2(1): 77-101.

Mill, J. S. 1911. *The Subjection of Women.* New York: Fredrick Stokes Company.

Minnesota, House Bill 1078. 2007. Retrieved 8 September 2007, from http://www.revisor.leg.state.mn.us/.

Minnesota, Senate Bill 0167, 85th Legislative Session. 2007. Retrieved September 8, 2007, from http://www.revisor.leg.state.mn.us/.

Mississippi, Senate Bill 2448. 2007. Retrieved September 8, 2007, from http://billsta-tus.ls.state.ms.us/.
Nelson, L. H. 1993. "Epistemological Communities." In *Feminist Epistemologies*, ed. L. Alcoff and E. Potter. New York: Routledge.
Nevada, Assembly Bill 496, Seventy-Fourth Session. 2007. Retrieved September 8, 2007, from http://leg.state.nv.us/.
Newcomer, R., and T. Scherzer. 2006. "Who Counts? On (Not) Counting Occupational Injuries in Home Care." Paper presented at the American Public Health Association 134th Annual Meeting, in Boston, MA, November 7.
North Dakota, Senate Bill 2112, Sixtieth Legislative Assembly of North Dakota. 2007. Re-trieved September 8, 2007, from http://www.legis.nd.gov/.
Nursing Home Community Coalition of New York. 2003. *What Makes for Good Working Conditions for Nursing Home Staff: What Do Direct Care Workers Have to Say?* New York: NHCC.
Oregon, Bill 2244/ Senate Bill 202, Seventy-Fourth Oregon Legislative Assembly. 2007. Re-trieved September 8, 2007, from http://www.leg.state.or.us/.
Paraprofessional Healthcare Institute (PHI). 2011. "Facts 3: Who Are Direct Care Workers?" Retrieved October 3, 2011, from http://www.directcareclearinghouse.org/.
———. March 2011. "Health Care Coverage for Direct-Care Workers: 2009 Data Update." Retrieved January 12, 2012, from http://www.directcareclearinghouse.org/.
Parreñas, R. S. 2003. "The Care Crisis in the Philippines: Children and Transnational Families in the New Global Economy." In *Global Woman: Nannies, Maids, and Sex Workers in the New Economy*, ed. B. Ehrenreich and A. R. Hochschild. New York: Metropolitan Books.
Passel, J. S., and D. Cohn. 2009. *A Portrait of Unauthorized Immigrants in the United States*. Washington, DC: Pew Hispanic Center, http://pewresearch.org/.
Pennington, Karen, Jill Scott, and Kathy Magilvy. 2003. "The Role of Certified Nursing Assist-ants in Nursing Homes." *Journal of Nursing Administration* 33, no. 11: 578–584.
Salter, V., and M. A. Vilner. 2006. "Conversations about the Future of Direct-Care Workforce Research." PHI. Retrieved January 12, 2012, from http://www.directcareclearinghouse.org/.
Sandoval, S. 2007. "FB Immigration Law Wins Easily." *The Dallas Morning News*, May 13.
Sassen, S. 2002. "Women's Burden: Counter-Geographies of Globalization and the Feminiza-tion of Survival." *Nordic Journal of International Law* 71, no. 2: 255–274.
———. 2003. "Strategic Instantiations of Gendering in the Global Economy." In *Gender and U.S. Immigration: Contemporary Trends*, ed. P. Hondagneu-Sotelo. Berkeley: University of California Press.
Schrecker, T., and R. Labonte. 2007. "What's Politics Got to Do with It? Health, the G8, and the Global Economy." In *Globalization and Health*, ed. I. Kawachi and S. Wamala. New York: Oxford University Press.
Seavey, D. 2010–2011. "Caregivers on the Front Line: Building a Better Direct-Care Work-force." *Generations* 34, no. 4: 27–35.
Smith, Kristin, and Reagan Baughman. 2007. "Caring for America's Aging Population: A Profile of the Direct Care Workforce." *Monthly Labor Review* (September): 20–26.
Texas, Senate Bill 589, Eightieth Legislature. 2007. Retrieved September 8 2007, from http://www.capitol.state.tx.us/.
United Nations. 2005. "Human Development Report 2005." Retrieved September 9, 2007, from http://hdr.undp.org/.
U.S. Department of Health and Human Services and Health Resources and Services Adminis-tration (HRSA). 2004a. *Nursing Aides, Home Health Aides, and Related Health Care Occu-pations: National and Local Workforce Shortages and Associated Data Needs*. Washington, DC: HRSA.
———. 2004b. "Projected Supply, Demand, and Shortages of Registered Nurses: 2000–2020." http://bhpr.hrsa.gov/.
U.S. General Accounting Office (GAO). 2001. *Recruitment and Retention of Nurses and Nurse Aides Is a Growing Concern*. Washington, DC: U.S. GAO.
Utah, Senate Bill 103. 2007. Retrieved September 8, 2007, from http://le.utah.gov.

Weiner, T. 2002. "Manzanillo Journal; In Corn's Cradle, U.S. Imports Bury Family Farms." *New York Times*. February 26, http://www.nytimes.com/.

World Bank. 2007. "International Bank for Reconstruction and Development International Finance Corporation International Development Association: Executive Directors and Alternates." Retrieved September 9, 2007, from http://siteresources.worldbank.org/.

Young, I. M. 2000. *Inclusion and Democracy*. New York: Oxford University Press.

Chapter Eight

Hidden Data, Hidden Victims

Trafficking in the Context of Globalization and Labor Exploitation — The Case of Vietnam

Ramona Vijeyarasa

When discussing labor in the age of globalization, one of the most central themes is migration. A related phenomenon is that of trafficking. A growing body of authors has begun to question the image of the coerced, uneducated, naive, poor female victim of trafficking that has dominated trafficking imagery nationally and internationally for many years. To the contrary, trafficking is increasingly recognized as a case of an initially voluntary departure that is best understood within a broad spectrum of migratory movement—or what I call "migration gone wrong."

As such, some degree of voluntariness and knowledge is present in a majority of trafficking situations (Vijeyarasa 2010c). Research increasingly demonstrates that modern-day trafficking rarely corresponds to the image of the kidnapped and naive young woman (Banerjee 2006, 192–193; Chapkis 2003, 931–932), but more frequently involves the economic migrant, who may even know that the tourist visa on which he or she travels has been obtained without disclosure of the intention to work in the destination country (Vijeyarasa 2010c, 218).

Despite this voluntariness, given that the movement of victims is often undocumented and in light of the regulation or criminalization of sex work in destination countries, irregular migrants face the risk of exploitation, with little or no access to redress. While the movement may have been initially voluntary, upon arrival in destination countries, the individual may face conditions vastly different from those which he/she expected, including being forced to provide unprotected sexual services; being forced to work seven days per week; or the denial of freedom of movement from their place of work or residence. I have elsewhere called this phenomenon that of "unmet expectations" (Vijeyarasa 2010b). Therefore, while the word "victim" is often associated with naivety, lack of voluntariness or agency, I contend that to use the word "victim" reflects the violation of rights and right to redress for exploited migrants abroad.

Yet even this approach is plagued by the challenge of defining the phenomenon of trafficking, its scope and its victims. As Guri Tyldum and Anette Brunovskis note, trafficked persons are considered a "hidden population . . . for whom the size and boundaries are unknown, and for whom no sampling frame exists" (2005, 18). Elsewhere, trafficked people are described as "voiceless," whether because of fear of reprisals from traffickers, psychological trauma, or potential stigmatization (Brennan 2005, 43). On this basis, several authors have concluded that representative samples and credible estimates of the number of trafficked persons are impossible to obtain (Andrees and van der Linden 2005, 60; Cwikel and Hoban 2005, 306–307; Tyldum and Brunovskis 2005, 17). They rightly contend that inadequate data collection methods lead to descriptions of trafficked persons that are unreflective of reality, with resulting policies to address such exploitation (or prohibit irregular movement altogether) consequently ineffective (Tyldum and Brunovskis 2005, 17).

Despite the lack of evidence, numerous assumptions about global victims of trafficking persist. At the same time, there is far-reaching interest in the topic stirred by the apparent magnitude of the phenomenon. It is the vulnerability of women and girls and poverty-driven desperation that is assumed to compel movement across borders that fosters global interest in human trafficking, from policymakers to the press. Set against the lack of reliable data, these assumptions about victims and the causes of trafficking are reproduced and amplified. Trafficking discourse, and in turn, policy responses, focus on sexual exploitation and this "perfect victim" and further the common "slippage" between trafficking and prostitution so striking in the popular press (Chuang 2010). Consequently, current assumptions about which subgroups in the population are deemed vulnerable to human trafficking, often young, female, ethnic minorities, and what is considered the most pressing problem—sexual exploitation over other forms of labor exploitation—are left unquestioned.

These global challenges in establishing an accurate understanding of human trafficking as a form of labor injustice are exacerbated at the national level by a range of factors, as I demonstrate in this case study of Vietnam. In this chapter, I argue that a sounder approach is required, in which the existing data are reassessed in terms of their methodological reliability and the reasons for which they were collected. My purpose is to examine some of the methodological challenges in determining the socioeconomic characteristics of Vietnam's presumed trafficked population, as well as the scope of the problem. The primary objective is to encourage a reconsideration of previously held assumptions while making recommendations for a more nuanced and accurate approach to data collection that can improve global understandings of the exploitation involved in this type of irregular labor "migration gone wrong."

My intention in this analysis is to explore trafficking for both labor and sexual exploitation. The United Nations Protocol to Prevent, Suppress and Punish Trafficking in Persons (hereafter, UN Protocol) defines human trafficking as movement (recruitment, transportation, transfer, harboring, or receipt of persons), by means of the threat or use of force or other forms of coercion, of abduction, of fraud, of deception, of the abuse of power, or of a position of vulnerability or of the giving or receiving of payments or benefits to achieve the consent of a person having control over another person, for the purpose of exploitation (United Nations Protocol to Prevent, Suppress and Punish Trafficking in Persons especially Women and Children, supplementing the United Nations Convention Against Trans-national Organized Crime, Palermo, Italy, 2000, Article 3(a): United Nations 2000).

As I have argued extensively elsewhere (Vijeyarasa 2010a, 91; Vijeyarasa 2010b, 15; Vijeyarasa 2010c, 218), the protocol is far from flawless. In any case, at the time of print, the government of Vietnam had not yet ratified the UN Protocol. Moreover, while this study aims to explore trafficking of both men and women, until a legal amendment was introduced in 2010, the Vietnamese penal code only offered legal protection for women and child victims: Article 115 of the Criminal Code (1999) addressed buying and selling of a woman; Article 119 of the Penal Code (2001) made "trafficking in women" a crime; and Article 120 criminalized trading in, fraudulently exchanging, or appropriating children. Only since January 1, 2012, when a new law on trafficking entered into force, has the trafficking of men been penalized in Vietnam (Law on Human Trafficking Prevention, No. 66/2011/QH12).

As discussed elsewhere in this chapter, the previous legal focus on women and children has detrimentally impacted how trafficking and its victims are defined and understood in the Vietnamese context. Moreover, in practice, the notion of the "quintessential trafficked victim" in Vietnam continues to be promoted as the coerced, uneducated, naive, poor female victim in policy responses, NGO practice, and the popular press.

While reading the following pages it may seem that, again, the analysis tends to ignore trafficking of men. As stated above, the scope of this chapter spans trafficking of both women and men from Vietnam for labor and sexual exploitation. However, partly due to the aforementioned factors, much of the data collected focuses on trafficking of women for sexual exploitation, which necessarily has to be the starting point for this analysis. In the following section, I provide an overview of the methodology used to collect country-specific information for this chapter. I subsequently discuss what is known about trafficking in Vietnam based on current available data. In the main part of this chapter, I evaluate the key obstacles to more accurate and encompassing data collection on trafficking. I conclude with an analysis of the policy implications of basing anti-trafficking initiatives on biased and otherwise unreliable data for Vietnam and elsewhere around the globe. My main finding is that the barriers to victim identification and data collection in Vietnam create significant doubts as to the accuracy of the current profile of victims and in turn hinder policies aimed at reducing the global injustice of migrant exploitation.

METHODOLOGY

In this chapter, I explore the challenges of establishing the scope and nature of the trafficking of men and women for labor and sexual exploitation in Vietnam. My analysis is based on fieldwork conducted in Vietnam from December 2008 to October 2009 involving interviews with seventeen key informants. Informants were contacted via e-mail and provided in advance with a standard set of questions to aid a semi-structured interview.[1]

Face-to-face interviews were conducted with fourteen informants. A further three interviews were conducted by e-mail, two of which involved translation of the interview questions from English into Vietnamese, with responses later translated into English. Translation from English to Vietnamese and vice versa was provided by a Vietnamese translator.[2] While face-to-face interviews were preferred, the validity of e-mail interviews has been recognized (Bampton and Cowton 2002). Advantages of e-mail interviews include savings in time and financial resources (Bampton and Cowton 2002, 25), as well as creating more comfort for interviewees who are engaging in an interview in a foreign language than there might be in a face-to-face interview (Bampton and Cowton 2002, 19). E-mail interviews are also beneficial when interviewing subjects with closed or limited access (Opdenakker 2006), in this case, shelter management or staff. While I accepted these e-mail interviews as a valid reflection of the opinion of informants, I also recognize their shortcomings, including lack of spontaneity and the challenge of probing for further opinions.

Regarding the selection and scope of informants, interviewees were selected based on their expertise and competence in the field. Key informants spanned the directors, managers, and staff of some of the key organizations, both intergovernmental and nongovernmental, working on trafficking in Vietnam. I also explored my research questions with staff from government, donor organizations, and a number of United Nations agencies.[3]

Efforts were taken to ensure a cross-section of expertise given that human trafficking is a multidimensional and multicausal issue (see figure 8.1, in which informants have been classified based on their primary area of expertise). Informants were selected from lists of organizations working on trafficking in Vietnam, and contact was also made with people identified in the literature. I also followed referrals made by those individuals who had already been interviewed or contacted for this research, adopting a form of snowballing technique. Stakeholders comprised both Vietnamese nationals and non-nationals.

In terms of this selection procedure, it is particularly important to note the lack of freedom of association in Vietnam, including freedom of expression among NGOs in what has been called a "state-led civil society" (Lux and Straussman 2004). This is reflected in the large number of informants in Vietnam who chose anonymity, with ten informants choosing complete anonymity and two choosing partial anonymity.

The existing body of literature was consulted extensively in the development of the interview questions, although the primary focus was on the causes of human trafficking and the degree to which the scope of the problem and the demographics of its victims has been accurately identified in Vietnam. In my interviews, I discussed with informants the so-called causes of trafficking, as well as the typical profiles of victims and traffickers. I sought interviewees' thoughts on the government of Vietnam's approach to the problem of human trafficking and the challenges faced by victims involved in the process of reintegrating into their former or a new community upon return. I also served as an active participant in five meetings of the reintegration network, a monthly meeting of a coalition of NGOs and international organizations working on reintegration in Vietnam.

An observation made throughout the interviews was the tendency for views to be repeated by key informants in a way that raised doubt as to

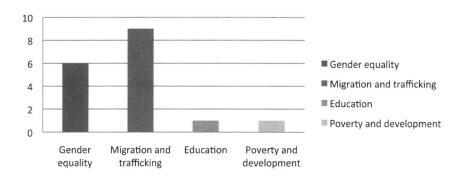

Figure 8.1.   Key Informant Expertises. *Source: Author created.*

whether they had been informed by the same source. This might include reading the same report or piece of research, listening to the same speech or attending the same workshop or training. Indeed, the anti-trafficking community in Vietnam is sufficiently small that there is a large amount of information sharing, particularly through the NGO reintegration network, whose members work in partnership with the government and international organizations. This potentially suggests that the breadth of knowledge is fairly limited, and obtaining diverging opinions is a challenge.

This limitation relates directly to the fear expressed by several informants to openly critique the government of Vietnam. Despite the fact that all participants received a participant information statement and consent form, and were offered anonymity, reluctance was still evident, both in the physical demeanor of participants, their occasional hesitations, and in two instances, requests to turn off the tape recorder at various points during the interview.[4] This reluctance was evident not only among informants of Vietnamese nationality but also non-Vietnamese nationals. However, this similarly reflects the value of this research in contributing to the body of knowledge on human trafficking in Vietnam, particularly given the lack of open critique of the government when particularly in relation to the issue of exploitation of Vietnamese migrant workers.

The results of this fieldwork have been complemented by government data and reports from key stakeholders working on this issue. I additionally attended conferences, including on the international and academic perspectives concerning human trafficking, organized by the Institute for Social Development Studies in Hanoi and a sharing workshop on the results of a trafficking survey by ActionAid Vietnam. I also draw on existing literature in this field and data on the scope of human trafficking from Vietnam, including statistics released by the government itself.

Given the challenges in obtaining firsthand data on trafficking from Vietnam and independent evaluations of an issue that is closely guarded by the government, the data collected represents a diverse cross-section of perspectives on the phenomenon of human trafficking. It is important to note that many academics caution against generalizing qualitative data beyond those of the research informants. While this is not the goal of my qualitative analysis, I do conclude this chapter by coupling the qualitative research findings with existing studies, to contribute to my critique of the mainstream approaches to trafficking, how such approaches fail to reflect an accurate understanding of the profile of victims, and how such assumptions act to undermine policy responses to address the exploitation of migrant workers abroad.

CONTEXT: EXISTING DATA AND GAPS IN KNOWLEDGE

Vietnam, a communist country bordered by China to the north, Cambodia to the southwest and Laos to the northwest, underwent market liberalization (*doi moi*, or renovation) beginning in 1986. The effects of economic expansion created closer economic ties with other nations and expanded destinations for documented and undocumented migrants. A latecomer to the Asian regional labor market, Vietnam favored ex-socialist countries in Eastern Europe during its early stages of exporting labor (Dang et al. 2003, i, 12). This movement continued until the collapse of the former Soviet Union, with new labor migration flows initiated in 1994 from Vietnam to Kuwait, Lebanon, Saudi Arabia, Libya, Japan, and Korea. By 2002, Taiwan and Malaysia had become the most significant destinations (Dang et al. 2003, i; Hoang 2008).

Currently, trafficking flows from Vietnam reflect the ease of cross-border movement, predominantly and unsurprisingly in the direction of China and Cambodia. The majority of data concerns these two destination countries. According to the SIREN (Strategic Information Response Network) Human Trafficking Data Sheet, a research and information initiative of the United Nations Inter-Agency Project on Human Trafficking (UNIAP), China was at that time the destination of 70% of the total number of trafficked Vietnamese women abroad, but the "nature and numbers remain difficult to determine" (SIREN 2008a). Women are trafficked to Cambodia from the southern provinces of Vietnam largely for sex work (Marshall 2006, 13; Duong and Hong 2008, 197–198). Estimates in this case vary, with one literature review on trafficking to and from Cambodia suggesting that between 15% and 32% of sex workers, not necessarily victims of trafficking for sexual exploitation, in Cambodia are of Vietnamese origin (Derks, Henke, and Ly 2006, 22–23). Data from the Cambodian Ministry of Social Affairs, Veterans and Youth Rehabilitation suggests that 50% of the trafficked persons of Vietnamese origin identified in Cambodia come from An Giang province in the south of Vietnam (SIREN 2008a, 2). Stakeholders also indicate some evidence of Vietnamese victims in other destination countries, including South Africa, the Czech Republic, and United Kingdom, but there is limited information documenting new routes (A. Bruce, IOM, personal communication, 21 September 2009). Nicolas Lainez's most recent study (2011) finds that mobility from southern Vietnam (namely An Giang) to Cambodia is no longer relevant as new Vietnamese migrants are traveling to different areas to engage in sex work and those Vietnamese from An Giang working in Cambodia are not new migrants.

Even a small collection of statistics reveals the range of numbers often quoted in regard to migration broadly and trafficking specifically from Vietnam. Released by governments and NGOs, or cited by the popular press, these estimates encapsulate data on undocumented migrant sex workers (although they are frequently—and inaccurately—conflated with trafficking data) and victims of sexual exploitation, forced marriage, and labor exploitation, whether smuggled, trafficked, or documented. In general, a comprehensive, countrywide and gender-disaggregated data set does not exist to facilitate an accurate discussion on the nature of trafficking and the demographic of its victims across Vietnam.

Government estimates concerning human trafficking are generally low, driven largely by concerns about Vietnam's international reputation and the government's interest in export labor as a form of income and to address the domestic labor surplus (Dang 2008, 2). In this respect, the reliability of these statistics, frequently cited in the popular press, is questionable. The Ministry of Labour, Invalids and Social Affairs (MOLISA) is the key government ministry responsible for human trafficking, although as I discuss later in this chapter, the issue is treated as less of a "labor" issue and more as a "social affair." The Ministry of Public Security (MPS) also investigates human trafficking and smuggling cases, in cooperation with the Border Guard Command (BGC). MPS is also responsible for the registration of temporary migrants and directly manages the household registration system for mainly permanent and official migrants, with spontaneous and undocumented migrants often excluded (Dang et al. 2003, 5).

According to police data cited by the MPS, 2,269 cases of trafficking were discovered during the period 1991–2001, with 3,787 people arrested on charges of trafficking. Of these, 1,818 cases involving 3,118 offenders were brought to court for trafficking of women under the former Article 119 of the Penal Code (2001). A further 451 cases, involving 672 offenders, involved charges of trafficking in children under the former Article 120 of the Penal Code (2001) (Government of Vietnam n.d., 7). For the period 1998–2002, MPS and the BGC pursued 921 cases of trafficking involving 1,087 accused persons (Government of Vietnam n.d., 7). Compared to the number of arrests and prosecutions, it appears that the number of victims is significantly higher. One report from 2000 by MPS indicated that between 1991 and 1999 at least 22,000 women and children were illegally sent to China as domestic workers and sex workers or as forced wives. For the period 1996–2000, the BGC documented 7,918 trafficked women returning from China (Dang et al. 2003, 14).

The popular media, about which we should be cautious in light of government controls over freedom of expression, similarly reports a diverse range of statistics. According to a report on 14 July 2009 by the *Xinhua News Agency*, the press agency of the government of China, citing "official" statistics from the government of Vietnam indicated that for January to July 2009, 191 trafficking cases were detected, involving 417 women and child victims, predominantly trafficked in the directions of Cambodia, China, and Laos. Consistently, *Viet Nam News* reported on 8 January 2010 that at the end of

2009 nearly double the number of cases had been identified, with 395 cases and 869 victims of trafficking detected by Vietnamese police in that year by December 2009.

The US State Department also provides an array of statistics on Vietnam in their annual Trafficking in Persons report, although neither the origin nor methodology of the data collection is provided (see Agustin 2009). Ranked by the United States as a "tier 2" country, the report states that there are an estimated five hundred thousand Vietnamese workers abroad facing conditions of forced labor and debt bondage (US TIP 2009).

A further issue is the large number of Vietnamese women marrying men in Taiwan, China, Korea, Japan, and Singapore. The complexity of marriage migration cannot be adequately addressed in this chapter. Reported data on Vietnamese brides is again inconsistent and unreliable, and there is a clear divergence between those authors who consider marriage migration a legitimate decision made by Vietnamese women and those who see it as a form of trafficking that should be stopped (Duong and Hong 2008, 198; see also Dang et al. 2003). With regard to Vietnamese brides in Taiwan, it has been recognized elsewhere that these women are "not necessarily in servile marriages and not trafficked victims" (ActionAid International Vietnam 2005, 7). Few in-depth quantitative or qualitative studies on "marriage migration" exist, and data remains anecdotal.

Finally, internal trafficking has been identified from rural to urban areas of Vietnam (SIREN 2008a), for commercial sexual exploitation, forced begging and labor exploitation of domestic workers and of workers in the construction industries. I was informed by one interviewee of the government's increasing reluctance to work with the international community to collect the necessary data to profile the situation of internal trafficking and the informal labor market generally in fear of such data being seen as a "sign of underdevelopment" (Senior Economist, Donor Organization, personal communication, Vietnam, 13 October 2009). This is arguably also related to evidence concerning labor market segmentation between informal and formal internal migrant workers and significant wage disparities (ODI 2006, 3). This evidence gap was reiterated in a UNFPA study, which noted the failure of studies to capture those most vulnerable, including short-term and seasonal migrants (UNFPA 2010, 5).

Overall, we can see great divergence in the data released by the government of Vietnam, researchers, and that which is published in the popular press. While we are able to establish a general picture of the patterns and purpose of movement, as the following section will reveal, the data outlined above are undermined by the obstacles I discussed below to more accurate, consistent, and unbiased gathering of data on patterns of labor migration broadly and trafficking specifically.

CHALLENGES TO VICTIM IDENTIFICATION

In the following section, based on empirical evidence, I aim to identify some of the major reasons for the pervasive absence of accurate and transparent data on trafficking in Vietnam. I analyze these data in the context of the existing research from government, academic, nongovernmental, inter-governmental, and UN sources. My goals for this section are twofold. First, I aim to identify several of the factors that act as challenges to accurate data collection in Vietnam. Second, I intend to analyze some of the existing stereotypes regarding the demographic of trafficked victims that continue to persist despite lack of an evidentiary basis or even in the face of contrary evidence.

A "Social Evil" Rather Than Labor Issue

One of the most important determinants of the treatment of trafficking in Vietnam is the approach of the government to the issue. What we know of trafficking and how it is understood in Vietnam, particularly where it involves women and children for sexual exploitation, is directly implicated by the state's approach to sex work as a "social evil" and by the naming of the Department of Social Evils Prevention (DSEP) as the agency responsible for trafficked returnees. This approach stigmatizes victims and implicates them for "involvement" in the criminal and social demise of the country (Vijeyarasa 2010a, 6).

Elzbieta Gozdziak and Elizabeth Collett point to the "lack of a critical attitude towards the state" in anti-trafficking campaigns, which instead tend to look at individual acts of violent traffickers (Gozdziak and Collett 2005, 101). In the case of Vietnam, I similarly contend that it is pivotal to critique the government's "strongly pejorative labelling of these groups of people considered to be morally corrupt or decadent" (Doussantousse and Tooke 2002, 2). Specifically, the government's approach raises questions about the extent to which victims of trafficking, returned through formal border controls, are deemed criminals as opposed to victims and channeled into "05" and "06 centers" (Vijeyarasa 2010a, 7; De Lind van Wijngaarden 2007, 43; Khuat 2007, 15). The "06 centers" are designed for drug users forced to undergo detoxification and rehabilitation, while the "05 centers" are for people (mainly women) involved in sex work. In a 2006 study, Phil Marshall attributes the apparent placement of victims in the government's "05 centers" to the lack of alternative shelters, rather than a policy decision (Marshall 2006); this argument is at odds with the relatively empty shelters discussed later in this chapter.

Although often referred to by the government as educational and vocational training centers for women, "05 centers" are essentially correctional facilities with limited freedom of movement for women involved in the sex trade. Marshall notes that special provisions are reportedly made for victims of trafficking, including arrangements for them to stay in a separate part of this facility, with more freedom (Marshall 2006, 21). Other stakeholders have recognized the relationship between the apparent placement of victims in "05" and "06" centers and inconsistent data on the number of victims leaving and returning to Vietnam. Several of my informants shared concerns about these centers as well as the process of determining who should be confined to them. Specifically on this point, Elena Ferreras, Programme Director for Multilateral Cooperation and Gender for the Spanish Agency for International Development Cooperation (AECID), in a long and passionate exchange, noted:

> There are a lot of re-education centers all around the country. It would be very interesting to see what is going on in those places. Who are going to those centers? The key moment is when the commander at the border decides whether he or she is a victim or a "criminal."

Explaining that it was a "supposition," Ferreras returned to this point at a later stage in the interview:

> If some report says there are 5,000 people trafficked per year and 300 are coming back as victims, I guess more are coming back and are being identified as criminals and going to re-education centers. (E. Ferreras, AECID, personal communication, 9 October 2009)

One informant, noting the lack of respect for the confidentially of detainees, drew a link to risks of re-trafficking: "[T]hey are equivalent to detention, they do not preserve your safety, they are often publically named, so if anyone wanted to find you and re-traffic you they could . . . they out you to your whole community [even] if you were in a position where no one knew what happened and wanted to preserve your privacy and reintegrate" (Anon., gender expert, United Nations Country team, personal communication. 20 October 2009).

What is clear is that the inaccessible nature of these "rehabilitation" centers and anecdotal stories about their residents raise important questions as to the whereabouts of Vietnam's "missing" victims and victim confidentiality.

Who Are the Victims? Male Victims, Labor Exploitation, and the Vietnamese Penal Code

As many individuals working in this field note, trafficking in Vietnam is largely associated with the sex industry and exploitation of women and children (Anon., program officer, international organization, personal communication, 5 October 2009). As noted above, a major influencing factor has been the lack of recognition by domestic legislation of the existence of male victims of trafficking until recent amendments.

The exclusion of male victims of trafficking was a stark omission in the former Penal Code. Further, Article 1 of the Law on Child Protection, Care and Education (2004) define children as persons under sixteen years of age, not those under eighteen years of age as defined by international law (UN Convention on the Rights of the Child, Art. 1). Therefore, male children aged sixteen to eighteen were excluded from the protection of Vietnamese trafficking laws.

Despite the enactment of the new law, the legislative focus on women and children to date has had a significant impact on how trafficking is conceptualized, particularly in its association with sex work. Political, legal, and social attention as a result is largely focused on trafficking for sexual exploitation over labor exploitation. Yet trafficked women are frequently forced to provide sexual services in conjunction with other exploitative labor (Kelly 2005, 235). Labor trafficking also implicates men. Anecdotal evidence of trafficking of men for labor exploitation has been documented, particularly from Lao Cai, a northern mountainous province of Vietnam, to China (Hoang 2008). Trafficking of male Vietnamese labor migrants has also been documented by Duong and Hong (2008, 119), who note that men who become involved in trafficking-like recruitment practices pay large fees to work in factories, mainly in Taiwan, South Korea, Japan, and Malaysia, with the promised contract later not coming to fruition. Many leave these factories, abandoning their original paperwork, and end up residing with irregular migration status in the destination country (Duong and Hong 2008, 119).

The absence of attention or data on male victims of trafficking is not unique to Vietnam but is a problem facing many countries with regard to the formulation of their anti-trafficking legislation. In the case of Vietnam, the formerly narrow approach will continue to inhibit the accuracy and success of screening of male victims if practical measures are not taken to specifically ensure their identification. A UN official I interviewed, speaking broadly of the challenge of victim identification, noted: "There is no standard definition in this country and people have a different understanding of screening. When it comes to trafficking, it is very hard to classify whether someone is or is not a victim" (Counter-trafficking program coordinator, United Nations, personal communication, 16 October 2009).

Two major challenges exist in relation to how "trafficking" is understood in Vietnam, first regarding the legal definition, and second, its interpretation. While the possibility of Vietnam's ratifying the UN Protocol has been raised by the government, it is unclear whether the government will actually take this step and accept the UN Protocol's definition, the best example of a global consensus on the meaning of trafficking in recent times (see discussion in Vijeyarasa 2010b). Even if the UN Protocol's definition were adopted, significant work would be required to create an understanding at the national level about which returnees fall within the definition, particularly for screening purposes by the Border Guard Command and other service providers.

A further challenge is that of the lay understanding of human trafficking. One informant drew attention to the lack of acceptability of the word "trafficking" in Vietnam, which is understood to denote the "wholesale" trade of people. Rather, there is a preference among some stakeholders for using the words "buy and sell," which are understood as referring to as few as one victim (counter-trafficking expert, international organization, personal communication, 12 October 2009). Once again, these definitional challenges are not unique to the Vietnamese language, with many languages failing to accurately define trafficking and reflect the relationship between traffickers and trafficked persons (Kelly 2002, 17–18).

Empty Shelters: Where Are Vietnam's Victims?

From a methodological research perspective, several academics note the limited means of access to returned victims of trafficking. As a result, the majority of research on trafficked persons is based on samples of "survivors" who have been identified by law enforcement, through prisons, immigration authorities, lawyers, NGOs, and international organizations (Laczko 2005, 8; Cwikel and Hoban 2005, 311). However, one feature of the reintegration process in Vietnam is the relatively small proportion of victims who opt for shelter rehabilitation. This creates a major limitation on the amount of data that can be collected through the support of these shelters and also poses the question of whether victims accessing reintegration shelter support are representative of the broader trafficked population.

At the time of research, there were five main shelters operating in Vietnam:

- The Peace House Project operated by the Center for Women and Development (CWD), a local NGO established by the Vietnam Women's Union[5] in July 2002.
- Two shelters operated by AFESIP (Agir pour les Femmes en Situation Précaire, or Acting for Women in Distressing Circumstances) in Ho Chi Minh City and Can Tho City in partnership with the Vietnam Women's Union.
- An "open house" operated by US-based Pacific Links (operating in Vietnam as ADAPT, the An Giang Dong Thap Alliance for the Prevention of Trafficking) in An Giang, for women from Kien Giang and An Giang who

have returned to Vietnam as trafficked victims or for those considered at "very high risks of being trafficked."
• A shelter in Hue operated by Nordic Assistance Vietnam (NAV).

Each of these organizations adopts different approaches when it comes to researchers' access to returned victims undergoing shelter rehabilitation. This impacts the amount of data that is collected and released about their demographic profile and, therefore, the extent to which data exist and are available on these returned victims.

During the course of my fieldwork, the number of returnees housed in these shelters ranged from zero to ten, staying for a period ranging from several months to over one year. NAV's shelter in Hue, with a capacity for twenty residents, housed only one returnee, which partly reflects the lack of interest of returnees to that region in shelter rehabilitation (Vijeyarasa 2010a, 9). In the case of AFESIP, its 2006 Annual Report documents twenty-eight residents in Ho Chi Minh City and thirty-three residents in Can Tho in 2006 (AFESIP 2007, 4; see discussion in Vijeyarasa 2010a, 8–10). AFESIP also reports that in 2006, 36.5% of returnees housed in the Ho Chi Minh shelter stayed for longer than nine months, whereas just over half of victims in Can Tho stayed for a period of less than three months (AFESIP 2007, 5). As of October 2009, the CWD shelter had housed a maximum of twelve residents during the course of its operation, despite having capacity for twenty persons.

There are number of factors that could be involved in the low numbers of shelter residents compared to the presumed number of victims. First, in light of the nature of the borders of Vietnam, unofficial returns are significantly higher than official returns (Anon., counter-trafficking expert, international organization, personal communication, 12 October 2009). Other authors note that the majority of returnees enter Vietnam by their own means, after having worked off their "debt," fallen ill, and subsequently been released, or after escaping (Marshall 2006, 7, 15). For returnees from Cambodia, the process of family tracing is reportedly slow; this waiting period creates an incentive to self-deny one's status as a trafficked person and be returned through faster deportation processes instead (Marshall 2006, 19). An array of reasons for low shelter populations was provided by one UN staff member whom I interviewed:

> The shelter service providers do not make themselves known to the victims, so other agencies do not provide referrals. There could also be some policy issues involved. For example, the AFESIP supported shelter in HCMC only receives residents from HCMC, not from other provinces. Also, from my understanding, in order to be accepted to those shelters, you have to be referred by a government agency. Quite often, victims do not want to be known and want nothing to do with the government. Sometimes when they come back, they

move to another area to start a new life. And also, there are some issues of quality. (Anon., counter-trafficking program coordinator, United Nations, personal communication, 16 October 2009)

With regard to the quality of shelter services, there is no standard set of guidelines in practice across all shelters, with one shelter, for example, prohibiting the use of mobile phones by residents and visits from family and friends (Vijeyarasa 2010a, 9). Shelter quality was identified as a concern by several informants, although one informant noted that work specifically on this area was being done at the time of the interview to evaluate and improve shelters-based reintegration support. I contend that the types of controls that presently exist, the lack of understanding of the rights of residents and inadequate psychological support offered to returnees through shelters (Taylor et al. 2009, 5; Marshall 2006, 21) mean that seeking shelter support may in fact not offer sufficient benefits, in terms of aiding reintegration, for a returnee to choose this option, hindering our improved understanding of the experiences of these victims of labor and sexual exploitation.

Self-identification is also an issue. This involves not only the question of whether victims are actually able to identify the concept of trafficking within their own experiences, but also the challenge of stigma. Explaining the factors that inhibit self-identification, one informant noted that victims "do not necessarily understand that they have been trafficked." The informant continued by noting "the limited benefits" available for those who identify as a victim such that "[o]nly in limited cases, where they know someone who trafficked them and they want revenge" will someone self-identify as a victim (counter-trafficking expert, international organization, personal communication, 12 October 2009). In this respect, the notion of "migration gone wrong" may better serve to reduce such stigmatization.

As a result, data collection from victims of trafficking housed in shelters, although valuable, must be scrutinized in terms of its representative value. The potential bias is reflected by Ferreras of AECID, the then principal donor to the CWD shelter in Hanoi during our interview:

> Most of the victims are not entering the social system and most of the cases in the social system, they are the worst cases. So we need to analyse if the clients in the shelters are really representative. They might be a minority of the big profile. What is the profile? It seems young women between 12 and 30 years old. It seems ethnic minorities, but is this the profile? (E. Ferreras, AECID, personal communication, 9 October 2009)

Ferreras's comments reflect a widespread concern among those on the ground about the accuracy of what is commonly accepted as the demographic of Vietnam's trafficked population.

Ethnic Minorities, Cross-Border Labor, and Trafficking

The shared history and ethnicity between populations living on either side of the Vietnam-China border is a historical fact, deriving from the days before national borders were firmly established. Populations continue to move fluidly across both sides of the border. NGOs such as Save the Children indicate that Mong Cai is a destination for many children looking for work (Save the Children 2008). Despite this evidence, there is a clear tendency to fail to distinguish between adult and child victims of trafficking and adult and child laborers engaging in cross-border migration from Vietnam to China. The cross-border trade is a significant and valuable source of empowerment. However, the literature, including NGO reporting, frequently refers to the trafficking of women and children into China from Vietnam's northern provinces which now extends beyond the border provinces of Yunnan and Guangxi to inland provinces such as Henan, Hebei, Anhui, Jiangsu, and Guangdong (Yi 2005, 7).

As a result, a strong connection is drawn between ethnic minorities status and trafficking; that is, it is presumed that the mountainous ethnic minority communities are particularly prone to trafficking. I argue that this assumption unjustifiably assumes that Vietnam's ethnic minorities experience patterns of trafficking similar to what has been documented in the past concerning Thailand's ethnic minority population, and in fact conflates migration among ethnic minorities to trafficking. Thailand's five hundred thousand hill tribe and ethnic minorities who do not hold Thai nationality are seen as more vulnerable to trafficking (Lyttleton 2002; SIREN 2008b, 1). Similarly, it has been noted that ethnic minorities in Vietnam "are very weak because the question of their citizenship is not very clear" (E. Ferreras, AECID, personal communication, 9 October 2009).

Ethnic minority movement is particularly difficult to grapple with in the age of globalization and for groups for whom "borders" may have little or no significance. This is not to say that ethnic minorities are not among those who are identified as trafficked. Instead, what is problematic is the framing of an ethnic minority as the "quintessential trafficked person" and the failure to distinguish between exploitation and cross-border labor. When I questioned a district-level government official on the profile of victims of trafficking, the respondent commented:

> The victim is a seventeen-year-old-girl of Tay ethnic community from a commune targeted by the Provincial Program 135 [a program to support especially difficult communes]. Her family's economic situation is very difficult. The majority of its earning comes from farm work. She is not able to go to high school and stays at home to help their parents with the farm work. (Anon., district-level official, DSEP, personal communication, 1 October 2009)

Taking a more nuanced approach to assessing the accuracy of studies that identify ethnic minorities as more vulnerable, one counter-trafficking expert referred to the long history between China and Vietnam. Given the nature of the geographic area and the fact that citizens from both sides of the border are frequently from the same local ethnicity, "it is sometimes easier for traffickers from the other side to talk to the people here and cheat them." However, the informant added that "this happens only along the border." The informant continued by noting how "[i]n other areas, like the central parts of Vietnam, ethnic minorities usually live in a group so it is very difficult for strangers to come into the area or community and to lure them because usually they believe only in what they can see." He also contended that "they are not adventurous people so in some ways their living conditions and habits protect them from being trafficked" (Anon., counter-trafficking expert, international organization, personal communication, 12 October 2009). While this comment also relies upon certain assumptions and stereotypes about ethnic minority communities, it also highlights the necessity for a more cautious approach to previous assumptions about minorities, as I will discuss in the following section of this chapter.

IMPLICATIONS FOR LAW, POLICY, AND PRACTICE

The uncertainty that exists regarding current global and national data on trafficking is widely recognized. Nonetheless, legislators, policy makers, and stakeholders developing programmatic responses to more effectively prevent trafficking, protect victims from exploitation, and prosecute traffickers face little choice but to rely on the data that currently exists. This results in shortcomings in policy responses. As an IOM report notes, "To talk of evidence-based policy making remains a target for now, which has not yet been achieved" (IOM and Federal Ministry of the Interior of Austria 2009, 5). In the following section, I discuss some of the implications of relying on such data and conclude by providing some recommendations on ways to move towards a more accurate and encompassing means of data collection.

The Approach of the Government

The government of Vietnam's approach is largely focused on the criminal justice aspects of human trafficking as opposed to the individual human rights violations involved in labor exploitation. This approach creates stigma and further hides an already often hidden population. The focus on trafficking of women and girls for sexual exploitation also leads to the neglect of other forms of trafficking in policy responses. The most pressing reform is the eradication of the language of "social evils" from policy and legislation, and the elimination of correctional facilities, for trafficking and nontrafficked persons alike (Vijeyarasa 2010a, 10). From a research perspective, a move away from this stigmatizing approach could greatly aid victims' self-identification and may foster greater willingness to cooperate with government authorities responsible for combating human trafficking.

The Law: Widening the Meaning of Human Trafficking

In addition to the implementation of Vietnam's new trafficking law from January 2012 onward, it is essential that policy and other awareness-raising efforts are used to give greater attention to the traffic of men and trafficking for labor exploitation. The exploitation of migrants moving within Vietnam's borders is a further neglected issue. In the words of one counter-trafficking program officer, "But if we ratify [the UN Protocol] and we accept internal trafficking and address men being trafficked, that would be good. All sectors can be addressed for all vulnerable people" (program officer, international organization, personal communication, 5 October 2009). Furthermore, greater focus should be placed on evidence showing a lack of awareness of risks and ensuring access to justice rather than on measures that have a punitive impact on trafficked persons.

Shelters, Data Collection, and Sampling in Vietnam

It is methodologically unsound to assume that samples drawn from victims housed in shelters are necessarily representative of the Vietnamese trafficked population as a whole. However, bearing in mind the rights to confidentiality of individual returnees, it is important that whatever data can be collected from shelters is shared with the wider public. This would allow us to better understand the relationship between victims and traffickers (personal contacts, friends, and family members), the markets in which the victims were exploited, and the nature of the forced work. In addition, aggregation of methodologically sound data collected from shelters across Vietnam would better inform counter-trafficking efforts in Vietnam.

Consolidation of Data

As noted by my informants during my fieldwork, Vietnam lacks a coordinating agency actively involved in human trafficking, despite DSEP's designation as having that role:

> Because of the way that the government is managing the situation, the statistics are not done properly and there is no government agency that is really managing and controlling all the information flow, especially on returns of trafficking cases . . . where that information is stored is the issue. Even though DSEP is responsible for trafficking, they have no statistics. (counter-traffick-

ing expert, international organization, personal communication, 12 October 2009)

Lack of coordination between BGC officials, the Ministry of Justice, and DSEP leads to a lack of consolidated data. If consolidation is attempted, careful attention must be paid to the different definitions of trafficking used in past data collection, the time periods for which the data exist, and the purposes for which the data were collected by the individual government agencies.

With a large number of stakeholders involved in data collection (shelters and shelter staff, local and international NGOs, and government agencies), a final challenge is whether coordination of data collection between the government and NGO community is actually possible. What is clear, however, is the need to couple NGO and government data and to undertake country-wide consolidation. Otherwise, we will continue to be inhibited in efforts to understand emerging markets, methods of transport, and new recruitment patterns, as well as the recruitment of men and boys who often (as in the case of Vietnam) fall outside of the reintegration services offered by NGOs and international organizations.

A Nuanced Analysis: The Situation of Ethnic Minorities

The limited ability to develop useful samples in Vietnam highlights the need for careful consideration of any data collected. This is particularly the case in regard to ethnic minorities in Vietnam.

A number of informants were critical of the tendency to assume a correlation between ethnic minority status and the risk of being trafficked. In this respect, a more nuanced approach to trafficking in Vietnam would recognize other factors that raise the risk of recruitment into potentially exploitative labor, such as geography:

> [S]ome communities are more vulnerable than other communities simply because they are close to the road, close to the trafficking route. There are some communities that are miles away, so they are not vulnerable to trafficking, because trafficking is just not an issue there. They have the same level of education, income and poverty but are less vulnerable based on their location. (counter-trafficking program coordinator, United Nations, personal communication, 16 October 2009)

To simply identify characteristics common to both trafficked and nontrafficked populations as a dispositional factor is erroneous and does not reflect the geographic element involved in trafficking, particularly in a country like Vietnam with high levels of cross-border movement. Therefore, the assumption of heightened vulnerability of ethnic minorities needs to be subject to increased examination.

The Stereotypical Portrayal of Trafficking

The common portrayal of victims of trafficking as a young female of ethnic minority status lured from her home stems largely from how key stakeholders on the ground describe identified or potential victims. There is a clear tendency in Vietnam to emphasize the stereotypical case, with the stories of other victims lost in reporting. As Ferreras noted, when stakeholders report cases, "they want the bad story, they want the stereotypical story. If you are talking about a woman of 35 years, it is not really interesting." To the contrary:

> [I]f you are talking about a girl 16 years, she talked to a false friend and the false friend sent her to a brothel in China and she was raped . . . if it is not this kind of story, it is not considered really interesting. It is not very "real." There is an impression that you need the worst scenario. (E. Ferreras, AECID, personal communication, 9 October 2009)

Given the current attention on young, female Vietnamese victims of trafficking, it is essential that reporting on the issue highlights the spectrum of experiences involved. With the amended penal code criminalizing the traffic of men, it is likely that stories of male victims will increasingly emerge, which must be given adequate attention in reporting from the ground.

CONCLUSION

This chapter has analyzed the global challenges that exist in relation to data collection about human trafficking, that are also frequently faced at the national level, through a case study of Vietnam. The ability to obtain accurate and unbiased data is inhibited by local political, socioeconomic, and cultural circumstances. In the case of Vietnam, victim identification is affected by the government's "social evils" approach that stigmatizes and criminalizes victims, inhibiting self-identification and raising questions about the whereabouts of victims. Shelters, although relatively empty, can provide a useful starting point in building a demographic picture, but the representative nature of such data needs to be questioned. This includes where it overrepresents ethnic minorities, and in the case of Vietnam, it only offers data on female victims.

Where data cited are not firsthand, the reliability of the original sources should be subject to scrutiny in all NGO, UN, and donors' reports. Distinctions need to be made between undocumented migrant women working in the sex industry in destination countries who may be vulnerable to labor exploitation and those who are trafficked for forced sexual exploitation. It is important to highlight marked differences between ethnic minority communities who experience heightened vulnerability to trafficking based on geographic location and those who do not. Finally, all published data needs to be considered with an understanding of the purpose for which it was collected and later published, and how this might raise questions of potential bias.

It is important that policies related to victims of trafficking be grounded in a better understanding of the conditions, needs, and priorities of the specific target groups, both in terms of raising awareness among potential migrants, as well as supporting returned victims of trafficking. However, to do this, it is essential that the data on which laws and policies are based better represents the demographics of victims, their experiences and needs upon returning home. Addressing the barriers to more accurate data collection is only a starting point to improved, evidence-based responses to trafficking. This reflects the important need for further research into the factors discussed in this chapter as well as ensuring these considerations influence the lens through which data are read, analyzed, and applied with the goal of reducing the risks of labor exploitation of Vietnamese migrant workers both within Vietnam and abroad.

NOTES

1. Approval was granted for this fieldwork by the Human Research Ethics Committee of the University of New South Wales on June 1, 2010. As required by the Human Research Ethics Committee of the University of New South Wales, a participant information statement (PIS) and consent form was distributed to all participants. This provided an explanation of the purpose, methods, and intended possible uses of the research; why the informant's participation in the research was requested; and the confidentiality of information supplied. Participant anonymity was offered, if desired.

2. Do Thi Thai Thanh holds a bachelor of English from the Hanoi Foreign Language College and has experience translating documents related to HIV and AIDS and migration for both local and international NGOs and international organizations in Vietnam.

3. Nine additional informants were contacted for potential participation in this research. This included four local NGOs, three of whom did not respond and one of whom responded by declining to participate on the basis of their insufficient depth of knowledge; one academic with a Hanoi-based research institution and two gender specialists at a multilateral donor organization, from whom no responses were received. Two staff working for UN agencies accepted to participate but were unable to do so due to personal circumstances.

4. As noted above, the ability to note these changes in demeanor and personal expressions is a valuable component of face-to-face research that unfortunately e-mail interviews do not offer.

5. The Vietnam Women's Union (or VWU) is a mass organization formed in 1930, the formation of which "effectively shut women out of full participation of the main arena" (Brownmiller 1994, 83). Still today the de facto national women's bureaucracy, the VWU is one of the largest women's mass organizations in the world, with an estimated 50% of women over eighteen years of age as members. With strong links to women at the village level and horizontally to trade unions, the VWU is a frequent partner for implementation of projects with the UN, international organizations, and donors. However, it is an underresourced entity that

"lacks mechanisms for coordinating policy with government units" (Goetz 2003, 77). As one informant commented, the "Women's Union does not exist to discuss emerging gender issues in the society of Vietnam. It exists to maintain the status quo" (Anon., Senior Economist, Development Bank, 13 October 2009; see also Vijeyarasa 2010d, 94, for a more detailed analysis of the VWU).

BIBLIOGRAPHY

ActionAid International Vietnam. 2005. "Synthesis Report: The Trafficking of Vietnamese Women and Children." Report.

Agir pour les Femmes en Situation Pre´cair (AFESIP). 2007. "AFESIP Vietnam 2006 general activity report." Academy for Educational Development, www.humantrafficking.org/uploads/publications/2006_AFESIP_Vietnam_REPORT.pdf.

Agustin, Laura. 2009. "TIP: Trafficking in Persons, the No-Methodology Report." Unpublished report.

Andrees, Beate, and Mariska van der Linden. 2005. "Designing Trafficking Research from a Labour Market Perspective: The ILO Experience." *International Migration* 43, no. 1/2: 55–73.

Bampton, Roberta, and Christopher J. Cowton. 2002. "The E-Interview." *Qualitative Social Research* 3, no. 2: Art. 9.

Banerjee, Upala Devi. 2006. "Migration and Trafficking of Women and Girls: A Brief Review of Some Effective Models in India and Thailand." In *Trafficking and the Global Sex Industry*, ed. K. Beeks and D. Amir. Lanham, MD: Lexington Books.

Brennan, D. 2005. "Methodological Challenges in Research with Trafficked Persons: Tales from the Field." *International Migration* 43, no. 1/2: 35–54.

Brownmiller, Susan. 1994. *Seeing Vietnam: Encounters of the Road and Heart*. New York: HarperCollins Publishers.

Chapkis, Wendy. 2003. "Trafficking, Migration and the Law: Protecting Innocents, Punishing Immigrants." *Gender and Society* 17, no. 6: 923–937.

Chuang, Janie A. 2010. "Rescuing Trafficking from Ideological Capture: Prostitution Reform and Anti-Trafficking Law and Policy." *University of Pennsylvania Law Review* 158: 1655–1728.

Cwikel, Julie and Elizabeth Hoban. 2005. "Contentious Issues in Research on Trafficked Women Working in the Sex Industry: Study Design, Ethics, and Methodology." *Journal of Sex Research* 42, no. 4: 306–316.

Dang, Nguyen Anh. 2008. "Labour Migration from Viet Nam: Issues of Policy and Practice, report prepared for ILO Regional Office for Asia and the Pacific." Working Paper No. 4, Bangkok: ILO.

Dang, Nguyen Anh, Tacoli, Cecilia, and Hoang Xuan Thanh. 2003. "Migration in Vietnam: A Review of Information on Current Trends and Patterns, and their Policy Implications," in *Regional Conference on Migration, Development and Pro-Poor Policies Choices in Asia*. Refugee and Migratory Movements Research Unit, Bangladesh, and the Department for International Development, UK. 22–24 June, Dhaka, Bangladesh.

De Lind van Wijngaarden, J. W. 2007. *Assessment of HIV/AIDS Vulnerability, Responses and STI/HIV Prevention, Care and Support Needs of Institutionalized Children Aged 14 to 19 in Selected Labour and Social Education Institutions and Reform Schools in Vietnam*. Hanoi, Vietnam: UNICEF.

Derks, Annusak, Roger Henke, and Vanna Ly. 2006. "Review of a Decade of Research on Trafficking in Persons, Cambodia." Prepared for the Center for Advanced Study, the Asia Foundation, and USAID.

Doussantousse, S., and L. Tooke. 2002. "A Cultural Approach to HIV and AIDS Prevention and Care for Sustainable Development in Ha Long City, Quảng Ninh Province, Vietnam." 14th International AIDS Conference, 7–12 July, Barcelona, Spain.

Duong, L. B., and Thu Khuat Hong. 2008. *Market Transformation, Migration and Social Protection in a Transitioning Vietnam*, Institute for Social Development Studies. Hanoi: The Gioi Publisher.

Goetz, Anne M. 2003. "National Women's Machinery: State-Based Institutions to Advocate for Gender Equality," in Shirin Rai (ed.), 2005. *Mainstreaming Gender, Democratizing the State: Institutional Mechanisms for the Advancement of Women*. New Jersey: Transaction Publishers.

Government of Vietnam. n.d. "Law on Human Trafficking Prevention." No. 2001/QH12.

Gozdziak, Elzbieta M., and Elizabeth A. Collett. 2005. "Research on Human Trafficking in North America: A Review of Literature." *International Migration* 43, no. 1/2: 99–124.

Hoang, Thi Tue Phuong. 2008. "Legislation to Combat Trafficking in Vietnam," in *17th Biennial Conference of the Asian Studies Association of Australia*. 1–3 July 2008, Melbourne, Australia.

International Organization for Migration (IOM) and Federal Ministry of the Interior of Austria. 2009. *Guidelines for the Collection of Data on Trafficking in Human Beings, Including Comparable Indicators*. Vienna, Austria: IOM.

Kelly, Elizabeth. 2002. "Journeys of Jeopardy: A Review of Research on Trafficking in Women and Children in Europe." IOM Migration Research Series.

———. 2005. "'You Can Find Anything You Want': A Critical Reflection on Research on Trafficking in Persons within and into Europe." *International Migration* 43, no. 1–2: 235–265.

Khuat, Thi Hai Oanh. 2007. "HIV/AIDS Policy in Vietnam: A Civil Society Perspective." Institute for Social Development Studies, report prepared for Open Society Institute, http://www.opensocietyfoundations.org/.

Laczko, Frank. 2005. "Data and Research on Human Trafficking." *International Migration* 43, no. 1/2: 5–16.

Lainez, Nicolas. 2011. *Prostitution Mobility and Representations: The Case of Vietnamese Prostitutes Going to Cambodia, Hô Chi Minh City and Bangkok*. Ho Chi Minh City, Vietnam: Alliance Anti-Trafic Vietnam and IRASEC/Observatory on Illicit Trafficking.

Lux, Steven J., and Jeffrey D. Straussman. 2004. "Searching for Balance: Vietnamese NGOs Operating in a State-Led Civil Society." *Publication Administration and Development* 23: 173–181.

Lyttleton, Chris. 2002. "Prevention of HIV/AIDS Among Ethnic Minorities of the Upper Mekong Region through Community-Based Non-Formal and Formal Education." Report prepared for UNESCO Asia Pacific Regional Bureau for Education—Bangkok, Sydney, Australia.

Marshall, Phil. 2006. "From the Beginning . . . Strengthening Return, Recovery and Reintegration Procedures for Trafficking Victims in Viet Nam." Unpublished report.

Opdenakker, Raymond. 2006. "Advantages and Disadvantages of Four Interview Techniques in Qualitative Research." *Qualitative Social Research* 7, no. 4: Art. 11.

Overseas Development Institution (ODI). 2006. "Internal Migration, Poverty and Development in Asia." Briefing Paper 11.

Save the Children. 2008. Vietnam field visit, http://crossborderprogramme.wordpress.com.

SIREN (Strategic Information Response Network). 2008a. "Human Trafficking Data Sheet." Hanoi, Vietnam.

———. 2008b. "Human Trafficking Data Sheet." Bangkok, Thailand.

Taylor, Raymond, Irene Stevens, and Nguyen Thi Thai Lan. 2009. "Introducing Vocational Qualifications in Care to the Socialist Republic of Vietnam." *Social Work Education* 28, no. 1: 29–41.

Tyldum, Guri, and Anette Brunovskis. 2005. "Describing the Unobserved: Methodological Challenges in Empirical Studies on Human Trafficking." *International Migration* 43, no. 1/2: 17–34.

UNFPA. 2010. *Internal Migration and Socio-Economic Development in Viet Nam: A Call to Action*. Hanoi: Vietnam: UNFPA.

United Nations. 2000. "Protocol to Prevent, Suppress and Punish Trafficking in Persons Especially Women and Children, Supplementing the United Nations Convention Against Transnational Organized Crime." G.A. res. 55/25, Annex II, 55 U.N. GAOR Supp. (No. 49) at 60, U.N. Doc. A/45/49 (Vol. I).

US Department of State. 2009. *Trafficking in Persons Report.* Washington: US Department of State.

Viet Nam News. 2010. "Human Trafficking on the Rise: Minister." January 8, http://vietnam-news.vnagency.com.vn.

Vijeyarasa, Ramona. 2010a. "The State, Family and Language of Social Evils: Re-Stigmatising Victims of Trafficking in Vietnam." *Culture, Health and Sexuality* 12, no. 1: 89–102.

———. 2010b. "Exploitation or Expectations? Moving Beyond Consent." *Women's Policy Journal of Harvard* 7: 11–22.

———. 2010c. "The Impossible Victim: Judicial Treatment of Trafficked Migrants and Their Unmet Expectations." *Alternative Law Journal* 35, no. 4: 217–222.

———. 2010d. "Scrutinizing Vietnam's Progress towards Gender Equality." *Development* 53, no. 1, 91–97.

———. 2012. "The Cinderella Syndrome: Economic Expectations, False Hopes and the Exploitation of Trafficked Ukrainian Women." *Women Studies International Forum* 35: 53–62.

———. 2013. "Stigma, Stereotypes and Brazilian Soap Operas: Roadblocks to Ending Trafficking in Vietnam, Ghana and Ukraine." *Gender, Place and Culture* 20, no. 8: 1015–1032.

Xinhua News Agency. 2009. "Vietnam Kicks Off Campaign to Curb Human Trafficking." July 14, http://www.china.org.cn/.

Yi, Wang. 2005. "Trafficking in Women and Children from Vietnam to China: Legal Framework and Government Responses." Written for Oxfam Quebec's Anti-Human Trafficking Programme in Vietnam.

Chapter Nine

Resistance to Work and at the Workplace

A Blind Spot for French Sociology of Work?

Stephen Bouquin

French sociology of work in the 1970s dealt with workers' resistance during the years of the crisis of Taylorist organizations. At this time, a high turn-over, sabotage, slow-down actions, as well as strikes expressed the workers' rejection of Taylorism. In the 1980s, most of the sociologists expected a lot from the post-Taylorist schemes. Moreover, they defended an interpretation that welcomed these changes as an element, together with post-Fordism, to resolve the crisis of work as well as the crisis of profitability. In the 1990s, the drive toward casualization, the flexibilization, and the growth of internal and external flexibility confronted mainstream sociologists with the limits of their views. A new critical stream developed a vision of the workplace where workers' resistance does not exist anymore and is not possible. In the place of workers' resistance, management dominated without contest nor conflict, and workers were subjugated and were volunteers of submission. A weak trade unionism at the level of the shop floor, as well as theoretical approaches and conceptual frameworks, gave more credibility to fieldwork depicting workers as isolated, in competition, without solidarity, and suffering. As author of several studies in the car manufactories (published as *La valse des écrous*, 2006) as well as in other areas (editor of the *Résistances au travail*, 2008), I was personally skeptical toward these approaches. This chapter will explain the origins of this skepticism and on which ground a different approach could be developed in order to take into account part of an apparent invisible reality. After a historical overview of the topic, we will present empirical data that demonstrates the existence of resistances as well as types

165

of misbehavior, and we will explain why resistance was so less used by French sociology of work, although it has always been influenced by Marxist conceptual frameworks.

The question of "resistance" has a long record in Anglo-Saxon sociology. History, sociology and labor process theory acknowledge the existence, or at least the possibility, of informal oppositional conduct at the workplace. From "workers' resistance" to "organizational misbehavior," the issue was (and is) a subject of controversy, but it was not denied as such (Brown 1977; Edwards 1979; Thompson 1983; Whiston 1997; Ackroyd and Thompson 1999).

Some may consider this behavior to be linked with the structural characteristics of wage labor, that is, being coercive and exploitative; others may consider it as the very truth of the Homo Faber, because living labor will never be completely mastered and objectified. In the Anglo-Saxon tradition, people at work are rarely seen as willing slaves, passive or dominated in such a way that they completely act according to management's will. Of course, some will argue that autonomous action in work situations is necessary in order for organizations to work well. Indeed, behavior such as workplace games (Burawoy 1979), coping attitudes or readjustments of job design are important. In these cases, human behavior stays within the boundaries of what is needed or expected to be efficient. But can we still consider them as part of "resistance to work"? I do not think so, and we will return later to this aspect of definition.

In French sociology, the issue of "resistance" is far from having the same presence in (academic) literature. As editor of a book (Bouquin 2008) about this subject, I started to analyze this relative absence as part of conceptual and theoretical differences between French and Anglo-Saxon sociology of work.

In the first section of this chapter I will present the history of this research in relation to the broader social-political background. In a second section I will confront empirical evidence with how French authors deal with domination and (or not) with resistance. In a last section I will explain the relative absence of "resistance" in sociological literature.

THE EBBS AND FLOWS OF WORKERS' RESISTANCE

The Years of Struggle (1965–1982)

In a country like France, with a weak system of industrial relations (outside the public sector) and a divided trade union landscape, one would expect a strong presence of informal ways of opposition. But this is not the case. Wage labor expanded after the Second World War, and the industrialization of rural areas integrated new layers into the working class, mainly women and former peasants. Production on a mass scale with Taylorist-Fordist methods grew fast as small-scale artisanal and familial capitalism reduced its share of economic output. The expansion of Taylorist methods led to a growth of the unskilled workforce, named *ouvriers spécialisés*, that is, task specialised workers. The skilled workers, *ouvriers professionnels*, were the main battalions of the trade unions, specially the CGT. But industrial and technological innovations led to the expansion of an unskilled and above all less-paid workforce. Skilled workers faced the growing presence of this segment of the workforce and feared being degraded in their professional status. In 1968, the first, hardest, and longest strikes were those among the new unskilled layers of the working class, outside Paris and its industrial belt. This was a concrete refutation of Serge Mallet's thesis about a "new working class" made of engineers, technicians, and skilled operators. The general strike was not a strike against Taylorist work systems as such. The sources of discontent were material (low wages in a wealthy France; the pay gap between Paris and province) and linked to the authoritarian management structures. The agreements of Grenelle increased the minimum wage (SMIG) by 30% and recognized trade unions in firms ("section syndicale"). Later on, in the early 1970s, a wave of strikes in the car-manufacturing sector expressed the aim of avoiding any segregation by job classification systems. Unskilled workers also wanted to have the opportunity to become professional (skilled) workers. This desire, combined with a high turnover, was the main symptom of a crisis of work relations. This crisis was interpreted by sociologists as a rejection of Taylorist works systems, which definitely was the case. According to Claude Durand (1978), fellow researcher of Alain Touraine, the second phase of technological development of industry could only lead to dissatisfaction, frustration, and a rejection of the strong division of labor, monotonous work tasks, chain work, standardized piecework, etc. Others, like Pierre Dubois (1976, 1980), as close readers of Harry Braverman, understood the crisis of work as part of a wider revolt against work degradation, with a large range of behavior, from attempts to win back control over the work situation (*freinage*, or slowing down, output restriction, or even sabotage) to ways of escaping out of these jobs.

According to sociologists, in order to solve the "crisis of work," Taylorism had to be replaced by new forms of work organization, recognition of tacit skills, job enlargement, and job enrichment. But the employers refused to do so during the whole of the 1970s. Some experiences, such as self-managed teams on a "carousel," were set up, but only on a small scale. An internal document of the employers' association of 1972 (Sudreau 1975; CNPF 1973) offers us an explanation of why these experiences remained so rare: according to the association, introducing new forms of work organization in the post-1968 context with low unemployment and a balance of power in favor of unions and workers would result in an increase of production costs (including the wages because of the recognition of "tacit" skills) and a shift of power to the shop floor. Therefore, any large-scale introduction of "sociotechnic" reforms, such as in Sweden, the UK, or Germany, had to be avoided. As a result, the employers' association advocated a further hiring of foreign workers from (northern) African countries as the best answer to the revolt against Taylorism. And indeed, until 1975, direct hiring of foreign workers continued on a high level. When these workers expressed their rejection of their unskilled condition, they did so with the aim of having access to skilled professional status. In 1973–1974, almost forty strikes occurred in Renault around this issue, and most of them were "wildcat strikes," more often recognized and supported by the CFDT than by the CGT. As a response to this protest, management created a new intermediate section of "quasi professionals." In a lot of cases, this was experienced as a threat to the status of "real" professional and skilled workers. These cleavages inside the "collective worker" often corresponded with differences in nationality or ethnic background. Trade unions also negotiated an agreement in 1974 with the metal-working industry, recognizing competencies acquired through work experience. This agreement aimed to end discrimination of workers who did not have the opportunity of a technical education through vocational education, or recognition of "on the job" acquired skills.

In the late 1970s and early 1980s, an economic crisis hit France very hard. Industry (i.e., garments, car manufacturing, and steel mills) was radically restructured, and unemployment was growing rapidly. In 1981, the new government of the united left faced a recession as well as the threat of an outflow of capital by the economic elites. The government made an attempt to democratize the economy through nationalizations and fostering collective bargaining (on the company level) as well as forms of workers' participation. During that period, sociological analysis ceased to deal with "resistance" and expressed the hope that new work schemes would develop in the aftermath.

The Years of Crisis and Restructuring (1983–1994)

Capital answered falling profitability, first with massive restructuring (layoffs) and then, starting in 1986, with a wave of technological innovations. Some of these were presented as an opportunity to change the division of labor and the nature of work. The fact that automation and new technologies were introduced at the same time as Japanese-inspired work schemes was seen as a single solution to a double problem, that is, restoring profitability and solving the crisis of work (namely, the dissatisfaction with and rejection of Taylorism). Work would change and cease to be a waste of energy and time; creativity would be used efficiently by organizations, and workers would make the best of their capabilities.

Most of French critical sociologists and economists (Coriat 1979; Zarifian 1993) adopted an analytical framework inspired by the "regulation school"

(Boyer). To them, a new regime of accumulation was "waiting 'round the corner": it combined the production of diversified goods for varying needs through a new productive model with higher skill requirements and therefore a different work organization with less division of labor. Some German authors (Kern and Schumann 1987) developed similar arguments. Generally, mainstream analysis expressed a strong dose of optimism that was very welcome in such dark times.

Unfortunately, organizational innovations inspired by the human relations approach developed by the Tavistock Institute only developed for a short period. The introduction of "quality circles" was limited to the steel and chemical industry, and other forms of participation had to fit with tight time management. At the end of the 1980s, most of these degenerated, and monthly meetings became less and less regular. Other institutional changes such as *groupes d'expression directe* (groups of direct expression) saw their agendas limited to immediate concerns and productivity issues. On-the-job rotation or job enrichment became a source of intensification and densification of labor. In 1987, the introduction of teamwork was limited to Renault under the name of *unités élémentaires de travail* (UET), and team leaders were established by the hierarchy. The other car manufacturer, Peugeot-Citroen, kept producing in the traditional way, with larger teams and a tight hierarchical chain of control (Durand and Hatzfeld 1998). In the early 1990s, it became clear that things did not change as expected. It became clear that Toyotism was mainly concerned with a higher return of invested capital through the reduction of production costs (lean manufacturing), externalization, and the system of "just-in-time" production (i.e., system where the size of stock or immobilized capital is reduced to the minimum). From the viewpoint of workers, the new organizations of production looked more and more like neo-Taylorism, since the use of the conveyor belt expanded, the amount of MTM devoted to tasks was shortened, and the prescription of how to work also reached subjective dimensions, that is, the relation to one's job (TQM, Kan Ban, zero defaults) (Bouquin 2006).

Of course, during the 1980s, the crisis of work faded away and was replaced by the "crisis of employment." The issue of informal workers' resistance disappeared from the literature. Some thought this was normal and unavoidable since its origins (Taylorism) had disappeared as well. Later on, when Taylorism was acknowledged as a work system that was still in place, sociological attention focused on the atomization of the collective worker and the willing submission to coercion.

The Years without Fairy Tales (1995–2008)

Halfway into 1990s, some authors started to reflect critically on the idea of a "new model of production" (Coutrot 1998). On the macro level of the labor market and society, the growing presence of precarious workers did not fit with the regulation school's expectations for a virtuous circle of growth based on new work with higher skills and increased productivity. Phenomena such as externalization or subcontracting, combined with temporary workers (contractual flexibility), created a periphery of impoverished and vulnerable workers around the core segment of stable workers. As an effect of this, thinking about a "productive model" as the "one best way," did not make sense, and models had to be pluralized. Most analysts of Gerpisa (M. Freyssenet; R. Boyer) took this road, focusing on distinctive profit strategies and industrial or productive models (Boyer and Freyssenet 2000). Others (Durand et al. 1998) developed a typology of the wage relationship (*relation salariale*) according to how collective bargaining, unionism, and HR policies interact with firms' industrial strategies. Such an approach tried to combine internal and external dimensions in the same analytical framework, which was a way to grasp all kinds of variations that did not fit in either the model of lean production designed by the International Motor Vehicle Program of Boston MIT, or the naïve idea of the early 1980s of a new regime of accumulation.

But, on the level of the firm or the network of firms (supply chain), the social balance worsened, despite the fact that the economic situation (profitability) improved in comparison with the 1980s. The phenomenon of permanent "downsizing" was seen as a consequence of corporate governance, with financial markets demanding a "return of own equities" (ROE) of 15%. More fundamentally, I would say that lowering the costs of production (capital and labor costs) was needed to restore profitability. This was obtained in the late 1980s. In the 1990s, the increase of productivity at a pace of 3 to 4% per year could only lead to reducing employment, since there was no significant reduction of working time and the global output hit the limits of the market (mainly the renewal of goods in the OECD countries and relatively small numbers of solvable consumers in the rest of the world). Most sociological analysis tends to forget that the "social return" of competitiveness and profitability (i.e., all anti-crisis policies on a firm level) was and is dependent on the presence of trade unions and the balance of power. Moreover, trade unions can take different orientations and may, in some cases, advocate these policies because they "are necessary to survive" under global competition.

Nevertheless, various surveys, such as the equivalent of WERS in France (DARES 1992), or the European survey on working conditions, demonstrated that work did not change as much as expected (Coutrot 1998; Gollac and Volkoff 2000). Intensification as well as a loss of control upon the pace of work—through short-term deadlines, an increase in the use of the conveyor belts, or the mobilization of client "awaiting"—showed a landscape where old-fashioned Tayloristic work systems were still very operative, while new schemes of mobilization, inspired by Toyotism, put the stress on the way of engaging in work through subjective, psychological means. As a result, more and more authors (Martucelli 2000; Courpasson 2002) started to speak again about "domination of labor" (*domination du travail*) or workers in "willing serfdom" (*servitude volontaire*) (Durand 2003).

The general situation depicted since the late 1990s, especially regarding the private sector, was very pessimistic. A general ebb of strikes expressed the "end of collectivism," as some would say in the UK. In France, it was seen as the end of the working class "for itself," that is, the end of class consciousness. Some case studies (Beaud and Pialoux 1996) even presented workers as being ashamed of their class identity, trying to escape their class by any means necessary. Since that period, most critical sociologists (Linhart, Boltanski, and Chiapello) have presented management as hegemonic, class domination as absolute (through symbolic violence), and the labor process as mastered and controlled by management (in France this is said as *le travail*, or the work being carried out).

Sociological reflection orientated itself to the questions of how management could be so successful and so uncontested. The answers lay in the objective situation (because of high unemployment, fear of precarity), in the subjective situation (the weakness of trade unions), and last but not least, in cultural trends marked by growing individualism. According to these sociologists, management had won the hearts and minds of the workers. Blue- as well as white-collar workers acted fierce fully accordingly to efficiency principles. The use of incentives (bonus schemes and variable wages) as well of the logic of competency (regular evaluations of one's engagement by direct hierarchical superior) sorted the effect.

In fact, the few sociologists still talking about "resistances" were pro-management. Organizational sociology, in particular authors such as Crozier and Segrestin, still stress "resistance to change" as a problem for management. Consultants still make money teaching "organizational learning" and psychological models that focus on avoiding or dismantling any disturbance or irregular behavior. Can we assume that these narratives are completely false, so much snake oil sold to management boards? No, personally I assume that there must be some truth in their models and PowerPoint presentations. If every five years the consultancy business can identify new "tools" and narratives to enhance performance, the topic of "resistance to change" obviously remains present (even as a best seller). I took this as an invitation to break from my colleagues and think differently about work situations.

Of course, inside the academic sphere, the debate (when it occurs) has some strange aspects: some are painting a very dreadful portrait of the labor market and work situations, while others are arguing that workers still have plenty of choices and include options that would lift them out of precarious social situations. These are positions that can hardly be brought into dialogue. If labor is an activity in which one can come to the realization of the self, it demands a strong work ethic and a strong commitment, even the ability to sacrifice leisure and family. High-performance work systems imply a strong corporate culture and carefully selected individuals. In this perspective, "resistance to change" acts as a mechanism of stigmatizing employees as "not motivated," "dysfunctional," or unable to fit into the organization. If this was subjected to a critical management analysis, do we have to assume that organizations are clean of discontent and that there is no room left for employees (blue-collar or white-collar workers) to think and to act in nonconformist ways? No, and for this reason in the last couple of years I have begun alternative fieldwork.

ALTERNATIVE EMPIRICAL EVIDENCE

Many of my students in sociology are from working-class backgrounds, and most of them work to pay for their undergraduate or postgraduate studies. They work in the summer or part time during the year. Some work in industry, while others work in food service or in call centers. For practical reasons, they use their workplace as a field for surveys or participatory observation.

My own PhD, published under the title "La Valse des écrous" (Bouquin 2006), contained three cases studies: Opel Antwerp, Volkswagen in Brussels, and Renault Trucks in Caen (Normandy). I was confronted with situations where informal workers' resistance was very present. In some cases, slowdown actions and sabotage developed because of the passivity of trade unions and agreements signed to guarantee jobs in exchange for increased productivity; in other cases, this informal resistance was part of a way of working and opposing foremen or hierarchy in general. I faced situations like assembly workers speeding up to make spare time to smoke a cigarette or play chess near the workstation. Sometimes there were "technical" incidents that indirectly expressed the polarization and tensions on the assembly line. These facts demonstrate that work relations and wage labor are always to some extent polarized by "structural antagonism" (Kelly 1998). Collective action is only the tip of the iceberg, and the fact that strikes do occur is important, but sociological analysis cannot limit its account to these dramatic events

In 2002–2003 some of my students started to echo my analysis with their own accounts about how things really happened at the workplace, and I tried to systematize all of our information and bring together different cases into a book published in 2008 (Résistances au travail). I give here a summary of some empirical evidence:

• In call centers, operators know how to use specific codes in order to keep someone on the line or to ask him/her to be called back later. These tactics explain and justify lower ratios of connection, selling, or survey response. Operators share this know-how via outside social networks, such as universities or pubs. They know they can be tracked by supervisors, but they also know how to negotiate supervisors' passivity or complicity.

- In electronic device stores, employees regularly steal "damaged" material (material that was put aside because of a small defect or because it was returned by a customer) and resell these products to increase their already low wages by 5% or 10% per month. In supermarkets, cashiers scan only one in two articles when a colleague comes for shopping, or they know how to keep goods out of electronic registration and therefore out of sight.
- In industry, cheating occurs sometimes with the consent of the employer since subcontracting produces solidarity between all parties involved. Here the same thing happens as when you bring your car to the garage and one problem is solved but another appears "by accident" a few weeks later. In the ICT sector and in many facility and maintenance services, contracts with suppliers try to avoid such malpractices through fixed prices covering all risks.
- Temporary workers tend to form small groups where one takes care of another; for example, pushing a colleague into a short mission that you do not need or like. As a result, a "moral economy" tends to develop solidarity through interdependency in order to reduce some of the professional insecurity.
- Output restriction appeared to be a common practice among high-level employees (such as sales managers) that work in large, multinational corporate organizations and have to cope with "targets" based on their earlier performance and results. In such situations they withhold some orders for the next period to avoid inflation of targets. I also observed new forms of slowing down or output restriction in traditional industry and in the transport sector. The motives seem to be less economic or material and more based on saving time for oneself or reducing the pressure and fatigue caused by intensification. Creative employees always find a good excuse.

WHAT'S IN A NAME?

Why should these practices be analyzed in terms of "resistances"? Indeed, they are useful for organizations since they create the possibility to cope with tense situations. For these reasons, we cannot disconnect such ways of conduct with others such as "adjustments" or singular forms of reappropriation of the work situation. At the same time, these forms of conduct have a group dimension, and they play a role in the informal recomposition of the collective worker. It is therefore problematic to analyze contemporary work relations as atomized and under complete control of management (see Linhart 1994, 2009).

Moreover, these forms of behavior have a group dimension: the group does not declare itself openly nor immediately, and when a new member is integrated they pass through evaluation and testing of their conduct, which can be analyzed as a form of peer socialization. It is the holder of semi-fragmented collectivism (Tilly 1978; see also Kelly 1998).

As we observed in the case of the maintenance workshop in the aircraft industry, these groups can correspond to trade union members, and they may share the same shop-floor culture. In this situation, the strength of a trade union is rooted in its proximity to the real, existing collective worker. But given the weakness of trade unions in France, in particular their divided and ideological character and the strength of managerial corporate culture and work ethics, most of the time these informal groups exist on a smaller scale and have to coexist with individuals and sometimes groups that tend to conform themselves to the dominant shop-floor culture.

The fear of falling into disgrace in the eyes of immediate superiors, the hope to obtain a better situation through promotion, the fear to be a part of the next cohort of redundancies and many other reasons still give management the advantage in implementing certain ways of conduct. Some authors (Jean-Pierre Durand) call this a kind of *servitude volontaire*, or "willing serfdom" (La Boétie) and the symbolic and material base of consent existing on a large scale. If this is the case, we cannot take for granted it will always remain true. As I demonstrated, employees act in accordance with what they understand as their interests. When there is no promotion, when management fails to deliver the promises that provide consent with a rationale, things change. People do "as if," and we can verify the existence of "hidden transcripts" of revolt, such as those identified in various situation by James C. Scott (1990), who noticed how dominated groups hide their own opinions but share these with others when those who do have power are absent or are not able to control subordinated workers. When the legitimacy of power is in crisis, people start to think again in a critical way, to disbelieve, and cease to collaborate in an active way. Then they go over to passivity, false collaboration, and active resistance.

If we evoke the notion of "interest," what do we mean by that? It is of course a question of perspective and therefore subjective. But even in the absence of a Marxist narrative held by trade union activists, employees may consider work to be a relation in which they do not receive enough in exchange for their efforts. Even in a liberal conception of labor as an exchange relation, there is an efficiency level of pay. Of course France has a Proudhonistic tradition that underpins its work ethic. Pride in a job well done is also something shared by the communist political culture, which developed a symbiotic relation with the professional ethos of craftsmanship. But nowadays, both are in crisis, especially within the younger generation where we can observe much more opportunism and utilitarianism regarding work and labor.

Moreover, we have to take into account that in a country such as France, where wages stagnated while productivity increased, the working poor are getting more numerous on both an objective and subjective level (people consider themselves as poor in comparison to others who are more wealthy), and last but not least the ideological legitimacy of income and wealth differences still relies upon the ideals of the republic and egalitarian individualism. Therefore, the feeling of injustice is something that spread among laboring people on a quite large scale, and some surveys recognize that fact (Baudelot and Gollac 2003).

When work is too tense and stressing, when pay is seen as unfair and employees suffer outside work from their labor, things are out of balance, and it becomes normal for "misbehavior" to occur. The purpose of this behavior is to put things back into balance through semi-informal clandestine means, hoping that change will eventually happen on a formal level thanks to better management or to a successful collective action by trade unions.

Some authors do consider "resistance" a real issue nowadays. But when they do, as is the case of Courpasson (2002), they see it as acting in favor of well-done work. The rebellion of the cadres, of white-collar managers, is seen as a revolt against bureaucratic and authoritarian structures that are ineffective regarding motivation and efficiency. By analyzing the question from this viewpoint, resistances can be seen as a symptom of badly managed and organized teams. This should pave the way to a pacification of the workplace that in the end never lasts. Such an interpretation fails to explain why work situations are never "a quiet frontline," and this is a reason to be skeptical of such "pro-work resistance." It may happen, of course, and employees may resist the fact that they do not receive the means to deliver quality work, but it can also be an attitude. When engineers, technicians, or managers refuse promotion, refuse to take responsibility, and refuse to give their best to their employer, or even toward their own work if they are freelancers, it has to do with the problematic centrality of labor in life. This is something that only becomes apparent when we develop longitudinal analysis or when people look back at their career. In their forties, people will see some conduct as vain, they will no longer expect as much recognition, and they will become more cynical about promises. At these ages, they will engage themselves in trade unions, in leisure and social activities outside work or into "quality time." The fact that such attitudes now appear among lower management also reflects the fact that these layers were submitted to a kind of "proletarization" in the recent period.

To me, "resistances" at work act against abstract labor and do not only occur at the workplace but can also be directed against work as such. There is a relatively invisible but real link between "resistances" and the structural character of the wage relationship and the rationality of a profit-based organization (driven by the accumulation of capital, in competition in a market). Even if "resistances" are just one of the kinds of behavior, even if it is often mixed or combined with others, it is considered disruptive by management. It cannot be recognized as functional by management (even though it sometimes is) but has to be stigmatized as an unreasonable, unqualified, and unapt way of working. Most of the time, when individuals are identified as performing such behavior, the sanction is hard and definitive.

CONCLUSIONS

To recapitulate, the relative absence of "resistances" in French sociology has to do with the overall social and economic evolutions of the last two decades. Wildcat strikes disappeared, and workers were anxious about employment. Turnover is at very low levels, and people more often express complaints than criticism. But as I have demonstrated, the situation at the workplace is more ambiguous than one would expect. These facts were not expected by those with a critical (Marxist) background. And to me, this is partly the result of a problematic early-Marxist and Proudhonistic conceptualization of work and wage labor. Early trade unionists as well as authors like Proudhon defined wage labor as a situation of alienation and subordination, of losing means of production and the control over the labor process. It obviously was (and is), but that is not the entire picture. They forgot to see that wage labor is also a commodified (economic) relation of exchange between an effort and pay. It is also a relation of co-dependency where the employer is never assured constant success in the surplus-extraction that has to be carried out. In the United Kingdom, common sense as well as sociological analysis did a much better job integrating the fact that wage labor contains such uncertainty (Biernacki 1995). In other words, culturally, in France, working badly when you are badly paid is simply "not done." Working for public services is working for the common good and delivering services of a high use value. For that reason, trade union activists evidently share a strong identification with their work tasks and their jobs; any kind of "resistance" that could be seen as sabotage is therefore rejected. Trade union culture in the private sector still bears the memory of rejecting Taylorism in the name of a culture of craftsmanship and professional ethos.

In France, sociologists as well as trade union activists have difficulties understanding that (young) people do act differently regarding their work tasks. One reason for that has to do with "projection": sociologists are in the situation to develop a strong identification to their work (in fact, more *oeuvre* than "labor") and think this should be the case for everybody. They develop the ahistorical viewpoint similar to the nostalgic craftsmen and find empirical confirmation in the social isolation and distress of unemployed people. Of course, without employment, one is lost. But does this mean that one cannot resist inside the sphere of work or regarding the wage relation as such? Common sense among sociological thinkers or in everyday life still opposes bad work to good work, bad jobs to good jobs, jobs with "suffering" (*souffrance au travail* is a successful theme in media developed by psychologist Christophe Dejours [1998]), and jobs that provide pleasure and the chance for self-realization. This common sense fails to question the roots of coercion that appear to exist more or less in all kinds of jobs, from skilled to unskilled, from "manual" to "intellectual" (emotional, knowledge) work. Since work is simply understood as an activity under constraint without taking into account the social form of labor (i.e., a commodified social relation linked to wage-relationship), mainstream analysis forgets to take into account the need to rationalize and to control human effort. Yet those two aspects are objective causes for the degradation of work and therefore are nourishing renewed forms of resistances to work and in the workplace.

BIBLIOGRAPHY

Ackroyd, S., and P. Thompson. 1999. *Organizational Misbehavior*. London: Sage.

Baudelot, Charles, and M. Gollac. 2003. *Travailler pour être heureux, Le bonheur et le travail en France*. Paris: Fayard.

Beaud, Stéphane and Michel Pialoux. 1996. *Retour sur la condition ouvrière*. Paris: Fayard.

Biernacki, R. 1995. *The Fabrication of Labor, Germany and Britain, 1640–1914*. Los Angeles: University of California Press.

Bouquin, S., 2006. *La Valse des écrous. Travail, capital et action collective dans l'industrie automobile (1968–2002)*. Paris: Syllepse.

———. ed. 2008. *Résistances au travail*. Paris: Syllepse.

Boyer, R., and M. Freyssenet. 2000. *Les modèles productifs*. Paris: La Découverte, La Repères.

Brown, G. 1977. *Sabotage*. Nottingham: Spokesman Books.

Burawoy, M. 1979. *Manufacturing Consent, Changes in Labor Process under Monopoly Capitalism*. Chicago: University of Chicago Press.

CNPF. 1973. "Le problème des OS." Mimeo.

Coriat, B. 1990. *L'atelier et le robot. Essai sur le Fordisme et la production de masse à l'âge de l'électronique*. Paris: Christian Bourgois.

———. 1994 [1979]. *L'atelier et le chronometer*. Paris: Christian Bourgois.

Courpasson, D. 2002. *L'action contrainte: Organizations libérales et domination*. Paris: Presses Universitaires de France.

Coutrot, T. 1998. *L'entreprise néo-libérale, nouvelle utopie capitaliste?* Paris: La Découverte.

Crozier, M. 1963. *Le Phénomène bureaucratique*. Paris: Seuil.

Crozier, M., and E. Friedberg. 1981 [1977]. *L'acteur et le système: Les contraintes de l'action collective*. Paris: Le Seuil.

DARES. 1992. *Conditions, organisation du travail et nouvelles technologies en 1991*. Paris: Masson.

Dejours, Christophe. 1998. *Souffrance en France - La banalisation de l'injustice sociale*, éditions du Seuil.

Dubois, P. 1976. *Le sabotage dans l'industrie, Calmann-Lévy*. Paris: Calmann-Levy.

———. 1980. *Les Ouvriers divisés*. Paris: FNSP.

178   *Stephen Bouquin*

Durand, Cl. 1978. *Le travail enchaîné: Organization du travail et domination sociale*. Paris: Seuil.

Durand J.-P. 1993. *Vers un nouveau modèle productif*. Paris: Syros/La Découverte.

1998. *L'avenir du travail à la chaîne*. Paris: La Découverte.

2003. *Travailler aujourd'hui: Flux tendu et servitude volontaire*. Paris: Seuil.

Durand, J.-P., and R. Boyer. 1993. *L'Après-Fordisme*. Paris: Syros.

Durand J.-P., and N. Hatzfeld. 1998. "L'efficacité de la tradition: l'usine Peugeot-Sochaux." In *L'avenir du travail à la chaîne*, ed. J.-P. Durand. Paris: La Découverte.

Duval, G. 1998. *L'entreprise efficace à l'heure de Swatch et Mc Donald's. La seconde vie du Taylorisme*. Paris: Syros.

Edwards, R. 1979. *Contested Terrain: The Transformation of the Workplace in the Twentieth Century*. London: Basic Books.

Gollac, M., and S. Volkoff. 2000. *Les conditions de travail*. Paris: La Découverte, La Repères.

Hatzfeld, N., and J.-P. Durand. 2002. *La Chaîne et le réseau: Peugeot-Sochaux, ambiances d'intérieur*. Lausanne: Page Deux.

Kelly, J. 1998. *Rethinking Industrial Relations: Mobilization, Collectivism, and Long Wave*. New York: Routledge.

Kern, H., and M. Schumann. 1987. *La fin de la division du travail? La rationalization dans la production industrielle*. Paris: MSH.

Linhart, D. 1991. *Les Torticolis de l'autruche: L'éternelle modernization des entreprises françaises*. Paris: Seuil.

1994. *La Modernization des entreprises*. Paris: La Découverte, La Repères.

2009. *Travailler sans les autres*. Seuil, Paris.

Martucelli, D. 2000. *Dominations ordinaires: Explorations de la condition modern*. Paris: Balland.

Scott, J. C. 1990. *Domination and the Arts of Resistance: Hidden Transcripts*. London: Yale.

Segrestin, D. 1992. *Sociologie de l'entreprise*. Paris: A. Colin.

Sudreau, P. 1975. *La réforme de l'entreprise*. Paris: F. Maspéro.

Thompson, P. 1983. *The Nature of Work: An Introduction to Debates on the Labor Process*. London: MacMillan.

Tilly, C. 1978. *From Mobilization to Revolution*. New York: Addison-Wesley.

Veltz, P. 1993. "Déstabilization et résistance du Taylorisme." In *Vers un nouveau modèle productif*, ed J.-P. Durand. Paris: Syros.

Whiston, Kevin. 1997. "Worker Resistance and Taylorism in Britain." *International Review of Social History* 42, no. 1: 1–24.

Zarifian, P. 1993. *Quels modèles d'organization pour l'industrie européenne?* Paris: L'Harmattan.

Chapter Ten

Global Justice Norms versus Interest Representation?

British Unions and International Solidarity

Charles Umney

Trade unions have an ambiguous relationship with the concept of global justice. On one hand, they are institutions of material interest representation that, when exercised by workers in the developed world, may be construed as self-preservation at the expense of workers in developing countries (e.g., Arrighi and Silver 2000; Silver 2003). On the other, this same sense of material interest, when considered in the longer term, may motivate unions to try to counteract such inequalities on the grounds that uneven conditions make it easier for capital to exploit workers everywhere (Croucher and Cotton 2009; Johns 1998). It may be that unions have normative commitments that fit closely with the idea of global justice; for example, they may be keen to campaign over issues such as freedom of association or labor rights. Alternatively, their emphasis on material gains may also conflict with the norms of identity-oriented social actors such as campaigning NGOs (Wade 2009).

When unions are considered as global justice actors, it is often in the context of mechanisms such as International Framework Agreements and corporate Codes of Conduct (e.g., Riisgard 2005; Wills 2002). In this chapter, however, I want to look at the experiences of domestic British unions under globalization and consider the ways in which their actions might be considered compatible with the notion of global justice. I will also address two further questions: What are the motivations for unions to act internationally? And what forms does such activity take? I will draw a distinction between internationalism motivated by material interest and internationalism motivated by trade union norms and will consider the possibilities and constraints contained within each model.

UNIONS AND INTERNATIONALISM

Unions have had a troubled recent history, which has led in some quarters to a renewed emphasis on the importance of international activity. They have been among the biggest victims of the decline of the welfarist consensus that characterized the "long wave" (Mandel 1978) of economic stability following World War II. For regulation theorists (e.g., Aglietta 1979; Lipietz 1986) this "Fordist-Keynesian regime of accumulation" entailed economic measures aimed at partially removing employment conditions from competition, and a normative consensus around the notion of "class compromise" (see also Harvey 2005, 10–11). Wage outcomes could be, to some degree, regulated collectively, with government intervening in and supporting the relationship between labor and capital (Howell 2005). Noteworthy here is the assumption of distinct national industrial relations regimes. Regulation theorists have been criticized for this (e.g., Collinge 1999), but ultimately this focus reflects an empirical reality: the Fordist era's emphasis on relatively closed national political regulation as opposed to the denationalized economic regulation that has superseded it under neoliberalism (Jessop 1997; Visser 2000). Now, instead, a hegemony of "regime competition" (Streeck 1998) subordinates national systems of political regulation to transnational economic integration. The enhanced spatial mobility of employers relative to workers means that the "credible threat" of practices such as outsourcing or whipsawing can strengthen labor compliancy (Cowling and Tomlinson 2005; Meardi 2007). In seeking to restrict this capitalist internationalism, unions may find themselves cast as protectionists or xenophobes.

The question to be asked here is what this transition means for the way trade unionists choose their targets and build their alliances. From more radical Marxian perspectives, it can be a significant opportunity, despite the traumas associated with the decline of national social contracts. Writers such as Moody (1997) or Waterman (2001) suggest the following logic: the breaking free of multinational capital from the constraints of national-level regulatory regimes represents a reassertion of class power by employers. This therefore rationalizes and necessitates a model of trade unionism that is both more militant and more internationalized, eschewing concepts such as the "national interest" in favor of the universalizing norm of class conflict. In accounts such as Moody's (1997), the idea of grassroots militancy is closely tied to internationalism, because the need for union leaderships to conciliate with employers prevents a class-based analysis, and it is only the latter that can be truly international in scope. Hence Moody's concept of "international social movement unionism" places grassroots union activists at the vanguard of a wider global justice movement incorporating social campaigners and NGOs.

The difficulty facing this argument is that there doesn't appear to be a naturally arising internationalism among trade union rank-and-file. There are glimpses of such a tradition: Thompson's (1963) classic history of the English working class, for example, argued that internationalism was an integral element of the early workers' movement, frequently incorporating appeals to political events abroad such as the French Revolution. But beyond these glimpses, the domination of international activity by union elites has generally been unchallenged from below. As Hyman writes:

> Increasingly, it would seem, the typical professional international trade unionist is a graduate with language skills, who having spent a few years as a researcher in a national labor movement has pursued a career at international level. Rarely does an international union leader have a background, however distant, as an agitator. (2005, 147)

While national labor movements have historically witnessed the development of stable institutions in response to popular movements, this sequence has generally been reversed at the international level. As Turner (1996) argues, on an international scale, institution building and contact making have driven grassroots protest, rather than the other way around. The latter must then enter to give the former legitimacy and power:

> Next to the proletarian internationalism predicted by Marx . . . cross-national labor protest and collaboration—aimed only at the regulation of an increasingly competitive and internationalist capitalist market economy—may seem quite tame . . . Reinforced by mass protest, however, such nascent structures may well bolster the contemporary social-democratic mission in the post–Cold War world: to bring a measure of justice and regulation to the no longer fundamentally challenged market economy. (Turner 1996, 389)

Whether or not unions fit easily into the role of global justice actors, there are important reasons why internationalism has so often failed among grassroots union members, instead remaining consigned to union elites. The first is structural, in the sense that union members are inevitably more severely menaced by potential threats to employment conditions than their leaders and hence more likely focus on immediate material priorities (Zeitlin 1989). The second, closely connected reason is that it is important not to underestimate the commitment of union officials to normative principles of workers' solidarity, which may transcend short-term interest representation. Kelly and Heery argue that "ideological conceptions of the aims and values of trade unionism . . . [and] an ethos of accountability to the membership" represent a strong "countervailing force" to the pressures toward conservatism placed on union officials by their role as bargainers (1994, 194–195). The latter point, though, remains an important one. As Hyman (1979) argues, union officials face the demands of maintaining an ongoing bargaining relationship with specific employers, which must surely to some extent impede the "class" based solidarity advocated by writers such as Moody. This conflict between values and position is also reflected in Watson's (1988) examination of officials' perceptions of their own role. Watson writes that the broader sociological controversy between "social structure" and "social action" is manifested explicitly in the daily role of trade union officers. Their closeness to managers is a hazard of the job that may compromise their role, and as such they may be bedeviled on a very personal level by the conflicting purposes that are inherent in trade unionism as a whole: between normative pursuit of the "sword of justice" and the pragmatic pursuit of "vested interest" (Watson 1988, 190).

The following examples illustrate the tensions between material interest representation and normative commitment among British unions. They also characterize the role of the union leader in developing internationalism in greater detail. The examples are drawn from qualitative research based on interviews and observation, conducted between December 2009 and March 2011. This research was conducted in two stages. The second stage was a comparative case study within the docks and seafaring sector, which I have discussed in detail elsewhere (Umney 2012). The first, upon which this chapter focuses, consisted of exploratory interviews at two large British unions, as well as at the Trade Union Congress, with NGO collaborators, and relevant Global Union Federation (GUF) operatives. Thus, the data presented is intended as the tentative first steps in inducing a broader theorization of international trade union activity, hopefully serving as a starting point for further investigation.

INTERNATIONAL ACTIVITY AMONG BRITISH UNIONS

The first and most fundamental question to be asked, then, is what is actually meant by "international trade unionism" in a practical context. Internationalism as "the spatial extension of trade unionism through the intensification of co-operation between trade unionists across countries using transnational tools and structures" (Greer and Hauptmeier 2008, 77) is a sufficient definition, but one that masks important distinctions. "International co-operation" could be between equal partners with common objectives, or it could refer to a situation where a stronger union seeks to aid a weaker one. As noted above, it could be aimed toward a very specific end, such as opposing whipsawing action undertaken by a particular employer, or it could be a more general commitment toward providing a union voice in international regulatory institutions. And it could be informed by a normative commitment to particular values, or by the furtherance of self-representative material interests. There therefore follows a brief discussion of three British unions, which showcase some very different approaches to internationalism.

UNISON

The British trade union with the largest distinct international department is the public sector union UNISON,[1] which has five members of staff based at their London office and (at the time of interview, 30 March 2010) an additional two people working on a Department for International Development (DFID) project in South Africa. UNISON has three rationales for the extent of its international activity. Firstly, as public sector employees, UNISON's members are clearly affected by the transference of political power to supranational institutions, most obviously the EU. As such, UNISON needs to cooperate with other unions in order to respond to and shape Europe-driven legislation. Secondly, UNISON aims to pursue and defend "trade union values" internationally, even where there is little direct connection to its members' material well-being. For example, UNISON undertakes solidarity work in countries such as the Philippines and Colombia, seeking to draw attention to the repression of trade unionists. This type of action is a manifestation of the normative principle that "solidarity knows no borders" (interview, 30 March 2010). Finally, UNISON tries to build capacity in developing world unions. This may revolve around more politicized subjects, such as support in opposing privatizations (where it will often work in cooperation with organizations such as Oxfam), but it is more often related to general development associated with DFID. The centerpiece of this type of internationalism is an ongoing three-year project on public sector trade union responses to HIV/AIDS in Southern Africa involving around thirty different unions and the Public Services International, as well as local and international NGOs (see UNISON and ACTSA 2009).

These objectives, particularly the latter two, mean that UNISON has expanded its collaborations in international civil society, including campaigning for anti-poverty organizations such as Oxfam and War on Want. The union collaborates with Oxfam to argue in favor of public service provision in the developing world, and a UNISON international official sat on the board of the Make Poverty History campaign. It also sometimes works with more overtly political organizations such as the Colombia Solidarity Campaign. UNISON may support ten to fifteen projects per year and receives requests mainly for backing on charitable endeavors. However, it generally only supports projects on the proviso that the work done pursues a purpose that is "neither purely charitable nor purely political" (interview, 31 March

2010), but which is instead connected to supporting trade unionists abroad. These collaborations are the result of the belief that trade unions are an essential partner in any social coalition, as well as the worry that specific union concerns—such as the concept of a "decent wage"—may be downgraded to niche or even protectionist interests rather than integral elements of a global justice movement.

One question asked of the UNISON interviewees was why their union was prepared to focus on these types of projects to such a degree. As they acknowledge, there isn't a clear "line of thought" connecting public sector UNISON membership to international labor markets, as would be the case if members were employed in multinational companies. Instead, UNISON's international activities are attributed to a normative tradition among members that extends back to the large international department at the National Association of Local Government Officers (NALGO), one of the unions that merged to form UNISON in 1993. The argument here is that this relative distance from direct international labor competition creates the space in which concerns oriented toward global justice norms can flourish.

How, then, does this normative element to internationalism take shape? The contours of UNISON's international activity can be better understood by roughly dividing the union's structure into layers. While UNISON's membership may take no more of an active interest in internationalism than any other union, it also has a strong lay activist stratum that is critical to international activity. UNISON's rulebook states that each branch should elect a Branch International Officer (BIO). While in practice fewer than half have done so, this still equates to approximately five hundred BIOs nationwide. The purpose of the role is to raise awareness of UNISON's international activity and its importance amongst membership who would otherwise have little interest or input. BIOs remain lay officers who retain usual local responsibilities in addition to their international role. Discussion seminars are held for all BIOs twice a year and constitute part of a consultative relationship between these activists and the central international office. It is through them that campaigning priorities are identified and reaffirmed. The international office consults activists on areas of interest, and consequently high-profile issues of political and human rights concerns—for example, campaigning over Palestine—tend to be strongly pushed "from below." UNISON's work on Burma, for example, has been driven by a small number of activists (two or three) who have been particularly interested in the issue and have pressured the international office into acting upon it. The international office, however, will also seek to identify new areas of interest—for example, it has recently suggested campaigning against trade union repression in the Philippines—in which analogous concerns apply. Such cases will then (the international official hopes) become as important to the BIOs as existing campaigns.

The practical business of establishing and administering campaigns is generally directed from the international office. BIOs, however, can be closely involved in such campaigns and are often highly important to them, depending on their levels of enthusiasm and the extent to which they are able to spread this interest among local colleagues. One interviewee had attended several trips to Southern Africa as a UNISON officer, sometimes as part of a broader campaign and sometimes as part of UNISON's own projects. The officer, while on the policy committee of UNISON's NEC, had individually volunteered to attend a delegation to Ethiopia, to observe a project for street children to which UNISON had donated money. The interviewee had then proceeded to play an active role in arguing for increased fundraising among UNISON members and securing delegate positions to events such as Amnesty International conferences. This was despite a degree of skepticism from other local branch members who may view such trips as "freebies" with little relevance to their daily working lives. The interviewee's involvement had been a case of self-volunteering for opportunities that were of political and compassionate interest, and because of this commitment he/she had become a valuable asset in UNISON's international activity.

UNISON's reliance on this type of activity to establish support for its international work means that, viewed from above, there are pockets of concerted interest among politically aware and active BIOs surrounded by large swathes of relative disinterest. As noted above, the contours of this activity can therefore follow high-profile international political concerns, operating in a mutually reinforcing arrangement with the international office. One BIO describes UNISON's annual delegate conference as being characterized by enthusiasm from delegates over particular high-profile issues, such as murders of trade unionists in Colombia, resulting in demands for action that are passed up to the international office. The latter then links it in to the priorities that are established annually by the NEC. "So [the international office is] very much tied—or should be tied—into what the activists want and take to conference" (interview, 16 April 2010).

UNISON is able to devote a substantial amount of time and resources to this sort of campaigning based on values and political concern because there is a level of distance between these issues and the working lives of its members. Because it rarely has direct representation in multinational companies, it is, to an extent, "liberated" from the accommodatory bargaining pressures placed on workers within those companies. As Hancké (2000) shows, where workers are exposed to international competition by the transnational reach of their employers, a focus on collaborating with managers to preserve local jobs may dominate, rationalized from the perspective of immediate interest representation. This could, potentially, develop into a protectionist or hostile attitude to workers abroad (Arrighi and Silver 2000).

By contrast, UNISON members' relative removal from the pressures of international labor competition means that there is a comparatively uncontroversial space in which the normative priorities of politically engaged activists and officials can achieve a fuller expression. Its development work also affords greater space for collaboration with NGOs because, much like the latter's value-driven social campaigning, it is not based around short-term material interest representation. It must be stressed that there are occasionally tensions between UNISON and NGOs. Such conflicts, however, tend to revolve around the types of issues prioritized in campaigning rather than the more fundamental disagreements over the union's self-representative (and therefore potentially "protectionist") role. The fact that internationalism is rarely presented as an issue of direct workplace concern also means that it tends to be official led, based around the central international office, excepting, of course, the role of engaged BIOs.

UNITE the Union

UNITE is Britain's largest union, formed in a merger between the Transport and General Workers' Union (TGWU) and AMICUS in 2007, and it claims to represent 1.5 million members across a wide array of sectors.[2] It places great emphasis on its role in international activity, citing internationalism among its three "key pillars" of work alongside political representation and organizing. The rationale for the primacy given to international activity is somewhat different to that of UNISON, rooted less explicitly in normative values. It reflects the increasing number of UNITE members incorporated into MNCs. The recognition that companies have expanded so dramatically on an international scale implies that union solidarity can itself no longer be contained within the nation state.

In other words, while the union (or in this case its constituent parts) has always recognized the principle of international solidarity, it is only now that employers have moved "through the roof," that these values have also become a practical imperative. UNITE's expanding international activity, particularly within the AMICUS section, reflects a general shift in strategy in response to material circumstance. AMICUS's membership base was severely impacted by the movement of financial sector jobs abroad, particularly to India, and at the outset of this process the union had sought to retain this employment in the UK. There arrived a point, however, at which this process appeared to be inevitable; in other words, the union's attempts to retain British jobs had been defeated. For one international official, this point coincided with the development of the Make Poverty History campaign and a growing public interest in development issues. Within the union there followed a growing emphasis on attempting to secure greater international regulation and to counter the company-driven "race to the bottom," perceived as a problem for all workers rather than particular national groups. This can be seen as somewhat similar to UNISON's experience; a normative reorientation toward global justice emerging in the space left by the lack of an explicit threat to material interest—even if, in this case, the latter was because the damage had already been done.

UNITE's international activities, however, are highly heterogeneous, encompassing a variety of strategies, some of which have progressed further than others. The most eye-catching move has been the formation of Workers Uniting—"the world's first global union"—in 2008, through the bilateral relationship between UNITE and the United Steelworkers (USW) in North America. This step grew out of UNITE leadership's apparent skepticism over the resourcing of GUFs, which led the union to pursue its own, more direct, links with unions abroad. USW is the United States' largest private sector union, with a membership spanning many more sectors than its name implies, following several mergers of its own. Thus it shares key parallels with UNITE and apparently also shares a political desire to construct a "proper international structure" (interview, 12 June 2010), which can challenge employers more directly on a transnational level without relying on umbrella organizations such as GUFs. Workers Uniting, however, also suffers from weak resourcing at present, in part because of differences in emphasis between sections of UNITE. The TGWU side may see more "organizing" American unions such as SEIU as more natural partners and may prioritize a revitalization of domestic strength over and above any extension of international activity. Thus there is a tension between revitalized local strength as an end to which international action is subordinate and the latter as an end in itself. This point will be returned to momentarily.

The purpose of pursuing more direct bilateral links outside of supranational institutions is to obtain a stronger grip on multinational companies themselves, thus enabling a mobilizing form of internationalism to emerge as a direct counterweight to global capital. One example from pre-UNITE AMICUS's recent history is the case of a two-year campaign for an international agreement with the Canadian company Quebecor, based around the core International Labor Organization conventions, which culminated in 2005. AMICUS pursued the company by trying to ignite organizing campaigns in four US sites, getting organizers to target workplaces in Latin America, as well as asking sites over the world to take short protest actions in sympathy. Finally, given the company's work for the Swedish firm Ikea, they asked Swedish colleagues to target the latter with information about abuses of labor rights at the company. This was the point at which Quebecor agreed to meet. Thus, while ideas such as directly coordinated industrial action remain a distant prospect, there appears to be some experience of coordinated global expressions of sympathy that UNITE hopes to build upon and that reflects the multidimensional campaigning model advocated by writers such as Jura-vich (2007) and Herod (2002).

While the integration of the AMICUS and TGWU sides remains an ongo-ing and politically sensitive process, both have sought to establish interna-tionalism as an integral part of union education. Both sides have run seminars on globalization targeting regional or sectoral steward committees, some-times extending to workshops specifically for groups of lay representatives within particular companies. Generally, the purpose of international educa-tion seminars is to encourage activists to better understand and become in-volved in the work UNITE does internationally, as an introduction to the concept of "globalization" and the questions it raises. This awareness raising initially takes a broad political form; for example, asking participants to brainstorm ideas associated with "globalization" and seeking to bring out particular issues and discussions—for example, the dangers and opportu-nities presented by labor migration and the emergence of China as an eco-nomic power. In addition, seminars sought to make workers aware of particu-lar solidarity campaigns it supports and to introduce its GUF affiliations.

Sometimes courses will also invite educators from GUFs, as well as bringing over trade unionists or NGO activists from the developing world, as part of raising the profile of "globalization" among UNITE members. In this sense the idea of mobilizing membership internationally does not proceed further than, as the interviewee says, trying to encourage attendees to "take ownership of that [international] agenda" (interview, 31 March 2010). Given the diversity of its membership, however, UNITE also has large numbers of members in multinational companies who may be covered by mechanisms such as European Works Councils (EWCs). There is generally a substantial gap between the workings of these institutions and the shop-floor level, in part because of the way in which collaborative international contacts tend to form naturally among international officials first and foremost, with no guar-antee of penetrating outside of these networks. Therefore, one more concrete measure that can engage members more directly with international activity is to seek to narrow this gap. Raising awareness of international political eco-nomic issues more generally can be a key preliminary part of this. But in addition, educators may also seek to emphasize the idea that the fates of workers in different countries are closely connected, thus trying to upgrade the basic solidarity that may exist *within* workplaces to solidarity *between* workplaces in different countries. Simply revealing the existence of institu-tions such as the GUFs can be a breakthrough in this sense, given that even local stewards who have been in their role for several decades are often entirely unaware of them.

Some of UNITE's education work has sought to go deeper, however, into stimulating a more radical grassroots-led internationalism. In one case, an educator had sought to encourage attendees at courses to form international networks within multinational companies in the same way that stewards' combines can be formed on a local or national level. The objective was quite explicitly to create more autonomous links between local activists on a global scale. Attendees (courses were typically attended by twenty to twenty-five people, generally stewards from within specific sectors or specific companies) were asked to draw up a global organizing strategy. While in most cases such networks were not developed, the educator argues that some participants went on to set up international committees and e-mail networks, enabling them to find out information that would otherwise have been completely unavailable to them.

Thus, while the courses introduce the GUFs to members, they may also try to encourage them to view these institutions critically and to demand a more active role within them as activists rather than leaving them to be channeled through official functionaries. A particular success one educator identified was a case involving a steward at a large multinational logistics company, whom he described as having developed a network of contacts to share information internationally as a means of rebutting management demands.

The optimism here must be qualified against the practical experiences of the particular steward mentioned above. The steward had undoubtedly been inspired by the education courses run in UNITE, stating that while he had previously sought to be involved in international issues, this had been in a broader political sense through membership of campaigns such as Justice for Colombia (comparable to the UNISON BIO discussed above). The education courses gave him a concrete impetus and vision of how internationalism could be approached on an industrial level as a mechanism of trade union interest representation. However, in practice he had pursued a slightly different course of action than that outlined by the educator above. A national, rather than international, combine for workers at a multinational logistics firm was formed at one of the courses; primarily an attempt to revive organizing traditions that had petered out in recent decades. The objective was to channel wider national support into specific disputes across the full range of sectors in which the company operated. It was clear that the steward saw the international dimension as an *extension* of this reinvigoration of national collective organizing, rather than a complementary process, and still less a prerequisite for it. Interviews with a leading international official and a key educator, by contrast, emphasized the importance of international expansion without viewing the rebuilding of domestic organization as a necessary first step; in fact, they argue that the reverse can be true, as international links can help to better leverage local sites.

For the steward in question, national revitalization remains challenge enough. Support for the combine remains limited to an ad hoc basis among the wider membership—"a leviathan that moves along at a snail's pace"

(interview, 22 May 2010)—which across the country remains generally atomized and apathetic. For the steward, therefore, "solidarity" needed resur-
recting as a local political project within unions before anything else could be
achieved on top of this. This is where the trade union as an international actor
fails in the face of local weakness and atomization. For the steward, apathy
can only be countered through the process of successfully pursuing material
conflicts: "[T]he one thing that members need to see being done is actually
getting results. Whether it's a knockback or whatever, they need to see you
having that fight" (interview, 22 May 2010).

The combine can therefore seek to involve themselves in small disputes,
bringing them together and associating them with each other, cementing the
relevance of the combine through a cumulative process of small battles rather
than large unwinnable ones. In this way external institutions such as GUFs
could potentially be used on an ad hoc basis as a resource, as ambitions
develop. This strategy had had limited success, for example, when the International Transport Workers' Federation's communication networks were
used to channel worldwide public support for a local dispute at a warehouse
in Northern England. Internationalism's success in the future, then, depends
on key local organizers successfully linking local disputes to mechanisms
such as GUFs. Thus, whereas at UNISON, a "global justice" unionism co-
alesces around key activists and officers in a relatively stable way, here a
more utilitarian internationalism develops disjointedly, depending on its value as a resource in local disputes.

What does the above tell us about internationalism and global justice at
UNITE? The first point is the key role of ideologically committed union
leaders in furthering internationalism. For the educator whose courses the
steward had attended, it had been a long-term objective to try to construct
these types of networks, and it was only upon arriving at UNITE that he had
sufficient resources to pursue this objective through education. The extent to
which the "message" about globalization is retained and can be built on, he
argues, depends on a number of things. Firstly, particular political-economic
developments raise the profile of the international environment. If a British
company is taken over by a MNC (the 2010 takeover of Cadbury by Kraft
was a high-profile news story at the time of the interview), then interest may
rise substantially, but this is, of course, also liable to subside again. A more
durable catalyst for the take-up of the ideas presented in the courses is the
political commitment of key activists, such as the steward discussed above.
Union members have to reach a conclusion themselves about the value of a
global union presence, and then international education can play a role in
facilitating the practical development of that objective. Political ideology
amongst key agitators is therefore a critical factor.

Therefore, internationalism at UNITE is a complex and sometimes
contradictory picture illustrating a tension between ideology and practicality.

Among key union's international officials and educators, a strong internationalist orientation can be discerned, which views international activity as a necessary response to the economic pressures of globalization as well as a normative imperative. They then seek to push this orientation downwards toward membership. This appears similar to the case of UNISON, which has sought to involve its BIOs in international campaigns (see above). The critical difference, however, is as follows: where for UNISON this process is a consequence of normative concerns and self-volunteering among key activists, for UNITE this is a part of getting to grips with a material environment in which companies have "gone through the roof" in terms of their command over space. Internationalism is not an external issue that requires a dedicated international office removed from the day-to-day concerns of membership, but something that, ultimately, is seen as being of direct material relevance to workplace life and that is hoped to become a part of activists' mobilizing repertoire. In consequence, as the UNITE steward's experience illustrates, internationalism can only develop on a constrained, ad hoc basis as a tool in particular conflicts. From the workplace activists' point of view, it is ultimately a subservient means to local strength that must continually prove its utility rather than a superordinate end in itself. Internationalism, if it progresses, will therefore develop disjointedly depending on the ability of key leaders and engaged stewards to manifest internationalist commitment as a practical asset.

The British Textile Industry

The tension outlined in the preceding sections is one with wider resonance.[3] For example, it might also be recognized in the historical decline of the British textiles industry, which can only be recounted fleetingly here. Here, a particular trajectory can be observed whereby explicitly anti-internationalist discourses initially emerged as a lever for grassroots, community-wide mobilization, which evolved into a more elite-led internationalism once it became apparent that preservation of British textile jobs was a lost cause. When global competition in the garment sector started to intensify in the 1970s, KFAT, the British textile workers' union, initially sought to pursue a protectionist "Buy British" strategy. As one former official describes it, the implicit attitude was one of "them that are pinching our jobs across the water versus us" (interview, 5 March 2010). This protectionist agenda was pursued, however, through a strongly mobilization-oriented approach, organizing mass marches down British high streets in which not just members but local communities were heavily involved.

A striking change occurred, however, when it became apparent that preserving British jobs was a lost cause. The tension separating local job retention and global interests was relaxed (albeit as a consequence of defeat rather than success). In response, the strategy of KFAT's leadership shifted substantially, moving toward heavier cooperation with the International Textile, Garment and Leather Workers' Federation (ITGLWF). The objective was to ensure that, even if British jobs were to be lost, British trade unionists were at least able to impose minimum standards on conditions internationally. A corollary of this process is that the strong mobilization of memberships and local communities that characterized the 1970s "Buy British" strategies had been transformed in a fundamental way. Union leaders' sphere of operation was transferred to Brussels, and a strategy of establishing minimum global labor standards has led to heavier involvement of unions in NGO-led consumer campaigns, associated with students and affluent consumers rather than the working-class community mobilizations of previous decades.

While in a very different context, this is an analogous process to the case of the AMICUS call center operatives discussed above, where a protectionist mobilization was eventually replaced by a more normative internationalism once tension over job losses had been defused (again, as a consequence of defeat for the union rather than success). It also mirrors another historical British case, that of the steelworkers, as narrated by Hudson and Sadler (1986). The latter showed, with reference to 1980s closures within the British steel industry, that the locus of contention switched from a class-based challenge to the Thatcher government's apparent anti-union program, to a place-based program of competing against other communities to save their local jobs once it became apparent that some closures were unavoidable. Except here, instead, initial strength led to a broader normative class commitment, and the replacement of that strength by the need for self-preservation saw it fractured into a narrower self-interest.

DISCUSSION AND CONCLUSION

A number of points can be drawn from the preceding. Most critically, there is clearly an important distinction to be drawn between internationalism as a normative project and as a means of material interest representation. In this sense, unions' capacity to fulfill the role of global justice actors reflects underlying material circumstances. If union members are directly caught up in multinational economic structures, workers abroad may be a source of solidarity, but they may also represent competition for jobs. In such cases, the subject of internationalism may be fraught with tension. If union figures—leaders or key activists with commitments to broadening solidarity— wish to strengthen international activity, it is necessary to do so by using international resources as a means of supporting local material disputes. While for these leaders, internationalism may be an end, to others involved in the dispute it may be a means to local preservation. Thus, "global justice" remains subservient to local priorities.

Where the global economy is not as directly linked to international economic structures, for example in the public sector or where labor market strength remains high (Umney 2012), internationalism is a less obviously conflicted issue. It may, certainly, be one of only limited interest to members. But this lack of interest among those for whom trade union involvement is a source of protection at work, without any higher normative importance, creates the space for politically engaged activists and officials to develop wider-ranging programs at a relatively elite level that are more compatible with the global justice model. It is in such situations that collaborations with other social actors such as NGOs are likely to be more common and durable.

In both cases, internationalism is to some extent driven "from above." The difference is that in the example of the UNITE educator and steward, there were stronger efforts to stimulate international networks among members. This partly reflects the commitment of the figures involved to grassroots models of trade unionism. But it is likely that such a model will only be possible if it is driven forward by the concrete need to defend material conditions, and if international levers can be successfully drawn into specific local conflicts. Thus, the role of unions as global justice actors progresses along two very different dimensions. A normative pursuit of international solidarity norms exists among key leaders and engaged activists, remaining relatively removed from the day-to-day business of union interest representation. An international union "movement," however, in which unions use global solidarity to counterbalance multinational employers, develops much more disjointedly. "Global justice" among unions was initially described at the start of the chapter as "ambiguous," but they might now be better termed "ambivalent"; torn between interest representation at the workplace level and more abstract normative projects.

NOTES

1. Unless otherwise stated, all information on UNISON is drawn from an interview with an international official (30 March 2010) and an interview with an international committee member (16 April 2010).

2. Information on UNITE is drawn from an interview with an international official (12 June 2010); an interview with a UNITE educator (31 March 2010); an interview with a senior steward (22 May 2010); a follow-up interview with a senior steward (22 May 2010); electronic education material provided by a UNITE educator.

3. Unless otherwise stated, information in this section is drawn from an interview with two ITGLWF officials (6 May 2010; 22 March 2010); an interview with an Ethical Trade Initiative coordinator (19 January 2010); an interview with a former KFAT and ITGLWF official (5 March 2010); an interview with a Clean Clothes Campaign organizer (14 December 2009).

BIBLIOGRAPHY

Aglietta, Michel. 1979. *A Theory of Capitalist Regulation.* London: Verso.
Arrighi, G., and B. Silver. 2000. "Workers North and South." In *Working Classes, Global Realities: Socialist Register 2001*, eds. L. Panitch and C. Leys. London: Merlin Press.
Collinge, C. 1999. "Self-Organization of Society by Scale: A Spatial Reworking of Regulation Theory." *Environment and Planning D: Society and Space* 17, no. 5: 557–574.
Cowling, K., and Tomlinson, P. 2005. "Globalization and Corporate Power." *Contributions to Political Economy* 24, no. 1: 33–54.
Croucher, R., and E. Cotton. 2009. *Global Unions, Global Business: Global Union Federations and International Business.* London: Middlesex University Press.
Greer, I., and M. Hauptmeier. 2008. "Political Entrepreneurs and Co-Managers: Labor Transnationalism at Four Multinational Auto Companies." *British Journal of Industrial Relations* 46, no. 1: 76–97.
Hancké, B. 2000. "European Works Councils and Industrial Restructuring in the European Motor Industry." *European Journal of Industrial Relations* 6, no. 1: 35–59.
Harvey, D. 2005. *A Brief History of Neoliberalism.* Oxford: Oxford University Press.
Herod, A. 2002. "Organizing Globally, Organizing Locally: Union Spatial Strategy in a Global Political Economy." In *Global Unions? Theory and Strategies of Organized Labor in the Global Political Economy*, ed. J. Harrod and R. O'Brien. London: Routledge.
Howell, C. 2005. *Trade Unions and the State: The Construction of Industrial Relations Institutions in Britain, 1890–2000.* Princeton: Princeton University Press.
Hudson, R., and D. Sadler. 1986. "Contesting Works Closures in Western Europe's Industrial Regions: Defending Place or Betraying Class?" In *Production, Work, Territory*, eds. A. Scott and M. Storper. Winchester, MA: Allen and Unwin.
Hyman, R. 1979. "The Politics of Workplace Trade Unionism: Recent Tendencies and Some Problems for Theory." *Capital and Class* 3, no. 2: 54–67.
———. 2005. "Shifting Dynamics in International Trade Unionism: Agitation, Organization, Bureacracy, Diplomacy." *Labor History* 46, no. 2: 137–154.
Jessop, B. 1997. "Capitalism and Its Future: Remarks on Regulation, Government and Governance." *Review of International Political Economy* 4, no. 3: 561–581.
Johns, R. 1998. "Bridging the Gap between Class and Space: US Worker Solidarity with Guatemala." *Economic Geography* 74, no. 3: 252–272.
Juravich, T. 2007. "Beating Global Capital: A Framework and Method for Union Strategic Corporate Research and Campaigns." In *Global Unions: Challenging Transnational Capital through Cross-Border Campaigns*, ed. K. Bronfenbrenner. New York: Cornell University Press.
Kelly, J., and E. Heery. 1994. *Working for the Union: British Trade Union Officers.* Cambridge, MA: Cambridge University Press.
Lipietz, A. 1986. "Behind the Crisis: The Exhaustion of a Regime of Accumulation. A 'Regulation School' Perspective on Some French Empirical Works." *Review of Radical Political Economics* 18, no. 1–2: 13–32.
Mandel, E. 1978. *Late Capitalism.* London: Verso.
Meardi, G. 2007. "Restructuring in an Enlarged Europe: Challenges and Experiences." *Transfer: European Review of Labor and Research* 13, no. 2: 253–266.
Moody, K. 1997. "Towards an International Social Movement Unionism." *New Left Review* 225: 52–75.
Riisgard, L. 2005. "International Framework Agreements: A New Model for Securing Workers Rights?" *Industrial Relations: A Journal of Economy and Society* 44, no. 4: 707–773.
Silver, B. 2003. *Forces of Labor.* Cambridge, MA: Cambridge University Press.
Streeck, W. 1998. "The Internationalization of Industrial Relations in Europe: Prospects and Problems." *Politics and Society* 26: 429–459.
Thompson, E. 1963. *The Making of the English Working Class.* London: The Camelot Press.
Turner, L. 1996. "The Europeanization of Labor: Structure before Action." *European Journal of Industrial Relations* 2, no. 3: 325–344.

Umney, C. 2012. "Managerial and Mobilizing Internationalism in the British Docks and Sea-faring Sector." *European Journal of Industrial Relations* 18, no. 1: 71–87.

UNISON and ACTSA. 2009. *Working Together to Defend and Strengthen Public Services: UNISON-ACTSA Southern Africa Delegation, 2009.* London: UNISON.

Visser, J. 2000. "From Keynesianism to the Third Way: Labor Relations and Social Policy in Postwar Western Europe." *Economic and Industrial Democracy* 21, no. 4: 421–456.

Wade, R. 2009. "Accountability Gone Wrong: The World Bank, Non-Governmental Organizations and the US Government in a Fight over China." *New Political Economy* 14, no. 1: 25–48.

Waterman, P. 2001. "Trade Union Internationalism in the Age of Seattle." *Antipode* 33, no. 3: 312–336.

Watson, D. 1988. *Managers of Discontent: Trade Union Officers and Industrial Relations Managers.* London: Routledge.

Wills, J. 2002. "Bargaining for the Space to Organize in the Global Economy: A Review of the Accor-IUF Trade Union Rights Agreement." *Review of International Political Economy* 9, no. 4: 675–700.

Zeitlin, J. 1989. "'Rank and Filism' in British Labor History: A Critique." *International Review of Social History* 34, no. 1: 42–61.

Chapter Eleven

Strike, Protest, Occupy, and Vote

Austerity Politics and Resistance to Neoliberal Social Engineering in Greece

Lefteris Kretsos

Since 2010 Greece has become an international point of reference and analysis due to its unfortunate pioneering role in the course of the ongoing economic crisis. The financial support to Greece (and gradually other EU member states) from the Troika[1] has been conditional on reductions in public deficits and public spending, initiating drastic labor market reform and a welfare state retrenchment unprecedented in the postwar period (Hall 2011). Not surprisingly, sweeping austerity measures have resulted in the upsurge of a serious humanitarian crisis in the streets of Athens and other urban areas. The therapy proved more dangerous than the disease, and most working people in Greece have seen their lives turned upside down in the matter of a few months. Homeless people were increased by more than twenty thousand; over 50% of young people and 25% of the workforce are unemployed according to the latest (October 2012) statistical data; at least sixty thousand small companies closed; thousands of workers are going unpaid for long periods of time; and suicides for economic reasons have taken place (Kretsos 2012; Matsa 2012). The pain caused by austerity packages is fast moving and approaching an economic abyss similar to that faced by the people of Argentina in 2001. The tough situation of ordinary workers, households, and communities has affected in turn trade union and social movement strategies. Community organizing, working with local assemblies and coalition building strategies with broader social groups and networks of activists are not anymore the abandoned children of union organization. Nevertheless, the resistance to ongoing neoliberal social engineering in Greece is half finished, unpredictable, and diffuse even if forced deregulation and structural reforms have their limits and risks. Sweeping austerity policies are still winning, but the rise of alternative unionism in the big urban areas and the leading of the political race by the Syriza (according to the latest polls)[2] are sunny images for more permanent radical political change in the near future.

The current chapter aims to provide new insights on the discussion on the Greek crisis highlighting the visible and nonvisible political dimensions of resistance to austerity politics. The chapter is organized as follows. The first section analyzes the conditions and the causal mechanisms of the Greek crisis and their associated perceptions in the public discourse. The second part discusses the impact of austerity policies on living and working conditions in Greece. The final section discusses the potential of restoring corporate power and smashing neoliberalism in Greece and consequently in other parts of Europe by the massive mobilization of working people and the articulation of different collective interests and new solidarities under the frame of social justice and democracy.

THE MISLEADING CLICHÉ OF THE OVERPROTECTED GREEK WORKER

An adequate assessment of the causes and consequences of the crisis is above all an issue with serious ideological dimensions. In the case of Greece the debate on what leads to and sustains economic crisis is heavily polarized and politicized. In general, two main explanations are observed, the radical and the conventional mainstream approach. The radical perspective examines the emergence of the Greek crisis as the result of structural weaknesses in the European monetary union project and the seismic failures and problems pla-guing modern capitalism across different national contexts. Such weaknesses are foundered on the rocks of the global financial crisis and the new stage of modern geopolitical antagonisms. National historical accounts and traits to economic development are necessary for exploring the reasons of the Greek crisis. But something bigger is at stake in the case of Greece. As it is stated in a recent ILO report (2011, 57), "[T]he crisis in Greece is not an exclusively Greek problem but a Greek manifestation of a global problem." For Zizek (2012), Greece represents one of the most critical laboratories of a new socioeconomic model with a global application: a nonpoliticized technocracy under the hegemony of financial institutions and elites that kill democracy. The new model of economic governance that promotes further the neoliberal project in Europe is based on three pillars:

1. the creation of specific economic support mechanisms at the European Union (EU) level (which is basically a permanent bank recapitalization mechanism);
2. the Fiscal Compact Treaty (which is basically a permanent austerity mechanism); and
3. the imposition of austerity measures has been associated with a clear-cut transfer of policymaking process from national to international actors.

Such mechanisms have gradually transferred the cost of the global financial instability caused by speculative financial institutions to the national governments, the same exact way it happened in United States with the Lehman Brothers collapse in 2008. According to this view, imposing austerity and saving greedy bankers who pawned off credit default swaps is necessary, while labor standards are subject to decline by a comprehensive system of economic and social policy driven by tough and ruthless austerity packages and privatizations. Greece was the first country in the old European Union (EU-15) that had to go through this painful trip to austerity and neoliberal social engineering.[3]

The conventional explanation of the crisis in turn puts the blame on Greek people. It analyses the crisis through the prism of long delays in modernizing the economy, widespread symptoms of tax evasion, and the low administrative capacity for policy implementation due to particular institutional and cultural deficiencies (the so-called Mediterranean syndrome). According to these narratives there is no big surprise for what is happening in Greece; "the country" (the whole country) has been irresponsible and is now paying the price for its "bloated public sector" and "culture of cutting corners." The mainstream idea of "Greek Exceptionalism" is based on various assumptions:

- Radical labor market reforms are necessary and urgent.
- Greek workers are overprotected.
- Strict employment protection legislation inhibits economic growth and undermines economic competitiveness.
- The "Mediterranean syndrome" (a low administrative capacity for policy implementation/negative attitudes and resistance towards structural reforms in the economy).
- It was a mistake to allow Greece to enter the Eurozone.
- The tax system is dysfunctional (Kretsos 2012).

In this framework it is not surprising that the dominant propagandists of laissez-faire approaches (IMF, OECD, World Bank) have systematically provided recommendations to the Greek governments during the last decade to promote the labor market reforms and regulatory changes that have gradually taken place in Greece and other Eurozone member states since 2010 (Koukiadaki and Kretsos 2011; Kretsos 2011a). Typical examples included proposals for adjustment in real wages in line to productivity outcomes; the promotion of flexible forms of work by changing legislation relating to temporary employment; the reduction of severance payments especially for white-collar workers; the abolition of the implicit permanent job status for the vast majority of public servants; and the provision of greater room for collective bargaining decentralization (Κουζής 2008). Within this approach, the employment protection in Greece has been considered a major obstacle to structural change and the liberalization of domestic markets.

According to studies prior to the upsurge of the economic crisis in 2010, Greece had one of the strictest employment protection legislation (EPL) amongst the OECD countries (Ochel and Rohwer 2009; Ioannou 2009). Nevertheless, beyond functionalist typologies and dichotomies between regulation versus deregulation there is a range of processes, spaces, and actors that interact both formally and informally in the institutionalization and standardization of the rules and conditions of the way labor markets operate. As Dedousopoulos (cited in Koukiadaki and Kretsos 2011) argues, if we dismiss the simplistic and misleading vision of a "natural" labor market, we come closer to a conception of the labor market as a social organization in which various types of trade-offs are established and function: trade-offs among forms of flexibility and among forms of job security as well as those established between flexibility and security. As such, a good understanding of regulatory change demands a broader conceptualization and definition of the notion of regulation and a stricter reference to the political and social context peculiarities (MacKenzie and Martinez Lucio 2005).

Nevertheless, cultural critiques and the "we are all part in this" argument[4] are inappropriate to explain the basic causes of the weaknesses of the Greek economy and the emergence of the current crisis in 2010, as they hide a basic truth: Greece has implemented key aspects of the neoliberal economic project since the mid-1990s, and the Greek labor market was not so rigid and heavily regulated as it was claimed by the domestic and international supporters of structural reforms. Further, labor market flexibility was a central point of reference of the policy agenda of all governments from the 1990s onward (Kouzis 2009; Tsakalotos 2010). Industrial relations in Greece before the crisis were highly structured and collectivized, but they were not always formal, with more and more workers not being protected by a collective bargaining system and labor legislation (Κουζής 2009; Kretsos 2004).

The emergence of a precarious workforce, composed mainly of young, female, and migrant workers, is a development observed in Greece long before the crisis.[5] The massive flows of undeclared migrant workers in the Greek labor market since the early 1990s provided a large pool of a reserve army for many employers, especially in the sectors that precarious employ-ment is usually popular (construction, agriculture, and the tourism industry). This condition should be linked to a further reflection of the relative impor-tance of undeclared work in Greece, as temporary and part-time employment was relatively less important in comparison to the OECD average.

The examination of precarious work in Greece has to be made into this analytical framework. Nevertheless, the situation has dramatically changed after the upsurge of the economic crisis in 2010. In the last two years more standard workers face significant challenges due to both ongoing austerity policies and radical labor market reforms. Such policies and reforms have increased the notion of job insecurity among the working population, as they have resulted in a dramatic increase in unemployment rates (almost 22%) and the expansion of nonstandard and atypical employment arrangements even in the public sector that was considered as a protective shelter of employment. Due to the fact that many third-country migrants in Greece are not declared, it is difficult to estimate their overrepresentation in precarious statistical employment figures. In contrast to this limitation, table 2 indicates the im-pact of the economic crisis in employment and the unemployment by age

Table 11.1. Key Employment Statistics Prior to the Crisis: Greece and OECD Countries.

	1999	2008	2009	OECD Total 2009
Temporary employment (% of dependent employment)	12.9	11.5	12.1	11.6
Part-time employment (% of total employment)	8.0	7.9	8.4	16.2
Average annual working time	2.107	2.116	2.119	1.739
Unemployment rate (% of labor force)	12	7.8	9.6	8.3
Youth unemployment rate (% of youth labor force)	31.7	22.1	25.8	16.4
Long-term unemployment rate (% of total unemployment)	55.3	47.5	40.8	23.6
Employment rate (% of working-age population)	55.4	61.9	61.2	64.8

Source: Data from ILO (2010)

group and between sexes. The impact of the financial crisis is dramatic in terms of job losses, especially among younger male workers.

Finally, it should be stated that labor market regulation did not affect economic growth in the last decades. Greece had one of the highest rates of economic growth across the EU between 1994 and 2008, a condition that is at odds with the parallel dramatic rise of public debt and deficit over the years. During 1994–2008 there had been a return of profits to levels approaching those of the early 1970s, while the share accruing to wages was continually contracting since 1996.[6] Further, between 1995 and 2009, the rate of labor cost per unit increased by 1%, while the level of competitiveness of the economy was reduced by 26.8% (INE/GSEE-ADEDY 2010). In addition, the tax burden to working and retired people before the upsurge of the crisis was more or less the same as the average for the EU-25 area (35.1% in 2007 and 36.4% in 2006, respectively), while the tax burden for corporate profits in Greece was almost half (15.9%) that of the EU-25 (33.0%) (Kretsos 2010). Such labor law regulation was not as influential in provoking the current twin problem of high public debt and deficit as other reasons, such as the inability of the state to increase public revenues, political and economic corruption, or the false bolstering of consumption and domestic growth through loans.

Such inequalities associated with a tradition of an inadequate welfare state and low social transfers (Karamessini 2008; Guillén and Matsaganis 2000) became more evident with the outbreak of the crisis. As a result the

Table 11.2. Changes in Labor Force Per Gender and Age Groups during 2008–2010.

	Labor force	Employed	Unemployed
Both genders	81.754	-155.135	236.889
15–29 years of age	-44.789	-108.437	63.648
30 years of age and over	126.543	-46.698	173.241
Men	-7.630	-143.954	136.324
15–29 years of age	-39.178	-74.329	35.151
30 years of age and over	31.548	-69.625	101.173
Women	89.384	-11.181	100.565
15–29 years of age	-5.611	-34.108	28.497
30 years of age and over	94.995	22.927	72.068

Source: Data from ELSTAT (Hellenic Statistical Authority), LFS (Labor Force Survey)

prospects for conflict-based alternative political and trade union formations became greater, including a restoration, or attempted restoration, of more radical social resistance to imposed austerity measures. The meteoric rise of the radical coalition party (Syriza) in the latest elections of May–June 2012 is indicative of this trend.

NEW MODEL OF ECONOMIC DOMINATION

The definition of precarious workforce has changed since the upsurge of the economic crisis in 2010. Young, female, and migrant workers are not the only workforce groups that are employed under precarious working arrangements. Other social groups, such as suspended public sector workers, joined the ranks of the army of precarious workers. Horizontal pay cuts in the public sector and thousands of workers in the private sector who were made redundant have dramatically expanded the precariat in Greece. The introduction of flexible work rotation schemes and the delayed payment practices in many companies in the private sector has become the norm for many companies in the private sector.

Further, through recruitment freezes and other measures, over 150,000 jobs will be cut by 2015 from 727,000 to 577,000. In addition to the pay cuts of 2010, other tough measures that haven been implemented include the increase in the weekly working hours for public sector employees from 37.5 to 40 hours, the reduction in overtime payments, the relaxation of the dismissal rules, the reduction of compensation payments, as well as the decentralization of collective bargaining and the ability of employers to impose lower wages and more flexible rules in work organization at the company level for reasons of economic difficulty. At the same time the Mediation and Arbitration Organization has lost its eminent power to act on cases of industrial dispute providing more flexibility to employers and undermining the right to strike by trade unions. Further measures in turn have downgraded the safety net young workers used to enjoy in the labor market. For example, the probation period was increased from two months to one year, and student work placement schemes were increased for young workers up to twenty-four years old.

Relevant studies have indicated the strong dynamics of labor market deregulation in Greece since the 2010 economic crisis and the implemented reforms imposed by Troika (Lampousaki 2011; Ghellab and Papadakis 2011). Nevertheless, for the Troika there is still plenty space for the implementation of greater austerity. To that direction, Act 4046/2012,[7] following the spirit of the 2012 Memorandum of Understanding on Specific Economic Policy Conditionality, the "(Greek) Government will take measures to foster a rapid adjustment of labor costs to fight unemployment and restore cost-competitivess, ensure the effectiveness of recent labor market reforms, align labor conditions in former state-owned enterprises to those in the rest of the private sector and make working hours more flexible."[8] Radical adjustment of the wage floors and far-reaching structural reforms (e.g., fast-track privatizations, dramatic welfare cuts, realignment and freeze of minimum wages) also constitute commitments undertaken by the Greek government for the disbursement of the second loan.

Such developments happen against a backdrop of labor costs and raising concerns over the health conditions of the population. For example, the recent study by Kentikelenis et al. (2011) indicated the tough situation many people face in Greece. According to the study findings, there was a dramatic increase in suicides by 17% to 25%, a significant increase in HIV diseases (with incidences of deliberate self-infection by individuals to obtain access to benefits and to get a faster admission onto drug substitution programs), and a dramatic rise in the proportion of the population seeking medical attention from their street clinics (from 3–4% before the crisis to about 30% in August 2011).

SHINES OF RESISTANCE UPRISING

The 2008 global financial meltdown and its repercussions on several indebted states and especially Greece have been used to promote the neoliberal project in Europe. The size and the characteristics of the Greek debt has been used by mainstream media as the new basis of labor market segmentation and the removal of basic workers' rights that constitute part of the national and European legal order. The governance of the Greek crisis provides an example of violating basic assumptions and functions of labor law in Europe, as established by the 1944 Declaration of Philadelphia and expressed historically by the gradual extension of the welfare state in the postwar period in Europe. Further, the sweeping austerity measures are not only unfair, but also ineffective. The national debt continued to follow upward trends since 2009 (from 115% of GDP in 2009 to 170% in October 2012). The Greek economy is still heavily trapped in a deep recession, and the austerity measures taken have failed to bring the country back to economic and social stability.

All-embracing and severe austerity packages and labor market deregulation initiatives have opened the window for widespread social unrest and political change. The tough situation that many workers, households, and communities have faced since 2010 has affected trade union and social movement strategies. The recipe for resistance in Greece is based on a complete course of anti-austerity action: strike, protest, occupy, and vote. Since 2010, twenty-two general strikes have taken place while numerous strikes and protests were organized at the company and sectoral level. Many strikes were accompanied by huge rallies across the country organized by trade unions.

Strikes and demonstrations were followed with the uprising of the Greek indignados movement in 2011 and a new grassroots social movement called "Δεν πληρώνω" (Don't Pay). Occupy and social disobedience movements organized huge demonstrations and numerous direct actions against the privatization of public services, the reduction of ticket prices in the public means of transport and the abolition of tariffs in the private-owned control checks on the national highways. Angry clashes between protesters and riot police and incidences of police brutality became endemic.

The characteristics and the influence of those movements in the battle against austerity in Greece demand special attention. First, Occupy and social disobedience movements received widespread support by broader groups of the Greek population. Second, such articulation and unity of collective interests among different groups of workers (male and female, young and old, public and private workers, etc.) gave rise to a higher level of consciousness and awareness about the reasons of the crisis. This development was reflected by the creation of a plethora of social network groups against austerity and Troika, the assembly-based democracy established in Syntagma Square between May and June 2011 and numerous expressions of social solidarity and radical grassroots-based actions. Third, strikes and protests became not only more passionate and frequent, but for the first time they were driven by a new actor of industrial relations in the post-IMF Greece: strong networks of rank-and-file activists and self-organized communities. Self-governed hospitals (General Hospital of Kilkis), occupied factories (Xalivourgiki), booming networks of part alternative currency/part barter system markets, local communities on the barricade (Keratea), and mass blockades of ministries and companies' headquarters left in their wakes a litany of promising woes for change. The decline of social democratic unionism in contrast to a stronger grassroots trade union movement with high mobilization and organizing capacities is another sign of the collapse of the old political order in Greece.

In this context the meteoric rise of the radical left coalition party (Syriza) in the two general elections of May–June 2012 (from 5.6% to 27%) was the final cut on austerity policies, as Syriza can be considered as the main agent of opposition to austerity in Greece and Europe. The radical left coalition is extremely popular to most frustrated and dynamic groups of the population (urban and working-class areas, young people, precarious workers) due to its anti-austerity agenda and its strong presence in street politics and grassroots community action. Syriza is now focusing on how to turn the electoral support for Syriza into a source of self-organized social power for change, as well as to build on it as the electoral path to government, leading at the same time the frontline of a struggle for a democratic Europe.[9]

EPILOGUE

The 2008 global financial meltdown and its repercussions on several in-debted states and especially Greece have been used to promote the neoliberal project in Europe. The size and the characteristics of the Greek debt has been used by mainstream media as the new basis of labor market segmentation and the removal of basic workers' rights that constitute part of the national and European legal order. The EU and IMF agreed on the imposition of neoliberal and socially unfair policies, and this is not a Greek phenomenon. Historically speaking, national debts have been used to serve the purpose of promoting the most offensive capitalist interests across the globe. The idea that there is no alternative to resolve the debt crisis is not just a myth, but also the ultimate foundation of the political and economic elites' hegemony over working people.

Not surprisingly, the crisis in Greece is presented by mainstream media as something peculiar—a case of "Greek Exceptionalism." For the labor move-ment, however, it is a manifestation of the structural weaknesses in the Euro-pean monetary union project, now exposed by the global financial crisis and renewed European tensions. As seen in the case of Greece, austerity policies bring about greater social injustice. The crisis acted as a catalyst for the implementation of neoliberal policies that promoted a serious humanitarian and political crisis across the country. The imposed austerity policies have made the future of Greek (and gradually European) economy and society totally dependent on international lenders, as the main outcomes of such policies were drastic welfare-state retrenchment, income and class polariza-tion, and increased poverty levels.

Nevertheless, forced deregulation and austerity have their limits and risks. People and communities frustrated by such policies have expanded social unrest and public anger at the mainstream political institutions. Since 2010 there have been twenty-two general strikes, numerous strikes and occupa-tions of government buildings, and the emergence of the "Don't Pay" move-ment. Further, more than forty-five new unions have been established in the last three years in urban areas of Greece, mostly based on young, immigrant, and leftist leadership. The crisis has allowed the growth of "real democracy" in the form of grassroots activism and leadership. The new unionist move-ment is also strongly based around social media and networking. Radical unionism and "street politics" can exert strong pressures on the existing bureaucratic trade union structures and reform social democratic unionism. Finally, Syriza, an amalgam of different political factions, and quickly be-come popular with dynamic groups within the population, such as urban groups, young people and precarious workers, and has become the main force for opposition to austerity.

To summarize, the numerous general strikes and protests that have taken place since 2010, the impressive actions of the Greek Indignados Occupy Movement in 2011 and the impressive rise of Syriza (radical left party) in the two general elections of May–June 2012 are simply parts of an almost complete puzzle of resistance to neoliberalism that sooner or later will bring about radical political and institutional changes. Optimism may be in short supply across the country, but so are anxiety and anger. You cannot really tell which spark will start a fire and when, as government and Troika still continue to tighten the screws and the anti-austerity movement is there to fight.

NOTES

1. Troika is the acronym for the European Commission (EC) on behalf of the European Union, the European Central Bank (ECB) and the International Monetary Fund (IMF).

2. See www.iskra.gr/index.php?option=com_content&view=article& id=9258:dimoskopisi-vprc-prwto-syriza&catid=82:kommata&Itemid=199 (accessed 8 September 2012) and tvxs.gr/news/ellada/pagionetai-dimoskopika-i-protia-syriza (accessed 20 October 2012).

3. In 2009, public debt in Greece stood at 127.1% of GDP while the average EU rate was 79.3% and the announced deficit stood at 12.9% of GDP. It was later revised upward to 15.4%, while the EU average stood at 6.3%. Following the lowering of the credit ratings and the subsequent rapid increase of credit default swaps (CDS), Greece was priced out of the international bond markets. As a consequence, a loan was advanced jointly by Eurozone states and the IMF and given to Greece in May 2010 in order to avoid a potential bankruptcy event that would result in the immediate collapse of the global financial markets. The loan stipulated the provision of eighty billion euros on the part of the Eurozone states and thirty billion euros on the part of the IMF. In exchange for the support mechanism, it was agreed that the EC, the ECB, and the IMF (generally known as "Troika") would prepare and oversee a program of austerity coupled with the liberalization of the Greek economy, aiming to bring the deficit to 3% of GDP within three years.

4. The vice president of the Greek government stated emphatically in the parliament in 2010 and at the outbreak of the crisis that both society and politicians are responsible to the same extent for the country's economic failure ("[W]e were all part of it"). According to his view this exchange of gifts and clientelistic mentality (votes to politicians in exchange of public sector jobs) resulted in the establishment of an unproductive and bureaucratic public administration and powerful trade union elites that blocked the reform capacity of the State and the necessity for sustainable growth regulatory changes.

5. There is no national definition of precarious work, and in most cases scholars refer to precarious workers as nonstandard workers. Nevertheless, prior to the economic crisis, the public debates on the so-called "Precarious Generation" or the "Generation of 700 (and even less in certain cases) Euros" resulted in a general acknowledgment that a growing and significant part of the young workforce is trapped into low paid and insecure jobs (Kretsos 2010). Similar narratives on precarious workers in the media and academic research referred to an unpleasant set of circumstances that many undocumented migrant workers usually face in Greece. The vicious acid attack on the Bulgarian immigrant union leader Konstantina Kounieva and the massive riots by young people that took place on the streets in Athens in December 2008 could be considered as critical events in the conceptualization process of precarious work and its social repercussions in the public debate.

6. See Yiannis Kouzis, "The Neoliberal Restructuring of Labor and the Crisis Alibi" (in Greek) in *The Map of the Crisis, the End of the Illusion*, ed. K. Vergopoulos (Athens: Topos, 2010), 82.

7. FEK A28/14.2.2012. Act 4046/2012 included as Annexes the MEFP, the Memorandum of Understanding on Specific Economic Policy Conditionality and the Technical Memorandum of Understanding. See also Act 6 of 28.2.2012 of the Ministerial Council (FEK A'38/ 28.2.2012) and Guidance by the Ministry of Labor and Social Security (2012) 4601/304.

8. See http://www.tovima.gr/files/1/2012/02/10/mnhmonioagglika.pdf, page 25.

9. See the thorough analysis of Hilary Wainright in http://www.redpepper.org.uk/greece-syriza-shines-a-light/.

BIBLIOGRAPHY

ΓΣΕΕ. 2008. "Trade Unions and Employees: Results from a Quantitative Survey." Συνδικάτα και Εργαζόμενοι: Αποτελέσματα Ποσοτικής Έρευνας. Athens: VPRC.

———. 2010. "The Agreed Action Plan of GSEE in the 34th Conference." Το Πρόγραμμα Δράσης της ΓΣΕΕ στο 34° Συνέδριο, *Ενημέρωση* 171 (April), Athens, INE/ ΓΣΕΕ-ΑΔΕΔΥ.

Carrera, L., M. Angelaki, and D. Carolo. 2011. "Do Cost-Containment Reforms Pay-off? Comparing the Cases of Portugal and Greece." 2011 European Union Studies Association Conference, Boston, March 3–5.

Economides, S., and V. Monastiriotis, eds. 2009. *The Return of Street Politics? Essays on the December Riots in Greece.* London: The Hellenic Observatory, The London School of Economics and Political Science.

Featherstone, K., and D. Papadimitriou. 2008. "The Limits of Europeanization: Reform Capacity and Policy Conflict in Greece." In *Palgrave Studies in European Union Politics*, ed. K. Featherstone. London: Palgrave.

Ghellab, Y., and K. Papadakis. 2011. "The Politics of Economic Adjustment: State Unilateralism or Social Dialogue?" Research Conference on Key Lessons from the Crisis and Way Forward, International Labor Office, Geneva, February 16–17. Accessed on November 14, 2011, from http://www.ilo.org/wcmsp5/groups/public/---ed_dialogue/---dialogue/documents/publication/wcms_172329.pdf.

Guillén, A. and Matsaganis, M. 2000. "Testing the 'Social Dumping' Hypothesis in Southern Europe: Welfare Policies in Greece and Spain during the Last 20 Years." *Journal of European Social Policy* 10 (2) 120–145.

Hall, D. 2011. "Greece: Cuts Watch November 2011." *Cuts Watch Brief.* Public Services International Research Unit, University of Greenwich, 2011. Accessed July 6, 2013, from http://www.psiru.org/cutswatch.

Hobsbawm, Å. 1994. *The Age of Extremes.* New York: Vintage.

International Labor Organization (ILO). 2011. *Report of the Committee of Experts on the Application of Conventions and Recommendations—Report III (Part 1A).* Geneva: ILO.

International Monetary Fund. 2007a. "Greece: 2006, Article IV Consultation—Staff Report." Country Report No. 07/26, January.

———. 2007b. "Global Financial Stability Report: Financial Market Turbulence: Causes, Consequences, and Policies." September.

———. 2008. Greece: Selected Issues May 2008, IMF Country Report No. 08/147, Washington, D.C.

INE/GSEE-ADEDY 2010. "INE Annual Outlook for the Greek Economy and Employment." Athens, INE/ GSEE-ADEDY.

Ioannou, C. A. 2009. "Employment Regulation and Labor Relations in Greece." Hellenic Observatory, LSE, November. Accessed February 21, 2012, from http://www.lse.ac.uk/.

Karamessini, M. 2008. "Still a Distinctive Southern European Employment Model?" *Industrial Relations Journal*, vol. 39, no. 6, pp. 510–531.

Kentikelenis, A., M. Karanikolos, and I. Papanicolas. 2011. "Economic Crisis, Austerity and the Greek Public Health System." *European Journal of Public Health*, 4.

Καψάλης, Α., ed. 2008. *Αδήλωτη Απασχόληση και « μονιμοποίηση » των μεταναστών: Η πρόκληση της μεταναστευτικής πολιτικής* [*Undeclared Work and Legalization Issues of Migrants: The Challenge of Migration Policy*]. Athens, INE/ ΓΣΕΕ-ΑΔΕΔΥ.

Κατσορίδας, Δ. 2008. *Βασικοί Σταθμοί του εργατικού συνδικαλιστικού κινήματος στην Ελλάδα (1870–2001)* [*Stages of Greek Labor Movement (1870–2001)*]. Athens: ΑΡ.ΙΣΤΟ.Σ./ ΓΣΕΕ.

Koukiadaki, A. and Kretsos, L. 2012. "The Case of Greece." In *What Social Law in a Europe in Crisis?* Eds. MC Escande Varniol, S. Laulom and E. Mazuyer. Brussels: Larcier. pp. 189–232.

Κουζής, Γ. 2007. *Τα χαρακτηριστικά του ελληνικού συνδικαλιστικού κινήματος: αποκλίσεις και συγκλίσεις με τον ευρωπαϊκό χώρο* [*The Characteristics of the Greek Trade Union Movement: Divergence and Convergence with Europe*]. Athens: Gutenberg.

———. 2008. *The Characteristics of the Greek Trade Union Movement—Divergence and Convergence with Europe*, (in Greek) Athens: Gutenberg.

———. 2009. "Το πανόραμα της εργασιακής ανασφάλειας και της επισφαλούς εργασίας [The Panorama of Work Insecurity and Precarious Employment]." *Epoxi*. Accessed December 11, 2009, from http://entosepoxhs.wordpress.com/.

Kretsos, L. 2004. "Industrial Relations and Undeclared Work." EIROnline. Accessed November 18, 2010, from http://www.eurofound.europa.eu/.

———. 2010. "The Effects of the Crisis on the Greek Construction Industry: From the Olympus Mountain to the Kaida Cliff." *Construction Labor Research News* 3. Accessed May 11, 2010, from http://www.clr-news.org.

———. 2011a. "Grassroots Unionism in the Context of Economic Crisis in Greece." *Labor History* 52, no. 3: 265–286.

———. 2011b. "Union Responses to the Rise of Precarious Employment in Greece." *Industrial Relations Journal* 42, no. 5: 453–472.

———. 2012. "Greece's Neoliberal Experiment and Working Class Resistance." *Working USA*, 14, 517–527.

Κρητικίδης, Γ. 2008. "Νέοι και Μισθωτή Απασχόληση' [Young Workers and Employment]." *Ενημέρωση* 148 (March), Athens: ΙΝΕ/ ΓΣΕΕ-ΑΔΕΔΥ: 15–22.

Lampousaki, S. 2011. "Sharp Increase in Flexible Forms of Labor." Accessed May 12, 2014, from http://www.eurofound.europa.eu/ewco/2011/05/GR1105029I.htm.

MacKenzie, R., and M. Martinez Lucio. 2005. "The Realities of Regulatory Change: Beyond the Fetish of Deregulation." *Sociology* 39, no. 3: 499–517.

Matsa, K. 2012. "Dramatic effects of economic and social crisis in population's mental health" (in Greek). *ΟΥΤΟΠΙΑ*, vol. 99, March-April 2012, pp. 7-10.

Ochel, W., and A. Rohwer. 2009. "Reduction of Employment Protection in Europe: A Comparative Fuzzy-Set Analysis." CESifo Working Paper Series CESifo No. 2828.

OECD. 2007. "Economic Survey of Greece." Paris, OECD. Accessed February 18, 2010, from http://www.oecd.org/.

———. 2009. "Economic Survey of Greece." Paris, OECD. Accessed February 18, 2010, from http://www.oecd.org/.

Tsakalotos, E. 2011. "Contesting Greek Exceptionalism: The Political Economy of the Current Crisis." Accessed March 27, 2013, from http://www.e-history.eu/files/uploads/Paper_-_2011.05.16.pdf.

VPRC. 2010. "The Greece Society and the Economic Crisis." Athens: VPRC. Accessed June 18, 2010, from http://www.vprc.gr/.

Zizek, S. 2012. "Save Us from the Saviours." *London Review of Books*, Vol. 34, No. 11, June 2012, page 13.

Index

Taylor, F. *See* Taylorism
Touraine, A., 167

White, S., 59, 65–67, 68–69, 76, 80n14,
    81n18, 81n22, 81n29

Zarifian, P., 168
Zizek, S., 198

COUNTRIES, STATES, ALLIANCES, AND REGIONS

Africa, 12, 106, 107, 117, 124, 126, 129,
    147, 168, 183, 185
Albania, 95
Argentina, 197
Armenia, 97, 117
Asia, 23, 40n6, 88, 101n4, 107, 117, 125,
    147
Australia, 115
Austria, 109, 157

Baltic States, 88, 93, 110
Bangladesh, 25, 27, 28, 35
Belarus, 97, 110
Belgium, 12, 19, 47, 48, 53n1, 109, 112,
    113–114, 114, 119n11
Bosnia-Herzegovina, 97
Brazil, 20
Britain. *See* United Kingdom
Bulgaria, 109–110, 110, 113, 114, 207n5
Burma, 184

Cambodia, 147, 148, 154
Canada, 115, 187
Cape Verde, 117
Caribbean, 124, 125, 126
Central America, 40n6, 124, 126
China, 11, 12–13, 23, 25, 27–28, 40n2,
    101n10, 110, 147, 148–149, 152, 156,
    157, 160, 188
Colombia, 183, 185, 189
COMECON, 89
Croatia, 95, 97
Cyprus, 120n14
Czechoslovakia, 95, 101n5
Czech Republic, 147

Denmark, 110, 116, 120n16

Egypt, 117–118
Ethiopia, 107, 185
Europe, 12, 15, 20, 23, 25, 37, 47, 48, 52,
    86, 88, 95, 100, 101, 102n11, 108, 109,
    112, 114, 115, 116, 118, 119n11,
    121n50, 170, 183, 198, 204, 205, 206;
    east-central Europe, 86, 88, 90, 92–93,
    93–95, 100, 101n10, 112, 147
European Union, 20, 37, 45, 86, 88, 89, 92,
    93, 94–95, 97, 97–98, 100, 105, 109,
    112, 114, 115, 116, 118, 119n2,
    121n37, 121n51, 170, 198, 199, 204,
    206, 207n1

Finland, 109
France, 12, 37–38, 93–94, 120n16,
    166–168, 170, 171, 174, 175, 176

Georgia, 10, 117
Germany, 14, 14–15, 20, 93, 102n12, 109,
    110, 168, 169; German Democratic
    Republic, 88; Nazi Germany, 11
global south, 19, 93, 125, 126, 135n8
Greece, 95, 109, 110, 114, 197–207,
    207n3–208n9

Hungary, 95, 98–100, 102n16, 109–110

India, 20, 38, 39, 60, 107, 110, 115, 119n7,
    186
Indonesia, 11, 13
Ireland, 109, 116
Italy, 94, 95, 109, 114, 143

Japan, 20, 115, 147, 149, 152, 168

Korea: North Korea, 11; South Korea, 11,
    147, 149, 152
Kuwait, 147

Laos, 147, 148
Latin America, 23, 89, 93, 117, 125, 187
Lebanon, 147
Libya, 147

Macedonia, 89
Malaysia, 147, 152

TERMS

About the Editors and the Contributors

József Böröcz is professor of sociology at Rutgers University. Böröcz holds a PhD in sociology from Johns Hopkins and a Doctor of Science from the Hungarian Academy of Science. His publications include *The European Union and Global Social Change: A Critical Geopolitical Economic Analysis* (2009), *Leisure Migration: A Sociological Study on Tourism* (1996), and numerous articles on the sociology of labor and economic sociology.

Stephen Bouquin is professor of sociology and director at Centre Pierre Navalle, Université Evry-Val d'Essone. He completed his doctoral work at Vrije Universiteit in Brussels and served as senior lecturer at Université de Picardie Jules Verne (Amiens) before joining the Centre Pierre Navalle. He is the author of *La valse des écrous: Travail, capital, action collective dans l'industrie automobile, 1970–2004* (2006) and the coauthor of *Résistance au travail* (2008), as well as the author of numerous papers on the sociology of work.

Edward S. Casey is distinguished professor of philosophy at Stony Brook University in New York. He served as president of the American Philosophical Association in 2009–2010 and as chair of Stony Brook's philosophy department from 1991–2001. Casey obtained his PhD at Northwestern University in 1967 and has taught at Yale University, the University of California at Santa Barbara, the New School for Social Research, and Emory University. Casey's published books include *Imagining: A Phenomenological Study* (1976; second edition, 2000), *Remembering: A Phenomenological Study* (1987; second edition, 2000), *Getting Back into Place* (1993; second edition 2009), *The Fate of Place* (1997; new paperback edition, 2013), *Spirit and Soul: Essays in Philosophical Psychology* (1991; second edition, 2004),

Representing Place: Landscape Painting and Maps (2002), *Earth-Mapping: Artists Reshaping Landscape* (2005), and *The World at a Glance* (2007). *Up Against the Wall: Re-Imagining the U.S.-Mexico Border*, written with Mary Watkins, is to appear in 2014, and *The World on Edge* in 2015. Casey's recent work focuses on borders and boundaries, including issues related to labor and migration.

Ronald M. S. Commers is professor emeritus of moral philosophy and value inquiry, and chairman emeritus at the Center for Ethics and Value Inquiry. at Ghent University. He was a professor of Moral Philosophy and Value Inquiry at Ghent University from 1986–2011 after serving on the faculties of the Free University of Brussels and Limburg University Centre. He was the founding director of the Center for Ethics and Value Inquiry at Ghent. He is the author of a dozen books, including *The Wise and the Foolish: Modernity and Its Philosophy* (1995; reprinted 2009), *Ethics in an Era of Globalization* (2008), and *Criticism of the Ethical Consciousness: Love Justifiably, Parts I and II* (2009 and 2010).

Tim R. Johnston received his PhD in philosophy from Stony Brook University in 2013, having written a dissertation on Bergson, affirmation, and LGBT identity. He now serves as the manager of Education and Training for SAGE (Services and Advocacy for GLBT Elders), the nation's largest organization dedicated to improving the lives of LGBT older adults. He writes and lectures on topics related to LGBT identity, aging, feminism, and care ethics.

Lefteris Kretsos is senior lecturer of employment relations and HRM and an active member of the Workplace Employment Research Unit (WERU) at University of Greenwich. Early in his career, Dr. Kretsos lectured and worked on various research projects at the Aberdeen Business School of Robert Gordon University and at Coventry University. Dr. Kretsos also worked for the Greek Trade Union Congress and the European Foundation for the Improvement of Living and Working Conditions as national correspondent for Greece. Dr. Kretsos's research interests are focused on the emerging trends and patterns of precarious employment, especially among young workers and on the impact of economic crisis on employment relations and trade unions. Dr. Kretsos's numerous articles have appeared in such journals as *Industrial Relations Journal, Industrial Law Journal, International Journal of Youth and Adolescence,* and *Labor History.*

Patrick Loobuyck is associate professor of religion and ethics at Centre Pieter Gillis, University of Antwerp. He studied religious studies at the Catholic University of Leuven and ethics at Ghent University. He is guest professor in political philosophy at Ghent University. His research focuses on liberalism, church state regimes, religion in the public sphere, religious education, multiculturalism, migration, Habermas, and Rawls. His articles have appeared in journals such as *Journal of Church and State*, *British Journal of Religious Education*, *Journal for the Scientific Study of Religion*, and *Ethnicities*.

Zahra Meghani is an associate professor in the philosophy department at the University of Rhode Island. She received her PhD in philosophy from the University of Michigan in 2006. Her areas of research are bioethics, feminist theory, and environmental ethics. Her articles have appeared in such journals as *Journal of Agricultural and Environmental Ethics*, *Developing World Bioethics*, and *International Journal of Feminist Approaches to Bioethics*.

John Pearson is associate research fellow at the Centre for Law and Cosmopolitan Values, University of Antwerp. John Pearson completed his PhD at the London School of Economics. He was a postdoctoral research fellow at the Social Law Unit, University of Antwerp. His research interests include global justice, republican political theory, human rights, and labor law.

Mary C. Rawlinson is professor of philosophy and an affiliated faculty in comparative literature and women's and gender studies at Stony Brook University. She is the coeditor of *Thinking with Irigaray* (2011), *The Voice of Breast Cancer in Medicine and Bioethics* (2006), and *Derrida and Feminism* (1997), as well as the editor of five issues of the *Journal of Medicine and Philosophy*, including *Foucault and the Philosophy of Medicine*, *The Future of Psychiatry*, and *Feminist Bioethics*. Her publications include articles on Hegel, Proust, literature and ethics, bioethics, and contemporary French philosophy. She is the editor of *The International Journal of Feminist Approaches to Bioethics* (*IJFAB*), as well as the codirector of the Irigaray Circle and the coeditor of the Section on Gender in the *Encyclopedia of Food and Agricultural Ethics*.

Franc Rottiers is a research associate at the Centre for Critical Philosophy and affiliated with the Centre for Intercultural Communication and Interaction, both at Ghent University. His philosophical work reflects his anthropological research with (undocumented) migrants and addresses the issues and philosophical questions that arise in this context by drawing on Adorno's critical theory and contemporary French thought. The protagonist throughout his research and writings has always been the figure of the refugee.

Charles Umney is lecturer in human resources and organisational behaviour at the Business School, University of Greenwich. He received his PhD from the University of Leeds in 2012. His thesis and related publications develop a theory of the ways in which trade unions collaborate across borders. Prior to entering academia, Umney worked for labor rights organizations such as Homeworkers Worldwide and the Worker Rights Consortium. Since joining the faculty at Greenwich, he has continued to work on research projects with trade unions. His primary current research is a four-year study, along with Greenwich colleagues, of the social effects of marketization policies across Europe.

Wim Vandekerckhove is Senior Lecturer in Organisational Behaviour at the Business School, University of Greenwich, Work and Employment Relations Unit (WERU). He obtained his PhD in Moral Sciences (Applied Ethics) from Ghent University, Belgium. He teaches organizational behavior and business ethics at the University of Greenwich. He is the coordinator of the special interest group on Teaching Business Ethics for the European Business Ethics Network (EBEN). His research and publications are on whistleblowing, philosophy of management, and global ethics.

Ramona Vijeyarasa is a human rights lawyer and activist who completed her PhD with the School of Social Sciences at the University of New South Wales (UNSW) in Sydney, Australia, in March 2013. Her research focused on challenging the mainstream assumptions held about victims of trafficking from Ghana, Ukraine, and Vietnam. Vijeyarasa has worked for a range of organizations, including ActionAid International, the International Organisation for Migration in Vietnam and Ukraine, the Center for Reproductive Rights, and the International Center for Transitional Justice. She earned her LL.M. degree (specializing in human rights) from New York University School of Law and a combined bachelor of arts (Politics and History)/Laws from the University of New South Wales. She has published extensively in international journals on reproductive rights, transitional justice, trafficking, sex work and feminist discourse, stigma and HIV, and the Millennium Development Goals.